Partnerships for Smart Growth

Cities and Contemporary Society

Series Editors: Richard D. Bingham and Larry C. Ledebur,
Cleveland State University

Sponsored by the
Maxine Goodman Levin College of Urban Affairs
Cleveland State University

This new series focuses on key topics and emerging trends in urban policy. Each volume is specially prepared for academic use, as well as for specialists in the field.

SUBURBAN SPRAWL
Private Decisions and Public Policy
Wim Wiewel and Joseph J. Persky, Editors

THE INFRASTRUCTURE OF PLAY
Building the Tourist City
Dennis R. Judd, Editor

THE ADAPTED CITY
Institutional Dynamics and Structural Change
H. George Frederickson, Gary A. Johnson, and Curtis H. Wood

CREDIT TO THE COMMUNITY
Community Reinvestment and Fair Lending Policy
in the United States
Dan Immergluck

PARTNERSHIPS FOR SMART GROWTH
University-Community Collaboration for Better Public Places
Wim Wiewel and Gerrit-Jan Knaap, Editors

REVITALIZING THE CITY
Strategies to Contain Sprawl and Revive the Core
*Fritz W. Wagner, Timothy E. Joder, Anthony J. Mumphrey, Jr.,
Krishna M. Akundi, and Alan F.J. Artibise*

Partnerships for Smart Growth

University-Community Collaboration for Better Public Places

Wim Wiewel and Gerrit-Jan Knaap
editors

LINCOLN INSTITUTE
OF LAND POLICY
Cambridge, Massachusetts

M.E.Sharpe
Armonk, New York
London, England

Published in cooperation with the Lincoln Institute of Land Policy

Library of Congress Cataloging-in-Publication Data

Partnerships for smart growth : university-community collaboration for better public places / edited by Wim Wiewel and Gerrit-Jan Knaap.
p. cm.—(Cities and contemporary society)
Includes bibliographical references and index.
ISBN 0-7656-1559-2 (cloth : alk. paper) ISBN 0-7656-1560-6 (pbk. : alk. paper)
1. Community and college—Case studies. 2. Regional planning—Environmental aspects—Case studies. I. Wiewel, Wim. II. Knaap, Gerrit, 1956– III. Series.

LC237.P37 2005
378.1'03—dc22 2004023627

Printed in the United States of America

The paper used in this publication meets the minimum requirements of
American National Standard for Information Sciences
Permanence of Paper for Printed Library Materials,
ANSI Z 39.48-1984.

∞

MV (c) 10 9 8 7 6 5 4 3 2 1
MV (p) 10 9 8 7 6 5 4 3 2 1

Contents

List of Illustrative Materials

Tables

Figures

Maps

Box

Preface and Acknowledgments

This book is the result of an initiative by the United States Environmental Protection Agency (EPA) to increase cooperation with academic organizations to highlight university-community partnerships related to smart growth issues. It was the EPA's hope that this project would encourage more universities to become involved in partnerships with community organizations and local governments. As the federal agency responsible for the protection of our natural environment, the U.S. EPA has a strong interest in identifying and promoting best practices; it will encourage universities and communities to use the material in this book to develop their own projects. The Association of Collegiate Schools of Planning, the learned society for university-based schools of planning, is committed to helping its members implement innovative programs of teaching, research, and professional practice aimed at improving our physical and social environment.

We solicited chapters through a request for proposals and were very pleased to receive more than seventy proposals. This testifies to the prevalence of these partnerships and the national concern about the nature of urban, suburban, and rural growth and development and its effect on the environment and quality of life. We chose projects that best exemplified an innovative practice, a long-term partnership, or a demonstrated impact, and that were likely to be replicable.

We appreciate the initiative, support, and substantive advice given by the EPA's Carlton Eley and Amber Levofsky, who moved on to other responsibilities before the project's completion. Kevin Nelson ably replaced them at the EPA, and we are grateful for his assistance, as well as that of Geoffrey Anderson, who contributed to the introductory chapter. We also thank Katie Petrone, at the National Center for Smart Growth, University of Maryland–College Park, and Kristen Kepnick, at the College of Business Administration, University of Illinois at Chicago, for their help in keeping the project moving forward.

The Lincoln Institute of Land Policy provided funding and editorial assistance in putting the manuscript into final form; we thank Rosalind Greenstein, Ann LeRoyer, and Julia Gaviria for their expertise and support.

At M.E. Sharpe, Harry Briggs made the publication happen, and Richard Bingham, as series editor, was supportive as always.

Most important, we thank the authors of these chapters, and all the faculty, students, community residents, and public officials who were involved in the projects highlighted in this volume. We hope that they continue to be proud of what they did—for the beneficial effects on their communities, for their contributions to students' learning, and, now, as possible models for others.

Wim Wiewel and Gerrit-Jan Knaap

Partnerships for Smart Growth

Introduction

Wim Wiewel and Gerrit-Jan Knaap

The subject of this book lies at the intersection of two topics of increasing interest. The first concerns recent attempts to improve urban growth decisions and practices. Often referred to as smart growth, efforts to create safe and convenient neighborhoods and to increase opportunities for walking, biking, and transit, as well as investing in existing neighborhoods before pouring money into new ones, have captured the attention of elected officials, businesses, and neighbors in communities across the country. The second topic relates to increasing interest in connecting universities' activities with their surrounding communities. Pressured by growing student interest in learning that is focused on real-world problems, by policy makers who view universities as catalysts for economic and social development, and by donors who want to see their contributions have impacts, universities have become increasingly involved in community outreach.

Universities occupy a significant position in many communities—as generators of economic activity, as land developers, as neighbors and property owners—so perhaps it is not surprising that, as universities have sought greater involvement in the community, they have chosen smart growth as a focal point. Nor is it surprising that communities have welcomed university involvement in land use development decisions. Universities and their respective neighborhoods strive for the same thing: an enhanced quality of life for residents, students, visitors, and workers. From the community's standpoint, the university can bring expertise, multidisciplinary resources, and academic rigor to the development discussion. The only real surprise, perhaps, is that more collaboration has not already happened between universities, with their planning departments, public policy schools, architecture studios, and economic development training, and the communities that have a need for these skills.

The Issue

Over the last fifty years, one pattern of development has dominated in the United States. Sometimes referred to as sprawl, it can be described as development that is spread out over large land areas, separating houses, offices, and shops from one another—leaving the automobile as the only practicable transportation option between them—and channeling investment to new communities and away from existing neighborhoods. Academicians and professionals have often raised concerns about problems associated with these development patterns. Lately, such concerns have reached the general public, as citizens have spent more time in clogged traffic, witnessed the loss of open space, and worried over tax increases and school crowding, while paying for infrastructure to support development outside their communities as their own infrastructure languished.

Often breaking down into a simplistic "growth versus no growth" debate, arguments have revolved around a number of issues. For some, concerns about the current development patterns are driven primarily by the perceived effect on the environment, as natural areas, agricultural land, and other open space are built up. Others focus on broader effects on the quality of life, such as the time spent in traffic, or an assumed loss of community. Inner-city advocates are usually more concerned with the equity consequences, as the ability of central cities to generate taxes is drained away by suburban growth. Yet others feel that the proliferation of separate municipalities associated with sprawl is inherently wasteful, or that the fragmentation of government will affect the economic competitiveness of a region. In each case, commentators, activists, elected officials, and policy makers are identifying areas where the costs of a given development pattern are not borne by the same people who reap the benefits, thus justifying public intervention.

Recently, however, the dialogue has changed. Communities are becoming more sophisticated, using smart growth strategies to catalyze job and revenue growth and to increase housing and transportation choices, while shielding them from negative impacts that can accompany new development. In essence, the debate has shifted away from dead-end growth versus no growth to new questions: How and where should we grow? How can communities grow so that they maximize growth's benefits and minimize its detriments?

The Role of Universities

Universities have become one of the major institutions addressing metropolitan development policy issues. Driven in part by the severity of urban problems, as well as increased calls for accountability and "engagement," institutions of higher education have started to play active roles in bringing their intellectual and institutional resources to bear on their immediate environment. This movement has been actively supported by the federal government through such programs as the Department of Education's university-community partnership program and the Department of Housing and Urban Development's Community Outreach Partnership Center program (COPC). Within universities, departments of urban or regional planning have often been leaders in creating partnership projects, involving faculty and students with community and civic organizations. This involvement often has been of very long duration, moving from project to project, enhancing the public debate while providing research opportunities for faculty and broad educational value for students.

For instance, in the early 1990s the Center for Urban Economic Development at the University of Illinois at Chicago conducted a study of the relative costs and benefits of brownfield redevelopment compared with greenfield development on behalf of the Brownfields Forum, a collaborative project involving the EPA, the city of Chicago, the MacArthur Foundation, and several civic organizations (Persky and Wiewel 2000). That project led to a joint conference on the interdependence of city and suburbs organized by the University of Illinois at Chicago, the Lincoln Institute of Land Policy, and the Brookings Institution (Greenstein and Wiewel 2000). This was followed by a request from the Civic Committee of the Commercial Club for the university to help produce an annual "regional report card" that measures progress on a range of sprawl-related indicators. A number of other policy documents, research papers, and articles were also published, all involving faculty, students, and civic organizations. The university also has been a participant in Chicago's Campaign for Sensible Growth. Thus, starting with one specific EPA-sponsored project, there has been a decade-long stream of policy-relevant research that has greatly contributed to the civic energy around the issues of sprawl, growth management, smart growth, and urban redevelopment in Chicago.

To explore these topics, this book contains case studies of efforts to promote smart growth at universities. The case studies were selected from a large number of submissions in response to a request for proposals. They provide examples from all parts of the country and different types of institutions, and involve university faculty, students, and staff. Despite their dissimilarities, however, they can be grouped into four categories: those that are embedded in university curricula; those that involve the work of a research center; those that result from collaborations; and those that involve the university as an integral member of the community.

Smart Growth in the Curriculum

The fundamental mission of universities is to educate students. And there is no better way to teach students than to involve them directly in real-world problem solving. To provide students with such an opportunity, most design-oriented programs—such as architecture, urban planning, and landscape architecture—offer or require pupils to take studio courses. In such courses, students often work directly with local governments, nonprofit organizations, or neighborhood associations dealing with the messy, complex issues of the real world. For many communities such problems involve some aspect of urban sprawl; thus, the remedy often includes smart growth.

The principles of smart growth are applicable not only in the design professions. Indeed, smart growth has become embedded in the curricula of programs in environmental studies, public policy, engineering, law, and others. Further, the nature of the studio course can vary a great deal. In some cases, the topics differ from semester to semester, problem to problem, site to site. In other examples, a sequence of studios can address the same problem in an ongoing relationship with one organization. Each approach has its strengths and weaknesses, but all can serve to promote smart growth.

Jim Cohen of the University of Maryland, College Park, writes about his studio course, in which he and his students worked with an advisory committee made up of residents and policy makers in Perryville, Maryland. Like many rural communities across the United States, Perryville suffered from the loss of manufacturing firms, a dying downtown, and haphazard, sprawling growth. To address these problems, the students referenced the smart growth principles espoused by Smart Growth America and the smart growth policies adopted by the state of Maryland. Based on these, the students offered the advisory group three scenarios—A Great Place to Live, A Great Place to Work, and A Great Place to Visit—and a specific set of recommendations for implementing each. In revisiting the community sometime later, Cohen found that the residents had implemented only a few of the recommendations. Still, according to the town administrator, the student report had so many useful references and innovative ideas that it has been used frequently as a guide and foundation for new policies and grant proposals.

Michael Greenwald and Nancy Frank of the University of Wisconsin–Milwaukee (UWM) write about a sequence of studio courses led by Peter Park, a recent graduate of UWM's joint program in architecture and urban planning, director of planning for the city of Milwaukee, and adjunct professor at the university. Park used these courses to explore and expand ideas about removing a freeway spur in downtown Milwaukee. This spur, once part of a large-scale plan to encircle the downtown in freeways, formed a major barrier between the downtown and otherwise healthy inner-city neighborhoods. In the studio courses, students constructed models and developed conceptual plans that showed how removal of the spur could help reconnect the neighborhoods with downtown, remove unsightly automobile infrastructure, and open up a large area for infill development. Through the persistent efforts of Park and the compelling evidence provided by students in his workshops, community leaders were persuaded, and the spur was removed. In its place there will be a revitalized, lively, mixed-use and pedestrian area—physical evidence of the power of students in promoting smart growth.

At the University of Oregon in Eugene, writes Robert Parker, the use of studio courses to promote smart growth is nothing new. In fact, the practice is older than the term *smart growth* itself. Oregon is widely recognized as an international pioneer in growth management. In 1973 the state adopted a land use program that featured farm- and forestland preservation, urban growth containment, and environmental conservation. Shortly thereafter, in 1977, the University of Oregon established the Community Planning Workshop (CPW), an experiential learning program closely allied with the Department of Planning, Public Policy, and Management in the School of Architecture and Allied Arts. Operating much like a consulting firm within the university, the CPW serves three basic functions: (1) it helps master's students meet their two-term practicum requirements; (2) it assists students by defraying their educational expenses; and (3) it provides professional-quality planning services to state and local governments at reasonable prices. Over the past twenty-five years the CPW has completed more than 250 projects ranging in focus from land use for transportation planning to affordable housing to rails-to-trails conversion and more.

Smart growth has also become an integral part of the curricula at the Conservation Clinic at the University of Florida, Gainesville. As described by Thomas Ankersen and Nicole Kibert, the Conservation Clinic was created in 1999 and is housed in the law school. The clinic became a formal component of the training and skills curriculum and the environmental and land use law certificate program. Launched with a donation from a generous former student, the clinic has developed a significant record of helping local governments meet the legal requirements of Florida's growth management system. The clinic helped the town of Marineland, for example, develop a sustainable tourism element as part of its comprehensive plan. It helped the city of Gainesville develop new policies for wetland regulation. And it helped the city of Cedar Key designate a community redevelopment area and a redevelopment plan to retain its traditional waterfront. Through these and other interdisciplinary projects, the clinic has helped train a new generation of smart growth lawyers and has shown graduate students in other disciplines how the law can be used to implement smart growth.

Smart Growth at Research Centers

Another fundamental mission of universities is research, some basic, some applied, and often conducted at research centers. Centers help universities pool resources and concentrate expertise on important and contemporary subjects. The National Center for Smart Growth at the University of Maryland is a prime example. But as the following cases make clear, a research center need not have "smart growth" in its title to promote its implementation. What centers often need, however, is funding from sources outside the university. With such financial support, they are able to apply highly advanced knowledge and technical skills to particular problems. For smart growth, this often means the application of geographic information systems (GIS). Because of its power to convey complex information in a simple visual format, GIS has the capacity to make urban problems better understood and amenable to various forms of analysis.

As described by Christine Danis, Laura Solitare, Michael Greenberg, and Henry Mayer, the National Center for Neighborhood and Brownfields Redevelopment at Rutgers, the State University of New Jersey, New Brunswick, is a prime example of a center that promotes smart growth. The center was established in 1998 in the Bloustein School of Planning and Public Policy at Rutgers. New Jersey is well known for its statewide land use plan, under which local governments in designated urban centers must collaborate to implement the plan. For local governments in Somerset County, the center helped them do just that. With assistance from center staff, local governments in Somerset County formed a steering committee and began collecting information. With this information the center was able to identify opportunities for infill and redevelopment and highlight challenges common to each jurisdiction. The center then developed a GIS model to evaluate redevelopment and rezoning impacts. Those results were then used to identify projects that required intermunicipal and county cooperation. Its use of GIS technology in assisting Somerset County demonstrated how the technological capacities of university centers can provide not only a clearer regional vision but also serve as a vehicle for promoting intergovernmental cooperation.

Another interesting example of how the research capacities of a center can be used to promote smart growth is provided by Greg Lindsey, John Ottensmann, Jamie Palmer, Jeffrey Wilson, and Joseph Tutterrow. In 1981 the Indiana legislature abolished the State Planning Services Agency, leaving few places for local governments to turn for help on land use issues. To fill this void, the Center for Urban Policy and the Environment at Indiana University–Purdue University, Indianapolis, has served as a proponent for smart growth in an otherwise unsupportive environment. It does so through collaboration with nonprofit organizations like the Indiana Land Use Consortium, and with such state commissions as the Indiana Land and Resource Commission. Working with these and other organizations, the center launched several major research projects to inform and promote smart growth in the state. One of these projects involves the mapping and monitoring of land use change in Central Indiana. This project has helped policy makers understand the extent and impact of urban sprawl. Another involved a smart growth audit of land use planning practices and policies, which provided current and comprehensive information about the state of planning in Indiana. A third project focused on the development of a land use forecasting model. This model gives state policy makers tools for exploring future development possibilities. While the work of the center has not moved Indiana to become a leader in land use reform, it has provided the foundation for improved state land use decision making.

Smart Growth by Collaboration

Universities are large, complex institutions. In many places they are among the largest employers in the community; in most places, they are communities unto themselves. Yet universities and their administrative units must collaborate with external organizations to succeed. They work, for example, with professional organizations on curricula, local governments on community development, and state and federal agencies on government policy. Universities also collaborate with a variety of organizations to promote smart growth. As the case studies demonstrate, this can occur through their work with nonprofit organizations, government agencies, and other universities.

As described by Priscilla Geigis, Elisabeth Hamin, and Linda Silka, Community Collaborative is an innovative partnership between the state's Executive Office of Environmental Affairs and the University of Massachusetts–Amherst. The seeds of the partnership took root in both organizations. They grew in part from the Executive Office of Environmental Affairs, which launched a Preservation Initiative in 1999 to provide tools and information to local leaders to help them make informed decisions about land use and growth. They also grew from the Citizen Planners Training Collaborative offered by the University of Massachusetts Extension and Department of Landscape Architecture and Urban Planning. Its mission is to provide training for members of official planning boards. With overlapping interests and the desire of both groups to expand their missions, the collaborative was formed and the Community Preservation Institute was launched. The institute provides education and training to local citizens, activists, and local government officials. Since its inception, it has trained 252 individuals from 136 communities.

A different kind of collaboration was formed at Cornell University, Ithaca, New York, according to David Gross and Edward LeClear. The Cornell case involves the university's Department of Natural Resources and the Edward L. Rose Conservancy, a land trust in Susquehanna County, Pennsylvania. As a nonprofit land trust, the goal of the conservancy is to protect natural resources, provide sanctuary for wildlife, and preserve the scenic beauty of the county. Susquehanna County, like much of Pennsylvania, is threatened by urban expansion, habitat fragmentation, and erosion of the agricultural economy. Together, the department and the conservancy have worked to conduct inventories of natural assets, develop resource conservation plans, and protect lands permanently from urban encroachment. In the process, this partnership provides real-world content for classes in conservation planning, senior practicum courses, and internships for master's students.

United Growth is the product of a collaboration between Michigan State University Extension, in Kent County, and the Michigan State University Center for Urban Affairs, in Grand Rapids. As a result, write Richard Jelier, Carol Townsend, and Kendra Wills, United Growth has an inherent urban and rural mission. Originally supported with a grant of $176,000 from the Frey Foundation, the project has since been able to generate over $800,000 from more than twenty-five funding agencies. With these funds, the project has provided training to rural audiences on farmland preservation, natural resource conservation, and alternatives for low-density development. It also has provided training on disinvestment and central-city revitalization to urban audiences. Funds were used as well to develop Michigan's first land use curriculum for elementary schools. This curriculum was piloted in fifteen classrooms in 2001 and served as the basis for teacher training in 2003. Finally, funds have been used to provide mini-grants and to support student projects, which include business district revitalization, neighborhood planning, crime prevention through neighborhood design, and historic preservation. As a result, United Growth has become a focal point for smart growth activities throughout Central Michigan.

Another example of intrauniversity collaboration is provided by the Community Design Team, which involves the Department of Landscape Architecture and the University Extension Service at West Virginia University, Morgantown. Modeled after the Minnesota Design Team, according to Christopher Plein and Jeremy Morris, the Community Design Team sends groups of faculty, professionals, and students into rural communities to help local residents address planning issues. Each team consists of twelve to twenty individuals with backgrounds in engineering, public administration, landscape architecture, forestry, medicine, public health, and other disciplines. Members of the team stay with host families on four-day visits, during which the team listens to presentations from local leaders, participates in walkabouts across the community, develops a set of community plans, and participates in an open forum to discuss the plans. Because the design team focuses on rural communities, plans often include presenting new ideas on how to protect farmland, safeguard historic commercial areas, and revitalize the community. Through this process, the Community Design Team has pioneered new applications of smart growth principles to rural areas.

Smart Growth in the Community

Regardless of their particular missions, universities are integral parts of their larger communities. As such, they occupy space, shape the character of neighborhoods, and participate in public policy decision making. Universities can help implement smart growth on campus, in the surrounding neighborhoods, and in the larger communities that they are intended to serve.

The University of North Carolina is the dominant institution in Chapel Hill. According to Richard Thorsten, it is home to more than 25,000 students and has over 11.87 million square feet of floor space. To accommodate an anticipated additional 8,400 students and employees over the next ten years, the university launched a major master planning process in 1997. With the aid of several consultants and extensive input from residents of the greater Chapel Hill community, the plan sought to enhance an environment that already embodied many of the principles of smart growth. To make the campus even more attractive, efficient, and sustainable, the master plan promotes many smart growth principles, including providing more infill housing, mixing land uses, making the campus more pedestrian friendly, and protecting open spaces and environmentally sensitive areas. Under a development ordinance and other agreements with the city of Chapel Hill, the university will cover 40 percent of fare-free bus service to students and Chapel Hill residents. The North Carolina master plan and planning process illuminate why universities remain leading examples of the principles of smart growth.

As described by Meredith Perry and John Schaerer, the University of Tennessee at Chattanooga (UTC) has been an instrument of smart growth even beyond the campus boundaries. UTC adjoins the historical and once-fashionable Martin Luther King District to form the urban core of Chattanooga. As part of the first phase of an ongoing urban redevelopment effort, UTC formed an alliance with the Martin Luther King Neighborhood Association, based on the university's need to grow in a landlocked campus and for the MLK district to stem its decline. Toward both ends, the university chose not to develop satellite facilities at the urban fringe, but to redevelop on the existing campus and its nearby neighborhood. Elements of the project included the construction of new university facilities, including student housing and two schools, and the rehabilitation of existing homes through the provision of neighborhood amenities and home ownership incentives. As a result, the MLK district has improved dramatically, the university has a more secure and prosperous environment, and the UTC's philosophical approach to its metropolitan mission—that people and partnerships matter more than projects and funding—has proved to be an effective way to promote smart growth.

Brian Ohm is a lawyer and member of the faculty in the Department of Urban and Regional Planning at the University of Wisconsin–Madison. In his case study, Ohm describes his role in the collaborative process that led to the passage of Wisconsin's comprehensive planning and smart growth law in 1999. As in many states, land use emerged in Wisconsin as a prominent policy issue in the 1990s. In response, Governor Tommy Thompson issued an executive order in 1994 creating a land use council comprised of state agency officials and a task force of various interest groups and local government officials. Like many such task forces, it produced a report that went nowhere. Subsequently, the Wisconsin Realtors Association approached Ohm to broker a meeting between the realtors and 1000 Friends of Wisconsin, a progressive interest group. Building on this alliance of longtime adversaries, Ohm enlisted the support of other stakeholders and eventually accumulated sufficient support for land use reform. As a result, in 1999 Governor Thompson signed into law Wisconsin's version of smart growth legislation. Though many challenges remain, Ohm helped build the constituency for new, smarter growth in Wisconsin—the first state in the Midwest to adopt smart growth reforms.

Summary

In their curricula, as part of a collaborative, as the home to a research center, or as a member of the community, universities across the United States are protagonists of smart growth. No two universities are the same, and no two promote growth in the same way. Still, evidence is ample in this volume's chapters that universities can promote the principles of smart growth.

The U.S. EPA has identified ten smart growth principles:

1. Mix land uses.
2. Take advantage of compact building design.
3. Create housing opportunities and choices for a range of household types, family size, and incomes.
4 Create walkable neighborhoods.
5. Foster distinctive, attractive communities with a strong sense of place.

6. Preserve open space, farmland, natural beauty, and critical environmental areas.
7. Reinvest in and strengthen existing communities and achieve more balanced regional development.
8. Provide a variety of transportation choices.
9. Make development decisions predictable, fair, and cost effective.
10. Encourage citizen and stakeholder participation in development decisions.

Including smart growth in the curriculum is an obvious way to promote it. Jim Cohen's studio at the University of Maryland was framed by Maryland's smart growth statutes and the EPA's ten principles of smart growth; it thus addressed every one of those principles. The Community Collaborative at the University of Oregon, because of its coevolution with Oregon's pioneering land use program, had long been promoting the principles of smart growth. The series of studios by Joe Park at the University of Wisconsin–Milwaukee led to the removal of a freeway spur; it thus helped direct development toward existing communities and promote transportation options. Finally, the law clinic at the University of Florida helped foster ecotourism and preserve wetlands, thereby enhancing distinctive, attractive places with a strong sense of place.

Collaborative efforts have been equally effective in promoting smart growth principles. Using collaborative training programs, the University of Massachusetts and the Office of Environmental Affairs directly encouraged community and stakeholder collaboration. Through the permanent preservation of rural land, the Department of Natural Resources at Cornell University and the Rose Conservancy have preserved open space, farmland, natural beauty, and critical environmental areas. In providing assistance to both rural and urban communities, United Growth at Michigan State University helps create a range of housing opportunities and choices to urban as well as rural residents. And via its Design Team, the Department of Landscape Architecture and the University Extension Service at West Virginia University helped to create walkable neighborhoods and foster unique, appealing places.

Research centers have both directly and indirectly facilitated smart growth. In providing advanced knowledge and technical assistance, both the Center for Urban Policy and the Environment at Indiana University–Purdue University, Indianapolis, and the brownfields redevelopment center at Rutgers University help make development decisions predictable, fair, cost effective, and better informed.

As integral members of the community, universities directly facilitate smart growth both on and off campus. The new master plan for the University of

North Carolina not only calls for more walkable environments, but also takes advantage of compact building design, preserves open spaces and environmental areas, and provides a range of transportation choices. Recent activities at the University of Tennessee at Chattanooga led to much of the same, but by investing in the historic Martin Luther King neighborhood it elicited community collaboration and directed development toward existing communities. Finally, through his active involvement in Wisconsin's land use statutory reform, Brian Ohm played a part in moving an entire state toward a smarter form of growth.

While all four approaches to promoting smart growth are within reach of every university, the studio approach is perhaps the easiest and least costly. As Jim Cohen's example makes clear, all it takes is a single instructor and a single class. Sustained efforts, of course, such as those at the University of Oregon and the University of Wisconsin–Milwaukee, will likely lead to greater impacts. Collaborative efforts, like any marriage, take more effort, but can be more fulfilling. Land trusts, state agencies, and extension centers have capacities that academic units do not. As shown in Michigan, New York, and Massachusetts, collaborations of these kinds can extend geographic reach, enlarge the scope of staff expertise, and expand the limits of legal interventions. The Indiana and Rutgers examples show that the best way to influence policy may be to bring knowledge and technology directly to policy-making bodies. Of course, this is easier with grant support. Finally, a university's influence on its environment is inevitable. Here, the choice is not whether to influence community character, but whether that influence will promote or inhibit smart growth.

References

Greenstein, Rosalind, and Wim Wiewel. 2000. *Urban-suburban interdependencies.* Cambridge, MA: Lincoln Institute of Land Policy.

Persky, Joseph, and Wim Wiewel. 2000. *When corporations leave town: The costs and benefits of metropolitan job sprawl.* Detroit, MI: Wayne State University Press.

Part 1

SMART GROWTH IN THE CURRICULUM

1

Using a Studio Course for Provision of Smart Growth Technical Assistance: The University of Maryland's 1999 Community Planning Studio in Perryville, Maryland

James R. Cohen

When a set of initiatives collectively known as "smart growth" was passed by the Maryland legislature in 1997, the acts became the latest in a series of laws, dating back to 1969, that distinguished the state as a leader in land preservation and watershed protection. Spurred largely by concern for the health of the Chesapeake Bay, the legislature had already established laws to purchase open space, farmland, and forests; protect tidal and nontidal wetlands; manage storm-water runoff; regulate development within one thousand feet of the bay and its tidal tributaries; require reforestation and tree planting as a condition of new development; and protect sensitive areas. The smart growth programs contained incentives and planning requirements aimed at curbing sprawl and revitalizing cities and inner suburbs.

To varying degrees most of the laws added planning and regulatory responsibilities to local governments. In early 1999 a faculty member in the University of Maryland's Urban Studies and Planning Program decided to focus his summer community-planning studio course on the challenges facing one of Maryland's small jurisdictions as it attempted to comply with its planning mandates and grow in a manner consistent with the state's smart growth program. The resulting course, What's Smart Growth for Perryville?, proved to be a rich learning experience for the students and a valuable resource for the town.

This chapter concentrates on how the 1999 summer studio course provided smart growth–related technical assistance to the town of Perryville. It gives brief profiles of the course and Perryville; discusses how the students approached the study; summarizes the major findings and recommendations of the final studio report; critically analyzes the degree to which the report has since been utilized by the town; highlights the students' reactions to the studio experience; and discusses the lessons learned from the studio.

Overview of the Planning Studio Course and Perryville

The Community Planning Studio is a six-credit "capstone" course for Master of Community Planning (MCP) candidates in the University of Maryland's Urban Studies and Planning Program (URSP). The one-semester course enables students to apply their knowledge and skills, analyze current, pressing planning issues in a selected community, and produce an oral and a written report containing recommendations for addressing those issues. In essence, the students act as a consulting team for a community client.

In early 1999 several MCP students requested a studio that would enable them to help a rural jurisdiction apply smart growth principles in dealing with new growth. Staff members of the Maryland Department of Planning were contacted for suggestions of possible case-study jurisdictions. James Cohen, the summer studio instructor, also consulted with Uri Avin, principal planner with HNTB, Inc., and member of the planning program's technical advisory committee, who recommended Perryville as the study site. Avin's firm had done a study on development opportunities and design options for Perryville's downtown in 1997 (LDR International 1998), and he thought that a studio report would be an excellent follow-up.

Located at the confluence of the Susquehanna River and the Chesapeake Bay, near the Delaware-Maryland border, Perryville (population 4,500) is the second largest city in Cecil County. During the 1990s the town's population grew by nearly 50 percent, while the state's population grew by less than 11 percent. First settled in 1622, for over two centuries Perryville consisted of just a cluster of residences and locally owned businesses along a postal road leading to the Lower Ferry crossing of the Susquehanna River. During the late 1880s the town grew because of its importance as a coach stop at the ferry crossing and as a busy railroad depot. Much of the old town's freight rail traffic was diverted to roads, however, following construction of major highways (such as State Routes 40 and 7, and U.S. Interstate 95) beginning in the 1940s.

Perryville's new growth occurred on converted farmland and forests away from the old town center, along Broad and Front Streets, and new, outlying subdivisions were annexed to the town. Further annexations occurred in the late 1980s and early 1990s. By the end of the 1990s the major employer in Perryville was the Veterans Administration hospital, situated on a peninsula

Map 1.1 **Perryville, Maryland, in relation to the University of Maryland, College Park**

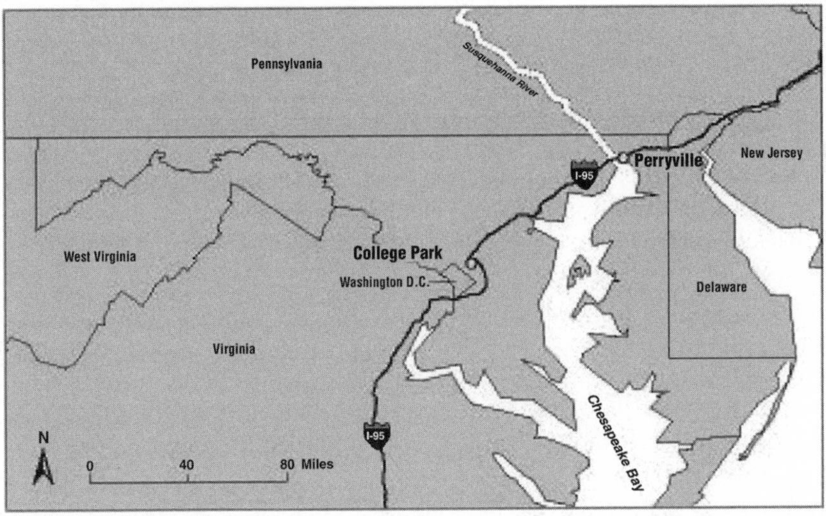

Source: Environmental Systems Research Institute, Inc. (ESRI) Data and Maps CD (2003).

just past the old town. Dozens of disabled veterans live in Perryville's old town in boarding houses that are privately operated. As Map 1.1 indicates, Perryville is approximately eighty miles north of the University of Maryland.

As with many of Maryland's rural towns, Perryville does not have a planning staff, yet it is responsible for most of the land use planning and regulation that addresses the state's environmental and smart growth legislation. About twenty-five smaller jurisdictions on the Eastern Shore of the Chesapeake Bay rely on the Maryland Department of Planning's "circuit-rider" planners for technical assistance in implementing their Critical Area land use program (discussed below), but this occasional assistance is constrained by limited state personnel and financial resources. Such limitations can hamper smart growth implementation in smaller jurisdictions, but create conditions suitable for graduate planning programs to offer technical assistance. For the above reasons, Perryville provided a studio opportunity with mutual benefits for the town and the students.

Perryville's town administrator at the time, Sharon Weygand, was grateful for the offer of planning services and technical assistance. The town commissioners subsequently endorsed the proposed studio. As is done with all URSP studio courses, an advisory committee was assembled comprised of major stakeholders at the local and county levels. Committee members would assist the students by identifying key issues in Perryville and Cecil County and by providing them with background information and planning documents. The nine members of the studio advisory committee included a town commissioner, the chairperson of the town's planning and zoning committee, the town administrator, the Cecil County planning director, the county's principal planner, the chairperson of the county economic development committee, two persons working with the Lower Susquehanna Heritage Greenway Project (which had economic and environmental importance to the town), and the Maryland Department of Planning's circuit-rider planner for Perryville.

After selecting the studio site, organizing the advisory committee, and compiling initial information and documents, the course instructor facilitated some of the student group discussions, acting sometimes as an ambassador between town officials and the students, and serving as occasional chauffeur (to take the eleven students on the 80-minute drive from campus to the town). He also exhorted the students to complete the written report by the end of the twelve-week summer session.

The town did not provide the studio with funding. Class expenses were supported with $600 from the Summer Programs division of the University of Maryland's Office of Continuing and Extended Education. The funds were used to pay for layout and printing of the final report. In addition, the Summer Programs division set aside $320 of the participating students' tuition, which was spent for the use of a van from the university's motor pool to make site visits to Perryville. For its part, the town gave the students the use of the Rogers Tavern, an historic landmark on the shore of the Susquehanna River, as a meeting place. The town also gave the students access to all documents needed for the study. In addition, town-elected officials and other stakeholders were very responsive to students' requests for interviews.

At a meeting at the beginning of the semester, each member of the advisory committee was given a chance to tell the students what he or she believed were the most compelling planning challenges facing the town. Following are the main issues raised by the committee:

- Perryville's comprehensive plan had been updated in 1997, prior to the full unveiling of Maryland's Smart Growth Initiatives; thus the plan needed to be reviewed to determine its consistency with the new initiatives.
- Neither the town's zoning ordinance nor subdivision regulations had been updated in decades; they were not consistent with either the 1997 plan or Maryland's 1997 smart growth legislation.
- Perryville does not have an easily recognized town center or even a landmark.

- There was a vacant, one hundred-acre industrial site in Perryville, formerly the location of the Firestone Plastics Company. It was unoccupied, due largely to poor access for trucks. Resident protests stopped a recent proposal to build an incinerator on the site, and the town was exploring other opportunities for the land's utilization.
- Commercial development in the area is found at the Outlet Mall off Interstate 95, on each side of Route 40, and (in small measure) in Perryville's old downtown. However, the town does not have a supermarket. Although an estimated 1,200 workers and visitors drive through the old downtown each day to reach the VA hospital, no attempt had been made to capitalize on the potential market created by the hospital-generated trips. Questions also arose as to how to bring the boarding homes for VA patients up to code. Some town commissioners were reluctant to put pressure on the boarding homeowners, but dilapidated properties were thought to undermine the old town's growth potential.
- The MARC train station in the old downtown was not being utilized for its commercial potential. (The MARC train connects Perryville to Baltimore and Washington.) The station could provide goods and services not only to daily commuters but also to downtown residents. Across from the train station and overlooking the Susquehanna is the historic Rogers Tavern, which was also underutilized. Because the population will increase within and near the old downtown, questions were raised about the kinds of commercial and/or tourism opportunities the town could pursue.
- The Lower Susquehanna Heritage Greenway Project was in its final planning stages and would create a corridor of protected open spaces along the Susquehanna River in Cecil County and neighboring Harford County. With its system of looping walking/biking trails, the greenway will provide recreational opportunities, habitat for rare species, and access to scenic views, historic sites, museums, local festivals, and cultural events. The town was deliberating the ways in which it could benefit from the greenway's economic development potential.

How the Students Approached the Studio Report

After the first meeting with the advisory committee and during the next twelve weeks, the students completed the following tasks:

- determined which of the above issues they could deal with in the given timeframe;
- organized their research agenda;

- read relevant literature, including state legislation, smart growth Web sites, and local, county, and state planning documents;
- collected data, conducted interviews with advisory committee members and other individuals with information and perspectives relevant to the studio topic;
- attended meetings of the Town Commission and the Planning and Zoning Commission;
- conducted extensive site surveys; and
- investigated potential sources of funding and technical assistance for implementing smart growth in the town.

The students gave an oral presentation to the advisory committee in September 1999, along with a written report. The written portion was intended to be a working document—something the town could use to manage growth in a way that is consistent with the major state legislation, including the Maryland Smart Growth Initiatives.

To guide them in their work, the students defined smart growth in two ways. One definition referred to local land use procedures and outcomes that are either mandated or encouraged via incentives. The mandates and incentives are established by four laws, collectively labeled as *Smart Growth,* which have been passed by the Maryland legislature since 1984 to prevent sprawl and/or protect environmentally sensitive areas. The second definition consisted of a set of general principles expressed in such Maryland legislation and in other local, state, and national antisprawl initiatives. These general principles were denoted as smart growth (lowercase *s* and *g*).

The first Maryland law that the students included under *Smart Growth* was the 1984 Critical Area Act, designed to improve water quality, protect habitat, and manage growth within a zone one thousand feet from the Chesapeake Bay and its tidal tributaries. The act mandates that jurisdictions inventory their Critical Area land into three zones, depending on the intensity of the actual land use. A one hundred–foot buffer from the shoreline is required for all new development, with exemptions for certain types of water-dependent uses. The local governments must then implement land regulations and performance standards specific to each of the zones, subject to oversight by a state commission. Because of Perryville's location, much of the town's land is subject to Critical Area Act requirements.

The Forest Conservation Act of 1991 constituted the second Smart Growth law under the students' classification. That act requires developers to replace some of the forests cleared for building and to plant trees on development sites that have few or no trees. Local governments are responsible for implementing, monitoring, and enforcing the act.

The third Smart Growth Maryland law, the 1992 Economic Growth, Resource Protection and Planning Act, is meant to facilitate economic growth and development that is well planned, efficiently serviced, and environmentally sound. The legislation required jurisdictions, by 1997, to incorporate the following seven visions into their comprehensive plans: (1) development is concentrated in suitable areas; (2) sensitive areas are protected; (3) growth in rural areas is directed to existing population centers, and resource areas are protected; (4) stewardship of the Chesapeake Bay and the land is a universal ethic; (5) conserving resources, including reducing resource consumption, is practiced; (6) to assure the achievement of the first five visions, above, economic growth is encouraged and regulatory mechanisms are streamlined; and (7) funding mechanisms are addressed to achieve these visions.

Under the 1992 act, new "sensitive areas" were to be included in plan updates. Each jurisdiction was allowed to define and determine the level of protection for steep slopes, streams and their buffers, the one hundred–year floodplain, and habitats of endangered species. Once the plan with the new sensitive areas element was adopted, the law required that zoning and subdivision regulations become consistent with the plan. Local planning commissions must review and, if necessary, amend their plans every six years.

Certainly the most nationally recognized of the four Maryland laws that the studio team defined as Smart Growth was the bundle of five programs passed in 1997 under the leadership of former governor Parris Glendening. The stated goals of the Smart Growth Initiatives were threefold: "To save our most valuable remaining resources before they are forever lost; to support existing communities and neighborhoods by targeting state resources to support development in areas where the infrastructure is already in place (or is planned to support it); . . . and to save taxpayers millions of dollars in the unnecessary cost of building the infrastructure required to support sprawl" (Maryland Department of Planning 2003). At the time the Perryville studio was in session, the Smart Growth Initiatives consisted of the following five core programs:[1]

1. The Smart Growth Areas Act, which directs state funding into locations that meet one of several criteria. Some of the qualifying locations are a municipality, an enterprise zone, a certified heritage area, and locally designated growth areas (aka Priority Funding Areas) that meet specific state criteria. With certain exceptions, only Smart Growth Areas may qualify for state funds for water, sewer, transportation, housing, economic development, and environmental projects.
2. The Rural Legacy Act, which established a grant program enabling local governments and private land trusts to purchase easements and

development rights in rural areas with such important natural resources as prime farmland.
3. The Brownfields Voluntary Cleanup and Revitalization Incentive Programs, which attempt to stimulate the reuse of contaminated properties.
4. An updated Job Creation Tax Credit Program, originally established in 1996, that encourages businesses to expand or relocate in Maryland by providing tax credits for each new, full-time job a qualified business creates—with higher benefits available for business expansions or relocations in Smart Growth and Priority Funding Areas.
5. The Live-Near-Your-Work Program, which creates financial incentives for employees to buy homes near their workplaces. Only home purchases in areas that qualify as "designated neighborhoods" (because they are mixed-use neighborhoods in need of revitalization) are eligible for the incentives.

The second definition of smart growth used by the studio encompassed principles being espoused at that time by the Congress for the New Urbanism, the Urban Land Institute, and the Smart Growth Network. (The students did their study before the Smart Growth Network posted on its Web site its "Ten Principles of Smart Growth.") The students referred to those smart growth principles as the following:

- Residents live close to their employment.
- Building placement and scale are conducive to a pedestrian-oriented environment.
- Neighborhoods are compact and walkable with a modified grid street network.
- Transportation systems and transit hubs are centrally located and accessible by pedestrians.
- Public gathering centers, parks, and open spaces are located in accessible and practical locations.
- Civic buildings and spaces are promoted.
- A wide spectrum of housing options is available, enabling a broad range of incomes, ages, and family types to live within a single neighborhood or district.
- Infill development is pursued.

By using the two definitions, the students set out to help the town in fulfilling its requirements under Maryland's Smart Growth mandates and to grow (and revitalize) in a manner consistent with smart growth principles.

Findings and Recommendations of the Final Studio Report

In the ninety-eight-page final studio report, *Smart Growth for Perryville*, the students clarify its purpose:

> We sought to create a useful, action-oriented document that clearly outlines Choices, steps and resources necessary to plan for and implement future growth, as well as to enable the Town to discuss and make decisions based on a range of alternatives. (p. 6)

The report begins by analyzing the extent to which Perryville's planning/regulatory practices conformed with smart growth principles in general and Maryland's major environmental and Smart Growth laws in particular. That analysis concludes with thirty-one recommendations for improving those practices; twenty-three for the town, three for Cecil County, and five for the state of Maryland. The report then presents three potential scenarios for future growth in Perryville, based on three different "visions" that the students found in their review of the town's comprehensive plan and their interviews with local officials and residents. The scenarios are: "A Great Place to Live," where quality, small-town life, and residential development take precedence; "A Great Place to Work," where business and industrial development are the focus; and "A Great Place to Visit," where heritage-based tourism is the main goal.

Each of the three scenario chapters opens with a vision statement followed by a description of how the town would look and feel if the vision were realized using smart growth principles. Each chapter then provides an inventory of assets and constraints, suggestions for short-term and long-term actions for realizing the vision (in terms of land use and zoning, design, transportation, amenities and services, and so forth), and a listing of implications for major stakeholders. In all, there are twenty-seven suggestions for implementing "Live," twenty-four for "Work," and twenty-seven for "Visit."

The students point out that each of these visions could have differing implications for the town's soon-to-be-updated zoning ordinance, for its capital improvement plan, its use of vacant land, its designation of town centers, and other policies and regulations. For example, in the Great Place to Live scenario, the town would have two designated centers: one in the old downtown, on Broad Street (where new residential development would be attracted to infill sites); and the other at the intersection of State Routes 222 and 40, about a mile and half from downtown. In the Great Place to Work scenario, however, there is only one center, at the latter site, for the convenience of employees and/or customers of new commercial and industrial development located away from the old downtown. In Live, the vacant Firestone property is to be examined as a potential site for boat access to shallow water on the bay. In Work, that site is assessed for pollutant contamination and marketed for light industrial uses. In Visit, the town's historical buildings, MARC station, and a new greenway trail are exploited for tourist-related commercial development.

In an effort to clearly distinguish the differences among the scenarios, the report contains a table summarizing how each of the three visions addresses each of the eight smart growth principles, and compares them with then-current planning practice in Perryville. In their report the students emphasize that the vision chapters are meant to stimulate discussion and action regarding Perryville's future—not to be a directive. Accordingly, following the vision chapters, the report outlines a series of steps the town could take to decide upon and implement its own vision, beginning with the formation of a strategic planning committee, representing a range of community stakeholders who would then develop a vision for the town. Following the outline of the strategic plan process are twenty-nine recommendations regarding meeting town hall's personnel needs; improving communication between the town and other jurisdictions; updating town codes; mapping; annexation, infrastructure, and public facilities; and design guidelines, economic development, and neighborhood revitalization.

The report concludes with a table to assist the town with smart growth implementation. The table matches twenty-five specific planning goals to a short list of town actions or tasks that can be taken to address each goal, along with the names of organizations that can provide funding and/or technical assistance in relation to those tasks. For example, for one of the planning goals, commercial business development, the table lists four possible actions (such as conduct market research) and identifies five sources of technical assistance and ten sources of funding to facilitate the task.

Finally, a twenty-page appendix contains an annotated summary of each of the eighty-four sources of federal, state, and nongovernmental program sources of funding and/or technical assistance listed in the previous table—including a one-paragraph description and contact information. The appendix also contains an additional listing of Maryland Department of Planning publications and services; a list of six relevant planning publications (such as Ames 1998 and Daniels, Keller, and Lapping 1995); four sources of training for public officials and staff in smart growth; and seven references for grant writing.

Perryville's Utilization of the Report

The studio advisory committee expressed great satisfaction with the students' work. Nevertheless, there was no formal commitment on the town's part to use the report, nor any expectation that the students or instructors would assist with the report's implementation. The document simply was to be left with town officials and the advisory committee members.

In the four years following the studio report, there was only one occasion for continuity in the university's connection to the town. Three members of the town's planning and zoning commission participated in a two-day Planning Commissioner Certificate Program training in November 1999, sponsored jointly by the URSP and MDP in neighboring Harford County.

To ascertain the degree to which the studio report was helpful to the town, the author interviewed Eric Morsicato, current town administrator; Sharon Weygand, town administrator at the time of the studio; Mary Ann Skilling, the MDP circuit-rider planner for the Critical Area assigned to Perryville; Barbara Brown, chairperson of the planning and zoning commission at the time of the studio course and now a town commissioner; Anthony DiGiacomo, principal planner with Cecil County; and David Dodge, a developer who is also president of the Perryville Chamber of Commerce and a major player in the revitalization of downtown Perryville. Each of the six was asked to discuss the nature and degree to which he or she used the studio report and implemented its suggestions and recommendations. To determine how much the town had incorporated the students' suggestions and recommendations in their official planning documents, the author read the latest draft of the zoning ordinance, dated February 2003, as well as the minutes from meetings of the planning and zoning commission and zoning board of appeals since September 1999 to get a sense of how their deliberations reflected the kind of smart growth ideas in the studio report. A drive through Perryville was also conducted to get a firsthand look at any visible changes in the town.

Before discussing the impact of the studio report, it is necessary to consider Weygand's comment, "Change [in Perryville] is gradual." The town has not fully updated its comprehensive plan since 1997. None of the town's five commissioners receives a salary, nor do the planning and zoning commission members. Also, typical of small towns on the bay's Eastern Shore, the salaried town administrator has multiple responsibilities. In Perryville, in addition to administration, those roles include code enforcement officer, zoning officer, and financial officer. This means that championing change requires voluntary activism on the part of elected officials and extra effort by the town administrator.

Consequently, the impact of the studio is discussed here in three main ways: (1) how the town has addressed the report's recommendations for having planning/regulatory practices conform with what the students described as Maryland's Smart Growth program; (2) the degree to which the town has responded to students' recommendations for creating a visioning and strategic plan, fulfilling personnel needs, updating town code, and other recommendations contained in the report's final chapter; and (3) other ways in which the key informants say they have used the report. In some cases the noted impacts were a direct result of the report; in others the report reinforced actions that the town administrator and some other stakeholders were already contemplating.

Several of the students' recommendations were immediately implemented to strengthen the town's enforcement of Maryland's Smart Growth laws. The circuit-rider planner and the town administrator prepared checklists to be used by the town to enforce the Critical Area Act and the Forest Conservation Act. The minutes of the town planning commission and zoning board of appeals disclose the stringent enforcement of environmental laws over the past four years. It is not possible, however, to determine the degree to which the studio report influenced this increased vigilance.

Consistent with student recommendations, the draft zoning ordinance requires public access to the waterfront in residential developments, enables future development to include commercial centers and high-density residential nodes, and enables infill and compact development. The town is also involved in implementing and promoting the Lower Susquehanna Heritage Greenway and in investigating numerous funding options for smart growth projects.

Some of the students' Smart Growth recommendations that have *not* been acted upon are those that would derive from an updated comprehensive plan, such as annexing open space to create a greenbelt, better defining sensitive areas, and working with Cecil County to establish a transfer-of-development rights (TDR) program. The TDR program option is not being explored at the county level because infrastructure capacity is currently insufficient to support the more intensive growth that would be directed to "receiving" areas. The students urged the town to apply for "Designated Neighborhood" status that, if approved, would enable it to participate in the Live-Near-Your-Work Program. The students believed this program could stimulate home purchases in Perryville by VA hospital employees.

Perryville did not follow the students' suggestion to create a strategic planning committee that would review the contents of their report (and other documents), develop a vision for the town, and then create a plan for its realization. Instead, in early 2001 the town created a revitalization committee that is focused on the old downtown. Established by the town administrator, Eric Morsicato, the group includes the mayor, developer David Dodge, downtown property owners, and other interested stakeholders. At their April 2002 meeting the group produced the following mission statement: "We will make Perryville one of the best places to work, live and visit in Maryland.

Come see us grow." In other words, for the time being the town will embrace all three of the students' visions, but concentrate their focus on a targeted area. Three new residential developments have been built in the old downtown, and a few more are planned. Combining elements of the students' Live and Visit scenarios, the revitalization committee and town officials are planning to create a community educational and recreational center near Rogers Tavern and build a pier for water taxis. According to Morsicato, the goal is to eventually create a mixed-use downtown and a waterfront with promenades and restaurants so that people will want to come downtown for recreation and entertainment. The greenway will be an integral part of these Live and Visit scenarios. The Work scenario is being addressed by an event that was unrelated to the students' report. In 2000 the state, Cecil County, and the town were able to attract IKEA to build a 1.7-million-square-foot warehouse and distribution center on the Firestone Plastics site, made possible by construction of an access road to Route 40.

The draft zoning ordinance complements the mission of the revitalization committee and incorporates many of the student's recommendations, including the creation of a new, mixed-use zone for downtown. The draft ordinance has a new Town Center Mixed Use Zone that incorporates the students' design guidelines and standards for parking, street lighting, and street furniture. Other features of the draft ordinance include bed-and-breakfast facilities as a conditional use in some zones, landscaping and open-space requirements for residential developments outside of the downtown, and support for planned unit developments.

The students had suggested that the town create an annexation declaration, clearly defining what kinds of land uses would be considered for additions to the town. This recommendation has been rendered moot for the time being because the town is nearing capacity use of its water and sewer treatment plants and is targeting its remaining capacity for infill development, especially in the old downtown. The report recommended that the town develop a long-range plan for water and sewer needs based on population growth projections, but the town has yet to begin planning for longer-term services.

Other recommended actions that have not been taken by the town include hiring a town planner and a code enforcement officer; adopting an adequate public facilities ordinance; improving town entry signage at key locations; creating an economic development plan and utilizing various kinds of tools (such as tax-increment financing) to finance site improvement in specific revitalization areas; and strengthening code enforcement. Most of these recommendations have not been adopted because of insufficient funds or because town officials are preoccupied with other issues.

Key informants identify four reasons for the studio report's utility. First, the report did contain some new ideas. As one planning commissioner stated, "The ideas that the students added to our vision were invaluable, because they thought of things we hadn't considered." Second, and probably more important than offering new suggestions, the report consolidated a number of smart growth–related ideas that either had been contained in earlier reports or had been proposed previously by others in the town. As a result, it was a resource for citizens who already had an interest in the town's growing in a "smart" manner. Rather than being a revolutionary document, said Cecil County planner Anthony DiGiacomo, the report "gave momentum to smart growth ideas by putting them into clear form and at a good time." Third, the concepts in the report have given additional legitimacy to initiatives by the town's present and former administrators. Morsicato, who has been town administrator since 2001, states:

> When I got here it was one of the first documents I read. I can't measure it, but I fall back on the report as a resource more than any other document. We use it a lot as a reference. It legitimizes some of our proposals, gives us backup support.

Morsicato says that he has used concepts in the report for every grant proposal he sends out, including one that obtained funds to purchase property on the waterfront for the planned community activities center. Fourth, perhaps the most immediately utilized component of the studio report was the table of sources for technical assistance and funding, and the accompanying appendix with descriptions and contact information. Sharon Weygand says that this part of the report was a godsend: "For me, being new [in the town administrator's job], I didn't know all the agencies to contact. I kept the report in my notebook as a resource." The Maryland Department of Planning, in its instructional guide for local governments, *Revisiting the Comprehensive Plan: The Six Year Review* (2000), has a resource directory that concludes with a note that some of the information in the directory was derived from the 1999 studio report.

Student Reactions to the Studio Experience

In addition to interviewing key informants about the impact of the Perryville studio, the author e-mailed several of the participating students to inquire about the greatest challenges for them in conducting the study and the degree to which the studio experience shaped their professional careers. The students identified two closely related challenges: obtaining the information crucial for their study and producing the report within a relatively short time frame; and learning to work effectively as a team. One student wrote: "The greatest challenge in doing the studio was having only three months to do it, and with no prior knowledge of Perryville. In that short amount of time we were charged with the task of understanding exactly what was happening in the town in order to develop scenarios for the town's future." Another student wrote of his difficulty in getting timely cooperation from some state and county officials who could provide information about various capital improvement projects slated for Perryville and surrounding areas.

The challenge of learning to work effectively as a team was underscored by every student contacted. The following comments from two of the students nicely recall a group dynamic.

> I recall that the biggest challenge was getting consensus among the members of our group on how the studio project should work, how far we should go in our recommendations, and [what] was realistic to expect as an outcome. We all brought different expertise, personalities and assumptions to the process. . . . While this was technically "just an academic project" . . . we were all pretty passionate about it and really cared about the outcome.

> As with any team working on a tight schedule, it was important to try to be as efficient as possible, while maintaining a high level of quality by capitalizing on the team's assets and overcoming individual shortcomings. Unfortunately, but not unpredictably, this did not always occur for a number of reasons, not the least of which were different expectations, standards and approaches.

Many of the participating students indicated that the studio experience has had an impact on their careers.

> It was a great benefit being able to relate this real-world experience to my professional planning career in Florida. I can better understand the challenges of managing growth, and that has helped me as a planner for a small city near Orlando, Florida. Like Perryville, my city is finding it difficult to redevelop the downtown and utilize historic resources, the land development code needs to be updated and development decisions are often affected by small town politics.

> I really enjoyed the intensity and creativity of the studio. I also liked working on the local level with a great team and with the multidisciplinary, problem-solving nature of smart growth. . . . [I am] lucky enough to continue work in the field of smart growth, albeit on a broader national scale [with a national organization]. What I like about my job is basically what I like about smart growth: it makes sense, it makes communities more livable, and it's a complex, challenging issue.

> Since working on the Perryville studio team I have been on a number of multidisciplinary teams in my professional career in various capacities—member, facilitator, resource. Each time I am reminded of my experience with the Perryville studio and am better able to anticipate these types of challenges.
>
> In Perryville there were a number of key individuals who provided invaluable information unavailable from any other source. In my [current] work as a consultant to local governments, it is interesting to discover in each new community that there are usually a handful of people with a vast knowledge of the community's history, politics and economics, just as in Perryville. As an outsider to the community—as a member of a student studio or as a consultant—it is essential to find those key individuals. At the same time the studio highlighted the value of verifying and validating information. This has been an invaluable lesson and has been reinforced in my professional career time and again.

Lessons Learned

The experience of the 1999 summer studio suggests that a semester-long, community planning studio is not only a valuable learning experience for students but also a viable way for the university to provide smart growth–related assistance to a jurisdiction. In the Perryville case, however, the reason for the project's impact is that there were, and still are, town officials and activists who are very interested in applying smart growth principles in local planning. These stakeholders greatly appreciated having a group of bright, conscientious students take a fresh look at the town's past and present planning actions and their future options. As a result of town elections and changes in planning and zoning commission appointments, it is conceivable that, over time, the studio report will be forgotten should smart growth lose favor among the local electorate.

Even if those committed to smart growth retain influential positions in Perryville, it would be valuable for both the town and the university to have a follow-up planning studio by the year 2006. The purpose would be to examine growth patterns in the town since 1999, determine reasons for such trends, and make refreshed recommendations to the town, county, and state. The students would have the intellectual exercise of figuring out what smart growth planning and policy changes have and have not occurred since 1999 and why. Town, county, and state stakeholders would again benefit from getting feedback from a group of intelligent outside observers with focused vision. This follow-up should be a standard practice for any smart growth studio.

The recommendation begs the question, though, of what kind of assistance the university offers in the interim years. After all, students graduate and faculty members move on to other projects, so there is a loss of continuity once the report is given to the jurisdiction. The answer to the question will have to be the product of ad hoc negotiations between the university and the jurisdiction. Where appropriate, assistance could be offered by other units in the university. For example, in early 2003 Eric Morsicato inquired about additional assistance from the University of Maryland with design issues related to Perryville's community facilities planned for the old town waterfront. As a result of his request, the University of Maryland's architecture program chose Perryville as the focus for its spring 2004 senior student studio course.

Some recommendations in the 1999 studio report called on the state of Maryland to increase the amount of technical assistance given to local governments in their smart growth planning and implementation. Should budget constraints continue to limit the amount of the Maryland Department of Planning's provision of such assistance, the university planning programs could be called upon to help meet the need. The Perryville studio experience strongly suggests that such assistance can be richly beneficial to both students and community stakeholders.

Note

1. See Cohen 2002 for a discussion of each of the initial five programs along with more recently passed Smart Growth programs.

References

Ames, Steven. 1998. *A guide to community visioning: Hands-on information for local communities.* Chicago: APA Planners Press.

Cohen, James R. 2002. Maryland's "smart growth": Using incentives to combat sprawl. In *Urban sprawl: Causes, consequences and policy responses*, Gregory D. Squires, ed., 293–324. Washington, DC: Urban Institute Press.

Cohen, James R., and Amy McAbee Cummings. 1998. A case study of local government response to the Maryland Economic Development, Resource Protection and Planning Act of 1992. Paper presented at the Association of Collegiate Schools of Planning Conference, Pasadena, CA, November 5.

Daniels, Thomas, John Keller, and Mark Lapping. 1995. *The small town planning handbook.* Chicago: APA Planners Press.

LDR International, Inc. 1998. *A vision for the future: Development opportunities and enhancement concepts for Old Town.* Prepared for the Town of Perryville, MD (March).

Maryland Department of Planning. 2000. *Revisiting the comprehensive plan: The six year review* (June).

———. 2003. www.mdp.state.md.us/smartintro.htm.

2

Freeway Demolition on the Road to Smart Growth: A University-Community Partnership for Infill and Economic Development

Michael J. Greenwald and Nancy Frank

On June 5, 2002, the freeway running east along the northern border of downtown Milwaukee was closed. Typically, a highway construction closure in June is nothing extraordinary for Milwaukee—a place where freeway closures are considered a harbinger of spring. This time, however, was to be different—the freeway would never reopen. Instead, it would be demolished, and the land under the right of way would be reclaimed for downtown redevelopment.

Peter Park of the University of Wisconsin–Milwaukee presented the idea of removing freeway segments in downtown Milwaukee for his 1995 spring semester urban planning studio course. The idea seemed audacious when introduced at an urban planning faculty meeting. While the faculty expressed differing views of the feasibility of removing the freeway, they agreed that the proposed studio offered a number of elements that make a successful studio project. It posed an important question of public policy, which was likely to be politically controversial, and it offered an opportunity to broaden students' understanding of urban issues and alternative ways to deal with them.

That studio ultimately led to an ongoing collaboration between the School of Architecture and Urban Planning (SARUP) at the University of Wisconsin–Milwaukee (UWM) and the city of Milwaukee. This collaboration culminated in June 2002 with the demolition of the Park East freeway as one element in a larger mixed-use downtown redevelopment plan. The Park East redevelopment will invigorate Milwaukee's downtown by reconnecting it to adjacent neighborhoods and creating an exciting new neighborhood along a neglected stretch of riverfront. The redevelopment plan expands residential choice in the Milwaukee metro area and brings opportunities for more balanced growth to the region.

This case study documents how a partnership between the university and the community allowed a planner-scholar to explore a major change to the infrastructure and physical form of Milwaukee's downtown, exemplifying two important principles for smart growth. First, history is not destiny; urban form can be redefined into more efficient patterns. Second, universities can serve an invaluable role as laboratories for experimenting with physical design and policy concepts for achieving smart growth goals. Such experimentation will, in turn, improve the quality of strategies that are implemented (Carruthers 2002).

The Issue

From the mid-1930s through the 1940s, cities across the country undertook studies to investigate whether the construction of freeways might benefit declining downtowns (Fogleson 2001, 249–82).

> The freeways, the experts claimed, would stimulate residential dispersal, allowing even Americans of modest means to live in the suburbs. But they would also encourage the centralization of business. By providing uninterrupted movement from the periphery to the center, by relieving traffic congestion and thereby enhancing downtown's accessibility, they would anchor the central business district. (Fogleson 2001, 273)

In 1946 Milwaukee joined the growing number of cities proposing to build freeways to and through the downtown. From the start, traffic engineers in Milwaukee envisioned a system encircling downtown. The plan that unfolded over the next two decades proposed the creation of Interstate 794, skirting the city's south side, while the Park East freeway would skirt the north side. Each spur would connect to the Lake freeway running north and south from downtown along the Lake Michigan shoreline (Figure 2.1). Connecting the Lake freeway to the Park East would have completed the downtown loop (Gurda 1999, 332).

As the name might imply, the Park East was intended to connect to a segment called the Park West freeway. Starting at the connection with Interstate 43 (the north-south freeway to the west of Milwaukee's downtown), moving northwest and beyond the boundaries shown in Figure 2.1, the purpose of the Park West was to link downtown to the suburbs emerging along the northwest side of Milwaukee County. Construction began on the freeway in 1952, even while plans for the complete system were still on the drawing

Figure 2.1 **Multisegment downtown loop freeway system for Milwaukee by 1990, as proposed in 1965 by the Southeast Wisconsin Regional Planning Commission**

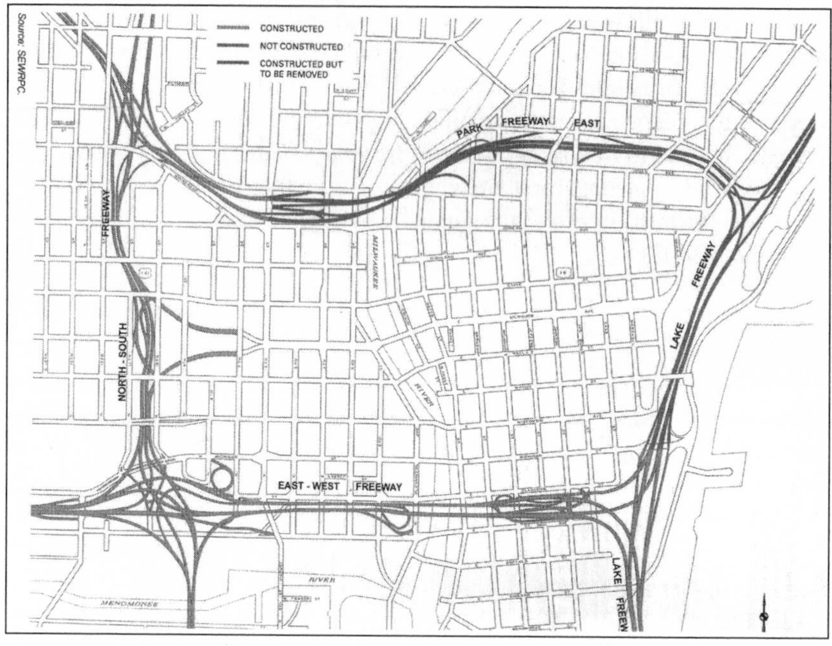

Source: Southeast Wisconsin Regional Planning Commission, in Cutler (2001). Used by permission.

board. As the initial phase of the downtown loop, the Park East freeway was completed in 1968.

Whether the traffic engineers' vision for downtown was ever the right vision became a moot point shortly after construction on the system began. Starting in 1965, strong public antipathy mounted against freeway development in general in the Milwaukee area (Cutler 2001, 70). Opponents were troubled by the disruption of traditional neighborhoods that the highway construction entailed. In addition, the Lake freeway was resisted for its likely negative impacts on Milwaukee's lakefront—as well as real estate values in the affluent neighborhoods along the bluff overlooking the lake. In 1971 an environmental attorney obtained a court injunction against construction of the Lake freeway on the grounds that the proposed right of way was on deed-restricted parkland; the Wisconsin Supreme Court upheld the injunction in 1973, ending the Lake freeway project (Cutler 2001, 76).

Almost immediately after the Lake freeway plan ended, the Park West also was challenged. In 1977 the U.S. Department of Transportation found the environmental statement deficient and refused to proceed any further with the venture (Cutler 2001, 89). Following the cancellation of these two projects, the I-794 and Park East freeways survived, but with little purpose. Neither facility carried anything near its engineered capacity, essentially functioning as mile-long off-ramps to the downtown. Built as elevated highways with three or more lanes in each direction, both spurs dramatically altered the connection between the downtown business district and nearby residential and commercial areas. A block-wide swath beneath the elevated spans lay fallow except for mostly underutilized parking lots.

Beginning in the 1980s the neighborhoods lying just beyond the freeway spurs experienced a resurgence of investment. However, the redevelopment of those areas was clearly in spite of, rather than because of, their proximity to I-794 and the Park East freeway. South of downtown and cut off from it by I-794, the Third Ward emerged during the 1980s as an area of loft condos, galleries, restaurants, and design firms occupying old warehouses in this historic industrial district. Somewhat later and on the other side of downtown, just to the north of the Park East freeway, Schlitz Park evolved into a successful adaptive reuse project that transformed the former Schlitz Brewery buildings into offices and condos. But all of this new investment was separated from downtown by the leftover freeway spurs. Thus, the continued presence of the Park East and I-794 freeway segments appeared to some planners and political leaders as the antithesis of smart growth. The freeway remnants had been highly disruptive to the urban fabric, resulting in lost tax base within the right of way, declining property values adjacent to the elevated roadways, and lost opportunities for revitalization.

The Partnership: Program Activity Planning and Collaboration

The partnership between SARUP and city planners working on the Park East freeway project hinged on the practitioner-scholar role of Peter Park in his capacities as both adjunct faculty and the city planning director of Milwaukee. An alumnus of the UWM joint degree program in architecture and urban planning, Park served as a bridge between the urban planning program and the city in relation to this important planning initiative. After receiving his dual master's degrees in 1991, Park joined a local planning and design firm founded by his mentor at UWM, Larry Witzling. In 1991 Park returned to SARUP as an adjunct faculty member to teach a single course. In 1994 Park was asked to increase his involvement with the university; in addition to teaching a lecture course and a studio each year, Park would spearhead the SARUP urban design program.

The planning faculty, in particular, made a major commitment to Park's association with their program. They appreciated Park's blend of theory and practice in both his professional work and his teaching. Park's preference for using real problems as the basis for course projects was a reflection of his own learning experiences at SARUP.

Studio projects in SARUP arise in two ways: either they are client-driven or they are problem-driven. In client-driven projects, students are presented with their task by a client who gives them an initial problem statement. He or she interacts with the students to refine the problem definition, goals, and values that should guide their solutions. Students are given the opportunity to take on the role of planning consultant and are reminded throughout the process of the real-world constraints within which their solutions must fall. As a result, while client-driven projects give students a healthy dose of urban reality, they may also discourage students from proposing bold solutions.

In contrast, in a problem-driven project, a problem is identified by the instructor and students are given a relatively free hand in designing solutions, without some of the constraints that client-driven problems entail. While problem-driven studios lack the real-world elements of communicating and negotiating with a client, projects that focus exclusively on the problem may allow students greater freedom to explore dramatically novel solutions.

The university-community partnership around planning the Park East freeway removal demonstrates the value of both models of service learning. Initially, the projects were problem-driven, selected by Peter Park from his read of the urban landscape. He presented students with a possible but, at the time, implausible scenario: What if a downtown freeway were removed? While Park provided the creative seed for exploring the potentialities involved in removing the highway, the university offered a protected environment in which the seed could take root.

When removal of the freeway was approved by the city, county, and state in 1999, the studio switched its focus to client-oriented program elements. By then, Park had been appointed to the position of city planning director. His studio then concentrated on translating his vision for the Park East corridor into a regulatory code the city would need to shape redevelopment following demolition of the freeway. Although the city relied on professionals to put together final proposals and drafts, Park used the studio as a way of conducting controlled experiments.

"What would you build," Park asked, "if the development controls looked like this? Is that the quality of development that the city needs in this neighborhood?" Park and his students explored different street configurations and varying densities of development. They asked, "What sorts of uncertainties remain in the development code? Will developers and architects understand the requirements and be able to meet them within a realistic budget? Is the development code too prescriptive, resulting in uninteresting and repetitive developments?" With his students, Park tested different urban design code provisions to ensure they were internally consistent, clear, and understandable in order to assemble a predictable regulatory process. Students explored alternatives to such conventional regulatory techniques as zoning. The urban design guidelines and form-based codes developed in the studios have significantly informed the real-world development code submitted for final approval by the Department of City Development to the Plan Commission and the Milwaukee City Council.

The Planning-Learning Feedback Process

Initially, Park approached the issues of Milwaukee's downtown freeways as academic exercises, at the same time hoping that demonstrations of the redevelopment opportunities that would be set up in the right of way would persuade policy makers to give his ideas serious consideration. Later, when the reality of the demolition was clear, Park's studio shifted to being more client-oriented, with Park serving simultaneously as client and instructor. As Park puts it, "Studios allow me to try out harebrained ideas with students. The 'aha's!' carry through to my work at the city."

Park offered the first of his series of studios on freeway removal in spring 1995, focusing on the I-794 spur. Milwaukee mayor John Norquist had long advocated the demolition of both the I-794 and the Park East freeways as part of a larger, pedestrian-oriented downtown revitalization strategy. During exploration of an alternative downtown site for a new baseball stadium, the possibility of demolishing the Park East freeway received substantial press and planning attention (Nichols 1996; Lamke 1996). It was in this context that Park introduced to a graduate design studio the idea of demolishing I-794. Mayor Norquist and Michael Morgan, the commissioner of city development, attended the students' presentation at the end of the semester. Park's vision for the downtown, as communicated through the students' studio work, was completely consistent with the mayor's own concept as a member of the Congress for the New Urbanism. Later that same year Park was offered a position as city planning director for Milwaukee.

In almost every year since then, Park's studios have focused on removal of Park East freeway and redevelopment of the corridor. Students have compared historic and current figure-ground analyses, examined traffic patterns and traffic counts, and researched historic and current land values. They measured and drew boulevards in the style of Alan Jacobs, showing the width of streets, sidewalks, and curbs and their relationship to the massing of buildings and traffic. They reviewed the literature on Boston, San Francisco, and other cities for precedents of freeway deconstruction. Each year students made models of the existing land use and planned land use, showing conceptual plans for how the downtown might be reconnected to surrounding neighborhoods and how new construction could be integrated into the preexisting street grid.

The studio work significantly influenced the Milwaukee downtown plan. The replacement of the Park East with an at-grade boulevard was one of thirteen catalytic projects recommended in the city's downtown plan adopted in 1999 (ANA Associates 1999, 4). During the preparation of the actual plan, the model that students built of the Park East corridor was moved from UWM to the city offices where consultants for the downtown plan were at work.

Smart Growth Outcomes

The downtown plan proposed increasing the variety and condition of the housing stock, adding to the number of entertainment amenities, and providing travel options to connect various downtown destinations through a variety of modes, with particular emphasis on the pedestrian environment. By recognizing the value of potential infill space in the central city and embracing concepts of pedestrian-oriented development, the plans that have emerged fulfill much of the promise of smart growth. Among the stated objectives of the plan are the following:

- To increase the amount and variety of downtown housing;
- To provide attractive options for travel within downtown;
- To make walking attractive, easier, and convenient;
- To take advantage of the special features found downtown;
- To promote residential, office, and mixed-use development;
- To incorporate the Milwaukee River as a visual feature of this district;
- To extend the RiverWalk in front of the new mixed-use buildings;
- To provide green open space;
- To enhance pedestrian connections across the Milwaukee River;
- To create a predictable regulatory process; and
- To generate consensus among businesses, property owners, residents, and associations.

Together, these objectives explicitly address almost all of the smart growth principles. More indirectly, this large infill project in the heart of Milwaukee will attract development that otherwise might have been located in outlying areas. In theory, more balanced regional expansion should result. In practice, what evidence can be cited to show that this is really happening?

Attracting Development

Twenty-six acres of land previously consigned to the freeway (twenty-three of which are directly in the right-of-way) will become available for development once the city and county of Milwaukee approve the area master plan and renewal plan. The master plan consists of the architectural analyses, street grid design, the identification of environmentally degraded sites within the project area, and the statement of project goals. The renewal plan contains the zoning, conformity with state regulations, and infrastructure improvements. Approval for both plans is anticipated in mid-2004. Planners expect assessed values in the entire sixty-four-acre redevelopment area encompassing the freeway corridor to increase from $58 million today to almost $500 million at build-out. Property in the immediate right of way, however, cannot be sold because it is owned by the federal government, and, therefore, projects cannot proceed until the land is transferred to the county of Milwaukee. This transfer will not take place until the necessary infrastructure improvements (e.g., street grid and sewer trunk line connections and traffic signalization) have been completed (Park 2003a).

Even though this deadline is several years away, the private sector is already pursuing new opportunities for the Park East corridor consistent with the renewal and redevelopment plans. These projects include mixed-use residential, office, and entertainment space. In the largest example to date, Wispark LLC (the property management division of Wisconsin Energy Corporation) and Ferchill Group (a Cleveland-based property developer) in September 2002 purchased the old Pabst Brewery site, located just south of where I-43 will be brought down to grade, for $10.3 million. The developers estimate the value of the project at $300 million (Daykin 2002a). North of the new alignment, along North King Drive, developers have bought a site for $2.15 million (Daykin 2002b). On the east side of the river, Mandel Group (a local condominium developer) has bought the abandoned and heavily contaminated Pfister Vogel tannery (located at the northeast part of the redevelopment area) for $3.4 million; the 560–unit project at that site is anticipated to have a final value of $90 million (Daykin 2002a). While none of these development projects is sited in the abandoned right of way, the removal of the Park East freeway was clearly an important factor in making the projects feasible. Given the developers' demonstrated enthusiasm to locate in areas immediately adjacent to the Park East corridor, demand for development sites within the corridor is likely to be vigorous.

Figure 2.2 **Proposed reconnections with street grid after Park East demolition**

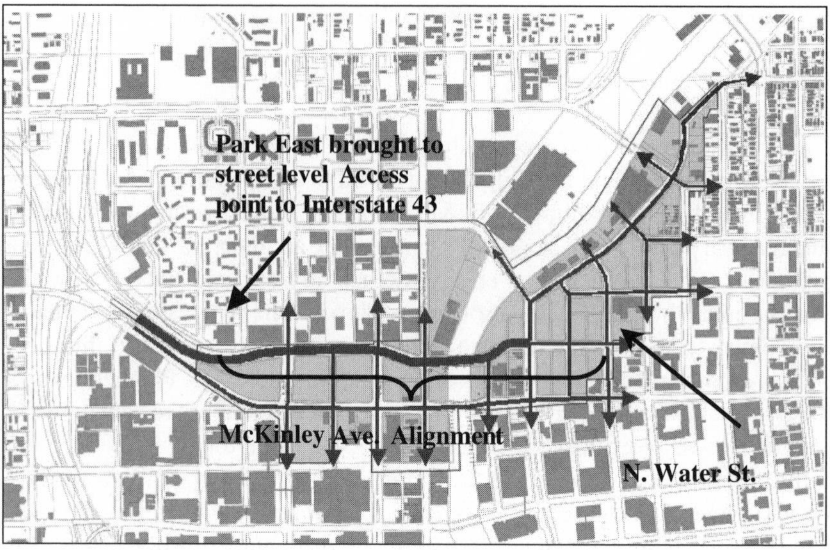

Source: City of Milwaukee, Department of City Development (2002). Used by permission.

Smarter Transportation

An important consideration of the Park East project is how to accommodate vehicle traffic while reconnecting the urban fabric once the freeway is removed. A new street, McKinley Avenue (the heavy line in Figure 2.2), will connect the freeway off-ramp to Water Street, where McKinley will feed into an existing east-west street. McKinley Avenue will need to be a six-lane artery to accommodate the traffic from the old Park East alignment and be populated with traffic signals to effectively integrate the new street into the existing network. Although this expansion will necessarily involve more cars on the downtown surface street system, the Southeast Wisconsin Regional Planning Commission (SEWRPC) stated in 2000 that "no significant change in traffic congestion may be expected." Initial estimates of the Park East removal suggested that travel times from the I-43 interchange into the downtown would increase from one to three minutes, although analysis of the final alignment adopted by Park's studio and the city of Milwaukee anticipated that the delays might be even less (WisDOT 2000; SEWRPC 2000). Such delays are more likely caused by lower speeds and stops for traffic signals on the arterial street that replaces free-flowing highway movement on the Park East, rather than resulting from induced traffic congestion.

Figure 2.3 **Architectural and urban design guidelines for structures in the Park East redevelopment area**

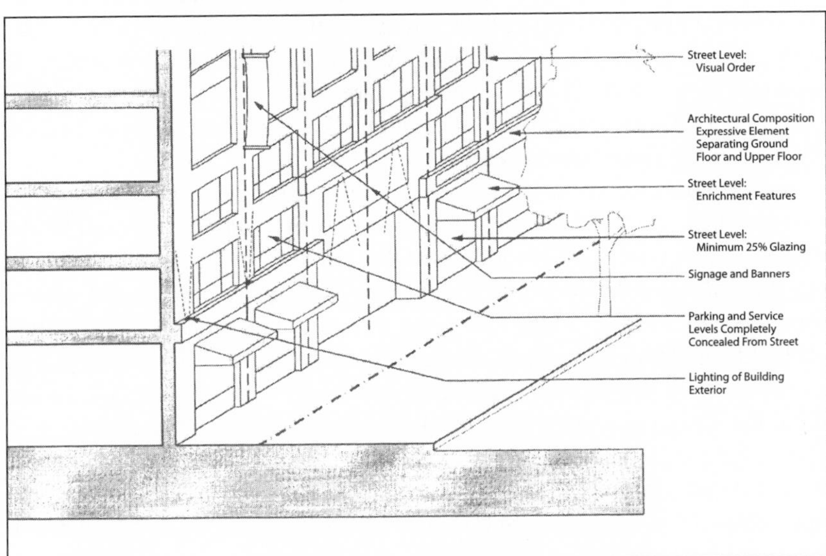

Source: HNTB Corp., Planning and Design Institute, Inc. (2002).

The plan recreates a fine-grained network of streets and blocks that pedestrians easily can move through. Development parcels have been designed to take up half a block, with new alleys inserted mid-block between parcels (City of Milwaukee 2002). In contrast to the pattern observed in many downtown areas, where daytime concentrations of workers are followed by deserted streets once rush hour has passed, the redevelopment plan envisions multiple mixed-use developments with twenty-four-hour activity. Extension of the downtown RiverWalk into the Park East area will provide an additional pedestrian route along the river (ANA Associates 1999, 24). As a result, walking will be a more viable alternative for travel between downtown areas.

The architectural code for the redevelopment area is consistent with Calthorpe's conception of an urban transit-oriented development node, emphasizing high-density, mixed-use development in close proximity to transit, supporting a variety of transportation modes (Calthorpe 1993). To promote the goal of a lively pedestrian realm within the Park East corridor, Peter Park, professional planners, and studio students developed a "form-based" code, as exemplified in Figure 2.3. Elements of the code are designed to enhance the pedestrian experience on the street. For example, the code requires at least 50 percent glazing of building facade (more in some areas), between two and eight feet from the street level (Park 2003a). No exposed parking is permitted within the first three floors. "Expressive elements" are required between the first two floors and the remaining floors to maintain a pedestrian scale, even in areas where buildings may be ten or more stories in height. To maintain a strong street edge, buildings are to be placed on lots in accord with the code's "build-to-line" stipulation. Build-to lines are specified for each lot in the redevelopment area.

An important consideration during the development of the code was whether such a rigorous definition of urban form would be opposed by developers. One way that Park addressed this concern was to have his students not only develop the code but also design buildings in compliance with it. Since 1999 Park has taught the studio in three units. During the first unit each student creates an overall design approach for the redevelopment area or subareas. In the second, each student develops a code that would implement the design approach. And for the third, students exchange codes with one another and each designs a building that meets an assigned construction program that complies with one of the student's codes. As a result, Park has been able to test the market and design feasibility of various code elements and combinations.

According to Park, developers actually welcome specificity in the codes. The high level of detail reduces uncertainty in forecasting what will and will not be approved by the city, which in turn expedites the design and construction process, saving developers time and money. It also helps them respond more quickly to changing market conditions.

Challenges

Despite the many smart growth virtues of the Park East redevelopment concept, the plans are not without critics. Open-space advocates have criticized the plan for reserving an insufficient number of acres for green space. The open-space element of the plan as it currently stands is a hardscaped river walk. Some argue that greater open space will translate into a premium feature for real estate with access to and views of green space. A coalition of community and labor groups has also faulted the plan for failing to require that any of the new residential units be affordable. In response to such criticisms, Park has argued that these issues are best addressed at the implementation rather than planning phase of the project (Park 2003b).

Although planners and city officials invested heavily in public participation to generate the momentum to obtain approval of the freeway demolition, public involvement in the preparation of the redevelopment plan was relatively limited to presentations to key stakeholders, including property and business owners, neighborhood organizations, and governmental bodies. A public open house was held at Milwaukee City Hall in November 2002, attended by roughly two hundred participants, who could view boards and an 18 x 10–foot model of the corridor.

Themes of the UWM–City of Milwaukee Linkages

This case study of the demolition of an urban freeway and its redevelopment into high-density homes, offices, and businesses highlights the role that universities can play in shaping the landscape of our cities. Looking at the relationship between the city of Milwaukee and the University of Wisconsin–Milwaukee suggests several instances that, at first glance, might appear to be unique to the project but in reality speak to larger concepts that must be addressed in any successful university-community collaboration regarding smart growth applied research.

Longevity

As demonstrated by the timeline of events, from Park's first studio to the actual demolition of the Park East freeway, achieving the outcomes described here required long-term commitments from both practicing professionals and the university. Individual faculty or an entire program can commit to work with practitioners on a specific planning area or issue over a period of several years. Such arrangements, however, may be prone to falling apart due to the inherent difficulties of maintaining communication and continuity.

In this case, a long-term connection was made possible by the urban planning faculty's commitment to retaining a planning practitioner on contract as teaching staff. Engaging planning professionals as long-term faculty is one of the surest ways to achieve continuity in a specific planning issue. Park's double role as planning director for the city and practitioner-faculty simplified what otherwise can be the weak link in university-community partnerships—continuous communication and sustained interest over time and over changing studio faculty.

The University as a Protected Environment

Like any land grant university, as part of its mission, UWM serves, as an unbiased venue where scientific approaches and public policy ideas can be studied to their fullest extent. Using university resources to investigate the impacts of Park's ideas on the Park East demolition and redevelopment is entirely consistent with the school's role. The resources and environment of

SARUP allowed ideas to incubate in a way that they could not have in a city planning department, which often is politically charged and budget constrained. SARUP's involvement did not totally eliminate these issues, but it did help minimize them. As Park explains, "What we do at the university helps people understand what the alternatives are. Partnerships with the city, like the work on the Park East, allow university resources to be used to educate the public and decision makers about what good planning and design can do."

The extensive testing and revision of the concepts and implementation codes for the Park East development conducted through the studios could not have happened alone in a traditional partnership between the city planning department and its consultants. Such testing and retesting would be too time-consuming without the aid of several students. As a result, future development in the Park East corridor will proceed in the context of a code explicit enough to provide predictability but without innumerable inconsistencies caused by inadequate pretesting.

The relationship fostered by Park between the city of Milwaukee and SARUP serves as a model for how the research mission of public universities can be incorporated into the smart growth debate. In terms of developing effective smart growth strategies, the creative freedom and associated changes necessary to develop consistent urban design-based public policy is too politically contentious and costly to sustain multiple revisions. Using university resources (both students and facilities) neutralizes some of those concerns.

Defining Success

However successful this collaboration has been, there are limits to what the university can reasonably expect to accomplish in fostering smart growth. While the university provides an environment for students and practitioners to offer their best thinking, implementation remains the prerogative of public agencies and elected officials. Even if recommendations are not adopted, however, such collaborations should not be viewed as failures, so long as the lines of communication between the public agencies and the university remain open.

Conclusion

Peter Park's studio, aside from posing an interesting urban design case study, gave the students the opportunity to creatively address a current public policy issue that, as Park's tenure in the studio continued, became progressively less hypothetical. One of the recurring themes that Park stresses in his studios is the way that changes to public infrastructure can enhance (or—as in the case of a freeway spur through the downtown—degrade) land values. This theme undoubtedly recurs in communities across the country. Although examples of freeway removal are few (the San Francisco Embarcadero freeway damaged by earthquake, Cleveland's freeway removal along the lakefront, and Boston's Central Artery, the "Big Dig," serving as prime examples), many cities have freeway links that are underutilized and might be reconsidered in light of current needs and opportunities.

In the end, the public and local leaders have responded favorably to the ideas developed in Park's studios. The redevelopment plan has been recognized by the Congress for the New Urbanism, garnering the 2003 Award for Excellence, and by the Wisconsin chapter of the American Planning Association, which recognized the plan as the best planning document from a large jurisdiction. If the gold standard for successfully achieving smart growth includes espousing public policies consistent with smart growth and training a new generation of architects, planners, and policy makers to understand the interactions between architecture and policy, then the outcome of Park's collaboration has been good for Milwaukee, for Park's students, and for society at large.

Acknowledgments

The authors would like to thank Peter Park and Allison Rozek for their time and effort in discussing the technical elements of the Park East project with Professor Michael Greenwald. Special thanks go to John Bratina for his valuable help in obtaining the technical documentation that served as the basis for discussing the traffic impacts. Thanks go also to the anonymous referees for their thoughtful and constructive criticism.

References

ANA Associates. 1999. *Milwaukee downtown plan: Catalytic projects.* Princeton, NJ: ANA Associates.

Calthorpe, P. 1993. *The next American metropolis: Ecology, community and the American dream.* New York: Princeton Architectural Press.

Carruthers, J. 2002. Evaluating the effectiveness of regulatory growth management programs: An analytic framework. *Journal of Planning Education and Research* 21(4):391–406.

City of Milwaukee Department of City Development. 2002. City of Milwaukee Park East redevelopment plan. Public meeting. Department of Community Development Building, Milwaukee, August 20.

Congress for the New Urbanism. 2003. *2003 Award of Excellence: Park East redevelopment plan.* Presented at the 11th Congress for the New Urbanism, Washington, DC, June 21.

Cutler, R.W. 2001. *Greater Milwaukee's growing pains 1950–2000: An insider's view*. Milwaukee: Milwaukee County Historical Society.

Daykin, T. 2002a. Developers circle as Park East falls: Boosters insist on value of project despite pullout of Harley Museum. *Milwaukee Journal Sentinel*, November 8, A1.

———. 2002b. Hot properties: Imminent demise of freeway heats up real estate market. *Milwaukee Journal Sentinel*, February 8, D1.

Fogleson, Robert M. 2001. *Downtown: Its rise and fall, 1880–1950.* New Haven: Yale University Press.

Gurda, J. 1999. *The making of Milwaukee.* Milwaukee: Milwaukee County Historical Society.

HNTB, Planning and Design Institute, Inc. 2002. *Park East redevelopment plan, document 3: Regulating plan-working draft.* Milwaukee: HNTB, Planning and Design Institute, Inc.

Lamke, K. 1996. Political, financial pitfalls have littered road to stadium. *Milwaukee Journal Sentinel*, October 6, B3.

Nichols, Mike. 1996. Downtown stadium fits Norquist vision. *Milwaukee Journal Sentinel*, April 11, B2.

Park, Peter. 2003a. Telephone interview with Michael Greenwald, October 8.

———. 2003b. Telephone interview with Michael Greenwald, October 7.

Southeast Wisconsin Regional Planning Commission (SEWRPC). 2000. *Staff memorandum: Evaluation of year 2020 traffic impacts of two new potential Sixth Street and Fourth Street termination options for the Park East freeway*. Waukesha: Southeast Wisconsin Regional Planning Commission.

Wisconsin Chapter of the American Planning Association. 2003. Memo to Peter Park regarding 2003 WAPA awards–Park East redevelopment plan, September 23.

Wisconsin Department of Transportation (WisDOT). 2000. *Environmental assessment for Park East freeway (STH 145), Hillside interchange to North Jefferson St., Milwaukee County: Project I.D. 1730–05–00, 1730–06–00, 1730–07–00.* County of Milwaukee: Wisconsin Department of Transportation.

3

Fostering Smart Growth Through Long-term Partnerships: The University of Oregon's Community Planning Workshop

Robert Parker

Oregon has more than thirty-year history in implementing statewide land use planning and growth management policies. Since 1973 the state has required all counties and incorporated cities to develop and adopt comprehensive land use plans and implementing ordinances. While Oregon's land use program includes many smart growth principles, it has also become increasingly complex in the years since it was adopted. Statewide requirements, coupled with economic and demographic changes, have left many Oregon communities without the technical resources to address land use planning and community development issues. The Community Planning Workshop (CPW) provides a bridge between higher education and Oregon communities dealing with land use and smart growth issues.

CPW is an experiential learning program within the Community Service Center at the University of Oregon, Eugene.[1] The CPW is closely affiliated with the Department of Planning, Public Policy, and Management in the School of Architecture and Allied Arts. CPW provides students the opportunity to address planning and public policy problems for clients throughout Oregon. Students in the Master of Community and Regional Planning Program work in teams under the direction of faculty and graduate teaching fellows to develop proposals, conduct research, analyze and evaluate alternatives, and make recommendations for possible solutions to planning problems in rural communities.

CPW's mission is threefold:

1. To provide educational opportunities in applied planning research to university students;

2. To provide professional planning assistance to communities, agencies, and organizations across Oregon; and
3. To provide paid research opportunities for students to help them defray some of the costs of their education.

Communities, agencies, and organizations contract with CPW to receive assistance with such planning and public policy issues as land use planning, community and economic development, economic and market analysis, facility management, tourism, social services, parks and recreation, housing, transportation planning, natural hazards, and energy analysis.

This case study provides an overview of the Community Planning Workshop. It begins with a brief history of the workshop, then describes the relationship of CPW to smart growth principles, the operational structure of the program, and how CPW implements its educational mission. It concludes with a consideration of lessons learned about university-community partnerships.

The History of the Community Planning Workshop

CPW has completed more than 250 projects for local governments, state agencies, nonprofits, and private businesses. Established in the early 1970s, CPW engages small teams of students, under faculty supervision, in community service projects. The program has a dual-mission: community service and education.

The first community service project—completed in 1973—produced *Activities of Statewide Significance,* a document that evaluated what might happen if Senate Bill 100 (the landmark land use planning legislation in Oregon) did not pass. In the early years projects were driven largely by faculty interests and the market: CPW worked with communities that had financial resources to support their projects. Early projects focused on energy resources, economic development, and tourism. In the late 1970s and early 1980s, though, CPW began expanding its interests.

CPW started an era of evolution in the late 1980s and early 1990s with a grant from the Fund for Improvement of Post-Secondary Education (FIPSE) through the U.S. Department of Education. The FIPSE grant helped fund the first CPW graduate teaching fellows (GTFs), who provided research and project management assistance. In 1990 CPW hired two full-time staff members, enabling CPW to expand its service areas and add a course specifically tailored to training students in project management. By 1995 CPW had six full-time staff members and was completing up to twenty projects each year. It also expanded and shifted the focus of services it provided between 1990 and 1995—completing larger and more complex projects that concentrated on land use, transportation, housing, and other social issues.

CPW and Smart Growth

The Oregon land use program is widely recognized for its commitment to statewide land use planning (Knapp and Nelson 1992; Abbott, Howe, and Adler 1994; Diamond and Noonan 1996). Recent efforts by the state's Department of Land Conservation and Development (DLCD) and the Transportation and Growth Management (TGM) program[2] have focused on development within urban growth boundaries (UGBs). These state agencies have pressed cities to adopt and implement smart growth principles.[3]

CPW, in partnership with the DLCD and TGM program, has worked with Oregon communities for more than ten years on many issues related to smart growth, ranging from land use plans that incorporate smart growth principles to economic development projections. For example, in 2001 CPW completed an update of the city of Eagle Point's comprehensive plan. Eagle Point is a small community (population six thousand in 2002) that grew more than 10 percent annually in the late 1990s and had more than two thousand vacant platted lots. CPW spent time with Eagle Point staff discussing such smart growth concepts as connectivity, mixed-use development, pedestrian linkages, and parks and open space. Many of these elements were included in the draft land use policies CPW developed for the city.

In 2003 CPW conducted a series of outreach meetings with planning commissions on the issue of smart growth. During the meetings planning commissioners were asked, first, whether they were familiar with the term *smart growth,* and second, what it meant to them. More than half of the planning commissioners had not heard the term, even though CPW was able to identify local developments that incorporated one or more smart growth principles in every community.

These examples underscore CPW's approach to applying smart growth principles in planning projects for Oregon communities. Moreover, CPW leverages contact with small communities through education and capacity building.

Implementing the Vision: The Structure of CPW

CPW's years of work with Oregon communities have yielded a wealth of understanding about the dynamics of developing and maintaining successful university-community partnerships. The CPW model is unique in many respects, but is transferable to any institution that wishes to link pedagogy with community service. Moving from a vision to a successful, sustainable program, however, is a substantial challenge that requires commitment and persistence.

Project Selection and Market Areas

A good starting point for this discussion is how CPW develops projects and determines which are appropriate. CPW historically has focused resources on rural Oregon communities for two reasons: (1) that is the area of greatest unmet need; and (2) those are communities that are least likely to have resources to hire consultants. In short, CPW identified a key market (rural Oregon) and implemented a series of strategies to build that market.

CPW operates on a twelve-month calendar that corresponds closely with the state of Oregon's fiscal year (July–June). While CPW is a year-round program, it operates in two cycles: the CPW class cycle that runs from January through June, and the summer/fall cycle that runs from July through December. One of the biggest challenges of managing the CPW is developing four to six appropriate projects for the required-course portion. The projects are for the class cycle that begins in January, and they should be completed in June. This project development phase can last anywhere from a few weeks to a year, depending on both the project and the client, and, thus, is a continuous process.

With respect to selecting projects, CPW applies a few basic rules:

1. *Projects must result in meaningful community service.* All CPW projects involve clients that are facing pressing planning issues. CPW prefers projects that will result in positive community change, thus, it largely conducts applied research rather than basic research.
2. *Projects must have a multifaceted methodology.* Projects that rely on a single research tool such as a household survey do not provide an adequate educational experience for graduate students. Minimum requirements for CPW projects are primary and secondary research, data analysis, client interaction, public meetings or focus groups, report writing, and oral presentations.
3. *Projects must be within the capabilities of faculty and students.* An obvious criterion, projects must be developed inside the participants' core area(s) of expertise. For example, CPW faculty and students do not have the capability to engage in such activities as botanical inventories, wetland delineation, and habitat assessments.
4. *Projects should enhance organizational capacity by partnering.* At the University of Oregon, CPW has partnerships with the

Infographics Lab (a program that specializes in geographic information systems), the landscape architecture program, and the environmental studies program. CPW also has partnered with state agencies, councils of government, and private consultants.

5. *Projects should address a range of topics.* CPW strives to develop projects that focus on multiple issues and provide students with a range of experiences. Many of the topical areas are selected because they represent emerging concepts within the practice—including principles of smart growth.

In summary, the types of projects that are most appropriate as service-learning experiences for graduate students in planning involve labor-intensive data collection and analysis. Focusing marketing efforts in areas that typically are overlooked by consultants can be fruitful in developing ongoing partnerships. Many partners are skeptical that academic programs can deliver useful products; therefore, establishing a track record of successful, high-quality projects is imperative in developing a sustainable program.

Staffing and Organizational Structure

The organizational and operational structure of CPW derives from its history as the required practicum of first-year graduate students in the community and regional planning program at the University of Oregon. It is the result of years of experimentation with approaches that yield a sound educational experience while providing professional-quality products to clients. The program uses an internal organization similar to many private consulting firms.

In 2003 CPW's staff consisted of a full-time program director, a full-time equivalent (FTE) planner, a grant administrator who also works with other programs within the Community Service Center, and a quarter-time FTE graphic designer. CPW also employs three to five graduate teaching fellows during the academic year (September–June). The number of student researchers typically ranges from eighteen to twenty-six and is determined largely by the number of students accepted to the community and regional planning program. Depending on the types of projects, CPW may recruit students from public administration, landscape architecture, environmental studies, and other graduate programs.

Each staff position plays an integral role in day-to-day operations. The program director is responsible for overall program administration, project development, quality control, and class activities. GTFs manage the day-to-day activities of student teams and serve as project managers. GTFs spend the

Table 3.1

CPW staff and faculty responsibilities

Position	Number of staff	Staffing level (full-time equivalents)	Role(s)
Program director	1	1.0	Program administration; project development; client relations; partnership development; budgeting; quality control; class sessions; student mentorship
Planner	1	0.5	Project development; project management; assistance with class sessions; student mentorship
Grant administrator	1	0.3	Accounting; proposal processing; fiscal analysis; budgeting
Graphic designer	1	0.25	Report and presentation graphics; document layout; design assistance to student researchers
Graduate teaching fellow	3–5	0.4	Project management; client relations; management of student researchers
Student researcher	18–26	0.25	Research; data analysis; report writing; client and public presentations

fall term participating in a project management seminar with the CPW director and assisting with project development.

To leverage limited resources and provide a sound learning environment, CPW uses a team approach to completing projects. The first-year graduate students are placed in teams of four to six and are assigned a specific project for the period from January through June. The teams work on all aspects of their projects from start to finish. Table 3.1 summarizes the responsibility of CPW faculty and students.

It is notable that the current CPW program director is not a tenure-track faculty member but rather is a practitioner with considerable experience in the consulting realm. From a programmatic standpoint, this has several advantages: the program director manages the financial elements of the program like a business; the students in the workshop not only gain practical experience on projects but get hands-on direction from a seasoned practitioner; and the presence of a practitioner on faculty complements the more academically oriented tenure-track faculty.

Funding

Funding university-community partnerships is a challenge. Projects cost money, and community partners should not expect to receive services without some type of financial commitment. While there are many approaches to funding such programs, CPW has used some creative funding tools.

The annual operating budget is approximately $250,000, with about $50,000 in direct support from the University of Oregon through three graduate teaching fellowships and a small amount of support for the class portion of CPW. Thus, CPW is largely dependent on soft money (e.g., grants and contracts). Its financial strategy has been one of diversification, based on partnerships with state and local governments. CPW staff has invested considerable effort in developing long-term partnerships with government agencies that have planning functions. These partnerships provide a diverse funding base and some stability to CPW operations and are essential in project development. CPW will not respond to Requests for Proposals unless specifically solicited—a policy that was established in the early 1990s after a consultant suggested that CPW unfairly competes with the private sector.

CPW also relies heavily on intergovernmental agreements. Such agreements do not differ substantially from those that local governments enter into with private contractors, with one key exception: in Oregon local governments can establish agreements without going through a formal bid process. This can substantially reduce the administrative burden on the local government and the university.

One of the unanticipated outcomes of operating over a long period of time is the large number of program graduates that go on to practice in Oregon. These former CPW participants recognize the benefits of experiential learning and are very supportive of CPW and its capabilities. Moreover, they provide excellent mentors for students participating in CPW. Since 2000, between 25 and 50 percent of CPW's projects have come directly or indirectly from program alumni. For example, CPW has completed three projects for a single jurisdiction in the past five years and at this writing is about to embark on another; the project proponent in all of these instances was a program graduate.

Institutional Structure

CPW has a unique relationship with the University of Oregon's administration. When the original program director retired in the late 1990s, there was considerable discussion about a successor to direct the Community Service Center and CPW. The staff had years of experience with the programs, but were not tenure-track faculty. Moreover, the significant reliance on soft money and the fiscal instability implicit in such funding required a series of discussions with the university's administration to ensure the program's continued sound management. Complicating these discussions was CPW's strong ties with the School of Architecture and Allied Arts (AAA) and the Department of Planning, Public Policy, and Management (PPPM). Because it is a required course in an accredited planning program, the AAA dean and the PPPM department chair felt that they needed some level of oversight of the program.

The management issue became clearer with the formal establishment of the Community Service Center, which acts as the umbrella organization for CPW. Research centers at the University of Oregon are typically independent from academic programs in most respects. The direct supervisor of the research centers is the vice president for Research and Graduate Studies. This administrative structure, however, did not fully address the concerns voiced by the AAA dean and the PPPM department chair.

The solution was a memorandum of understanding that was signed by all of the affected parties as a binding agreement. The memorandum defined the roles of the various players and how CPW would interact with those players. The key provision is that CPW reports to the vice president for Research and Graduate Studies on research and fiscal issues—including proposal review—and to the AAA dean and PPPM department chair on academic issues.

Leveraging Limited Resources: The Power of Partnerships

A key factor contributing to CPW's success is the many partnerships it has developed and maintained over the years, including those with campus organizations, state agencies, local governments, professional organizations—and with students and faculty. The partnerships shown in Figure 3.1 are central to CPW's mission and operations, but the graphic does not fully convey the complexity of the partnerships. In many respects, CPW serves as a catalyst for creating partnerships that occur at several levels and do not necessarily have to include CPW.

Because partnerships are pivotal to the success of CPW, it is worth describing them in more detail.

State Government

State government agencies are obvious targets for partnerships. They work across jurisdictions and frequently have access to funding sources that are not available at the local level. Moreover, many state agencies have grant programs that may be accessible to universities. CPW has sustained partner-

Figure 3.1 **Organizational partnerships of the Community Planning Workshop**

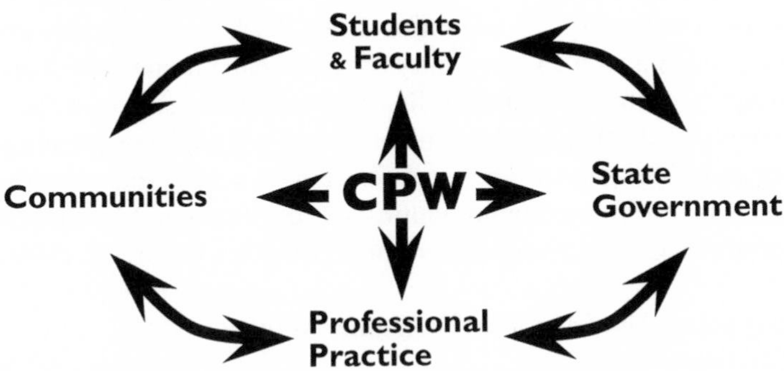

ships with several Oregon state agencies, including the Department of Land Conservation and Development (DLCD), Housing and Community Services (HCS), Economic and Community Development (ECD), and the Office of Energy (OOE). The most prominent relationship is with the DLCD, which oversees the statewide land use planning program. It has been a major player in CPW's efforts to promote smart growth principles. CPW has completed several projects for the DLCD or with DLCD grant funds. Partnerships with state agencies can provide more than project funding. For example, the Oregon Department of Housing and Community Services shared a high-level program executive with the Community Service Center for a period of three years.

Communities and Professional Practice

Communities are the foundation of CPW's partnerships. The number of communities and the range of planning and public policy issues faced by them demonstrate their natural linkage. CPW focuses on partnerships with rural communities because they tend to have fewer staff and financial and technical resources to address local issues.

CPW also has partnerships with practitioners. CPW does not generally compete with practitioners and consulting organizations; it has collaborated with consultants on several occasions, which can be particularly rewarding. Students get the opportunity to interact with practitioners, while practitioners get affordable support on labor-intensive activities. CPW serves as a subcontractor in most partnerships with private consultants. University administrative policies can make such collaborations difficult—particularly if the university takes the role of prime contractor. Moreover, university policies on overhead, billing, and accounting all make financial management more difficult.

Faculty and Students

CPW has a unique set of institutional relationships. It operates as one of several programs in the Community Service Center at the University of Oregon, and is a required course for first-year graduate students in the community and regional planning program run by the Department of Planning, Public Policy, and Management. These relationships benefit both students and faculty, as well as offer rich opportunities for collaboration. Moreover, campus organizations present ample opportunities for service learning projects.

Coping with a Dual Mission: Engaging Students in Service Learning

A prominent challenge of managing a service-learning program is coping with the dual mission of providing a sound educational experience to students and quality products to clients. The issue here is how to manage a group of eager—but relatively inexperienced—students to complete projects that in some instances are quite complex. The answer lies in building upon the theoretical framework of service learning and adding a healthy amount of personal experience. From a pedagogical perspective, service learning should focus more on the process than the topic. This has been a key axiom for CPW over the years and is reflected in the course syllabus:

> Completing one project in a six-month period will not teach you all there is to know about a specific aspect of planning. In other words, don't expect CPW to make you an expert in a specific area of planning. In our experience, it is the process of completing the project that is most instructive; the topic is of lesser importance.

This can be a tough sell to students, many of whom come to graduate programs with specific academic and professional objectives. Despite repeated reinforcement by CPW faculty that the process is more important than the topic, it is not uncommon for as many as half the students to select one project as their top choice.

Because of the unique structure of CPW—with paying clients that expect professional results—the balance between the pedagogical objectives and the practicality of getting projects done is challenging. Observations of students in CPW suggest that learning occurs at many levels (see Figure 3.2), each of which provides rich lessons. Many lessons, such as facilitating a public meeting, are fairly obvious, while others are much more subtle. For example, students can learn some important things about project management and

Figure 3.2 **Learning relationships at the Community Planning Workshop**

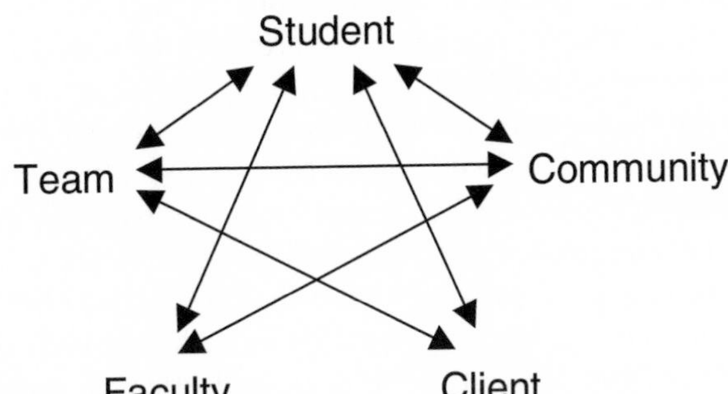

interpersonal relations from faculty and GTFs; such lessons may not be obvious, however, unless they are pointed out. Sharing the rationale for why certain decisions were made becomes an important part of the educational experience.

These interactions also provide a fertile environment for discussing the promise of planning theory and the realities of planning practice. Because CPW projects always involve paying clients with contracts, the degrees of freedom for what a team produces and how it is produced are significantly diminished. Timelines and budgets may preclude using innovative planning tools; clients may desire products that are not the appropriate ones; and clients have expectations for quality and performance. While some of these issues can be and often are negotiated in the development phase, project development almost always occurs before the student research team is assembled. Thus, students are confronted with a work program that typically provides a general description of methods and products, but does not always set out a detailed rationale for them. Student-faculty discussions about these issues offer excellent opportunities for reflection on planning theory and practice.

The Reality of Managing Student Researchers: It's Hard Work!

CPW is occasionally criticized for unfairly competing with the private sector. What the private sector does not realize is that a great amount of effort is required to teach students the skills necessary to complete a project. Most who enroll in CPW have never worked on a project with the components and complexity of the typical CPW project. Managing students presents many challenges—some of which are predictable and others that are not. In short, even graduate students behave like students—they are confronted with multiple priorities and will make personal decisions that may be in their best interest but not in the project's best interest.

CPW uses a tiered approach to managing students. Four to six students work in a team, with a graduate teaching fellow or staff person assigned as a project manager. Project managers go through a term of training in the fall and meet weekly throughout the year to discuss issues related to their projects and the management of their teams. Each project manager has a faculty adviser, usually the CPW director but occasionally other CPW staff. This tiered approach, combined with applications of basic project management and quality control, keeps students engaged and clients satisfied. CPW uses project management principles described by Moore (1991): manage for time, budget, and quality; aim research immediately and continuously toward a well-defined product; write early and often, in outlines and in standard formats; and document all data and assumptions immediately and completely.

These principles, along with such corollaries as the eight-hour rule (i.e., check in with students on progress for every eight hours of time they invest in the project) and internal deadlines (usually a week or two before actual deadlines), minimize some of the predictable friction points. Students will grow dissatisfied if they are not given sufficient direction to complete their tasks, and managers have to check progress constantly to ensure that students are producing useful output. CPW has found interim products to be useful in keeping clients pleased and for ensuring progress on work programs.

Quality control is one of the most difficult components of managing student teams. Again, CPW has used a tiered approach. Students typically work through their report outline and product in a meeting with their manager. A resulting annotated outline gives students the "big picture." Teams are required to present their work program in a class session in the fourth week. While many students do not perceive the broader agenda of these presentations—allowing managers and faculty to gauge their levels of understanding of their projects—the presentations are nevertheless useful exercises in communication skills. Managers debrief teams after the presentation and fill in knowledge gaps. They are also responsible for substantial editing to ensure quality control, since writing skills within a team can vary widely. Written products are given considerable attention and go through at least three rounds of editing—by peers, by the team manager, and ultimately by the CPW director.

Establishing expectations at the outset of service-learning projects is key to maintaining student engagement and ensuring high-quality products. That said, the challenges can bring out the best in students. CPW has seen some truly outstanding student efforts that have been recognized with various awards, including the national 1000 Points of Light award, several student achievement awards from the American Planning Association (APA), as well as from other professional organizations.

Lessons Learned: Practical Advice for Academics and Practitioners

Given CPW's years of university-community partnerships, what practical advice can be offered to academics and practitioners who want to engage in service learning? While one could fill a book with anecdotes about the various projects, successes, failures, and near disasters CPW has experienced, the foundation for success can be distilled into a few main points.

1. *Strong faculty commitment.* University-community partnerships take time and effort. Successful partnerships, particularly those involving students, require faculty commitment. The support that CPW gets from CSC faculty and the faculty in the Department of Planning, Public Policy, and Management are critical to success.
2. *Develop institutional support.* The importance of this point cannot be overemphasized. The literature suggests that academic credit is for learning, not for service (Howard 1993, 5–9). Academics should expect some level of disagreement concerning what types of experiences constitute learning; the ability to articulate the dual mission of service-learning programs to peers and administrators is crucial. Having strong institutional support—at the program level, the department level, the school level, and the administrative level—is essential in developing a successful program.
3. *Establish a niche.* Identify and develop areas of need out in the community and match university resources to those needs. Having several core areas will yield a greater mix of project topics and a richer experience for students.
4. *Understand your capacities.* Developing university-community partnerships that include students imposes inherent limitations. Projects involving complex technical analysis or a deep understanding of policies may not be appropriate for students.
5. *Charge fees for service.* CPW's experience is that many communities will not take complete ownership of projects without some financial stake. A disengaged client diminishes the learning experience and makes project management difficult. The fee structure should be on a cost-recovery basis.
6. *Provide practical results, not academic studies.* Our experience is that communities come with projects that address pressing community needs. This approach is consistent with the "basic policy analysis" approach described by Patton and Sawicki (1993, 52–65). The

applied research and products that communities desire do not preclude the use of results for basic research purposes.

7. *Make sure that your clients are supportive of the educational mission.* Having clients that understand the implications of working with student teams can make the process much more rewarding for students and can lead to better products. Students tend to have more ownership in their work when they perceive that clients value their efforts and are committed to the products.
8. *Establish partnerships.* Long-term partnerships with a variety of organizations will result in a broader range of projects; better relationships between faculty, students, and client groups; and a sustainable flow of work. Partnerships are the foundation that has carried CPW for more than twenty-five years.
9. *Develop diversified funding streams.* Most academic institutions will not be able or willing to fully fund programs like CPW. Developing diversified funding streams relates to the point made earlier on partnerships and will serve to even out cash flow and sustain staffing. Budget forecasting is essential in developing funding streams.
10. *Provide ample quality control.* Programs that engage students will have, at best, a highly motivated but relatively inexperienced labor pool. Expect students to make mistakes, which is a natural part of the learning process. Developing internal quality control systems will help to ensure consistent communication with clients and to avoid embarrassing mistakes or inadequate coping with difficult client or public-meeting situations. Applying Moore's principle of "write early, write often" has proven to be an essential quality control mechanism for CPW.
11. *Manage your time.* It is easy to underestimate the amount of time it takes to manage a service-learning project—much less a program. Faculty will need to develop mechanisms to provide a quality educational experience that includes basic components of thoughtful community service: community voice; orientation and training; meaningful action; reflection; and evaluation (Campus Outreach Opportunity League 1993). Each of these activities takes time and can easily become overwhelming when the project cycle nears the end.
12. *Provide engaging opportunities for students.* CPW faculty and project managers spend considerable meeting time discussing ways to keep students engaged in projects. Programs that involve students do not have the traditional system of rewards that exists in the workplace (good performance is rewarded with more responsibility and more money; poor performance can result in termination). Thus, project managers must find other effective mechanisms to keep students

engaged, such as continuous client contact and public meetings. Activities in the community make the project more "real" to students and result in a higher level of attention.

These are a few of the principles that have contributed to CPW's success. Academic institutions have much to offer communities in terms of applying smart growth principles and making sound planning decisions. Leveraging faculty expertise with student research has proven effective in the CPW university-community partnership. Moreover, the experience students gain through the field-based activities is invaluable as they embark on their planning careers.

Notes

1. The Community Service Center includes several other programs that complement CPW: the Resource Assistance for Rural Environments Program, which places students in communities for a period of one year; the Oregon Natural Hazards Workgroup, which coordinates public and private risk-reduction activities; the Proposal Writing Assistance Program, which provides communities with training and assistance in grant writing; and the Student Originated Studies program, which provides funding to students for thesis projects. See http://darkwing.uoregon.edu/~csco.

2. The Transportation and Growth Management program is jointly sponsored by the Oregon Departments of Land Conservation and Development and Transportation.

3. To that end, DLCD and TGM have developed a substantial library of outreach and technical assistance documents. See http://www.lcd.state.or.us.

References

Abbot, C., D. Howe, and S. Adler. 1994. *Planning the Oregon way: A twenty-year evaluation.* Corvallis: Oregon State University Press.

Campus Outreach Opportunity League. 1993. *Into the streets: Organizing manual, 1993–94 edition.* St. Paul, MN: COOL Press.

Community Planning Workshop. 2001. City of Eagle Point comprehensive plan update. University of Oregon. Unpublished.

———. 2002. DLCD technical assistance and outreach needs assessment. University of Oregon. Unpublished.

———. 2003. Integrating transportation and land use planning: Outreach to planning commissioners. University of Oregon. Unpublished.

Diamond, H.L., and P.F. Noonan. 1996. *Land use in America.* Washington, DC: Island Press.

Howard, J., ed. 1993. *Proaxis I: A faculty casebook on community service learning.* Ann Arbor, MI: OCSL Press.

Knapp, G., and A.C. Nelson. 1992. *The regulated landscape: Lessons on state land use planning in Oregon.* Cambridge, MA: Lincoln Institute of Land Policy.

Moore, T. 1991. A practical guide for managing planning projects. *Journal of the American Planning Association* 57(2):212–223.

Patton, C.V., and D.S. Sawicki. 1993. *Basic methods of policy analysis and planning,* 2nd ed. Englewood Cliffs, NJ: Prentice Hall.

4

Applying Clinical Legal Education to Community Smart Growth: The University of Florida Conservation Clinic

Thomas T. Ankersen and Nicole C. Kibert

The University of Florida Conservation Clinic brings applied legal and graduate education to the service of communities, nonprofit organizations, and individuals seeking to pursue conservation objectives. The Conservation Clinic is one of a growing number of environmental law clinics that has begun to use the policy planning tools of smart growth to address land use and growth management issues in communities. Law schools have long maintained a tradition of judicially sanctioned community service through student representation (under supervision) of underrepresented segments of society. Environmental law clinics arose in the wake of the environmental movement of the 1970s as a means of providing similar services in defense of the environment. Today, clinical environmental legal education has moved beyond the courtroom—and the law school—to offer a broad range of professional services in ways that represent the diversity, maturity—and interdisciplinarity—of this practice area.

The UF Conservation Clinic did not start with a specific mandate to emphasize smart growth and local government law. The legal enabling environment for smart growth in Florida, however, provides an ideal combination of practice and pedagogical opportunities for law clinics. The Conservation Clinic has taken advantage of this ambience to assist rapidly developing Florida communities with designing policy tools that apply principles of smart growth. Since its inception in 1999, the Conservation Clinic has worked with three communities in the formation of downtown redevelopment districts and one brownfield site; designed a community green building program and drafted its implementing ordinance; helped to designate a multijurisdictional heritage highway; drafted a community wetland policy and implementing ordinance requiring local watershed planning; drafted a sustainable tourism policy for a community comprehensive plan; and helped to formulate the legal and planning basis for a community air-quality program. The clinic has also conducted "conservation assessments" of property subsequently acquired for community parkland, helped to create an "ecocemetery," assisted with the creation of a local bond initiative for land acquisition and represented landowners wishing to sell or donate conservation easements over their property.

This chapter presents a brief history of clinical environmental law. It then discusses the UF Conservation Clinic's development in its university and law school setting, and the effect this has had on the nature of this law school clinic and its portfolio. The legal enabling environment for smart growth initiatives in Florida is considered, using selected case studies to illustrate how the clinic has taken advantage of this environment to provide service education.[1] These case studies illustrate aspects of the clinic-client relationship, the importance of the pedagogical feedback loop, issues presented by interdisciplinary professional collaboration, and difficulties inherent in "town-gown" collaboration.

A Brief Overview of Clinical Environmental Law Education

Traditional clinical legal education introduces law students to professional practice under the supervision of a practicing attorney-professor, focusing on litigation skills. In the past, clinical legal education was something of a stepchild of the law school system, which upheld a doctrinaire resistance to practice-oriented pedagogy. That changed in the mid-1990s as a result of a report by the American Bar Association, which grants law school accreditation (Joy 1994), that concluded that skills training should be an integral part of the law school curriculum and that instructors of legal skills should be included in law school faculties and governance. As a result, the number, nature, and diversity of law school clinics have grown.

Environmental law clinics began by following the traditional clinical model of a litigation firm (Gorovitz-Robertson 1998, 268). The first clinics emerged in the West in the late 1970s and focused on litigating under the citizen suit provisions of such newly minted federal environmental legislation as the Clean Water Act, the Clean Air Act, and the Endangered Species Act. Today, there are more than thirty environmental law clinics, nearly half of which were founded since 1995.[2] While the vast majority of these still describe themselves as litigation clinics, many have begun to diversify themselves. Some, like the UF Conservation Clinic, eschew traditional court litigation in favor of advocacy in other forums and other types of professional law and policy service. In addition, interdisciplinary environmental law clinics have emerged, pioneered by the Yale University Clinic, which began in 1994 (Esty 1999, 14). Of the existing environmental law clinics surveyed, four, including the UF Conservation Clinic, describe themselves as interdisciplinary, meaning that graduate students in other fields enroll and form teams with law students to work with clients on cases and/or projects.

Models of environmental law clinic governance vary. Some, such as the UF Conservation Clinic, are in-house clinics in which pedagogy and student representation are centered at the law school and the clinical director is a full-time employee and faculty member. In other examples, clinics are fully or partially supported by nonprofit organizations, often such public interest law groups as Earthjustice, in San Francisco, under whose auspices they operate. In some instances, law schools supply office space while the nonprofit organization provides the attorney, who is appointed to the law faculty as an adjunct or courtesy appointment. Sometimes the office is external to the law school, and students function as interns, with varying degrees of faculty supervision. Some of these permutations have arisen due to political backlash from clinics that take on activities that are unpopular with alumni or political bodies. There are recent and notorious examples of what clinicians call "political interference" at both private and public law schools, including Tulane, the University of Pittsburgh, and the University of Oregon (Kuehn and Joy 2003, 1981–987; Carter 2002, 24). Operating off-site and under the auspices of an independent organization helps to insulate both clinics and law schools from political interference, but no variation, including choosing not to litigate, can guarantee that a law clinic will not be scrutinized.

Clients of environmental law clinics tend to vary as well. Traditional clinics have focused representation on such nonprofit environmental advocacy organizations as the Sierra Club, National Wildlife Federation, Defenders of Wildlife, and their regional, state, and local analogs. With the changing nature of environmental practice, the increased emphasis on interdisciplinarity in legal education and the emergence of land use as a central theme in environmental protection, the variety of potential clients has widened to include the United Nations, local governments, federal agencies, state legislative committees, neighborhood associations, and foreign governmental and nongovernmental organizations. Clinical environmental law education has extended beyond traditional courtroom litigation, which has also dramatically expanded the range of potential clients. The Conservation Clinic, among others, has taken advantage of this development to offer students a wide choice of professional experiences with an increasingly diverse client base. Conservation Clinic clients have included the U.S. Fish and Wildlife Service, governmental agencies in Costa Rica (environment ministry) and Colombia (ombudsman's office), the Florida Marine Research Institute, the West Coast

Inland Navigation District, such Florida cities as Waldo, Sarasota, Flagler Beach, and Marineland, as well as the university's hometown of Gainesville and Alachua County. The clinic also has represented a variety of citizen groups, including neighborhood associations, nonprofit organizations, and individuals pursuing conservation objectives on private lands.

The University of Florida Conservation Clinic: Origins and Development

The UF Conservation Clinic began in 1999 in an effort to further integrate students into the contract- and grant-based work of attorneys at the University of Florida Levin College of Law's Center for Governmental Responsibility, and to create a pedagogical framework for their work. Center lawyers, including the clinic's director, have a long track record of assisting local governments in addressing their requirements under Florida's growth management system and in seeking grants to pursue smart growth initiatives. At the same time, professors in the College of Law and Center attorneys began discussing the need to develop a cohesive environmental law program that would include land use law and legal skills training as core features. This culminated in the creation of the College of Law's Environmental and Land Use Law Certificate Program, which includes a joint degree program with the College of Architecture's Department of Urban and Regional Planning.

These developments coalesced in a decision by the College of Law to establish the Conservation Clinic as a formal part of the college's skills-training curriculum and its environmental and land use program. A portion of the Center's space was given over to the clinic, and the Center's staff lends a hand to clinic projects, including accounting and administrative support. A generous donation from an interested alumnus provided start-up funding, enabling the purchase of office furniture, computers, and supplies.

Interdisciplinarity was enhanced when the University of Florida created a new graduate program in interdisciplinary ecology, to which students interested in policy have gravitated. The Conservation Clinic became a listed elective in the new curriculum and has benefited from the influx of ecology students, who bring such skills as training in geographical information systems technology and landscape architecture. The clinic's place in the law school was further secured by the faculty's decision to offer legal skills professors long-term contracts at the college and to include the Conservation Clinic director's position in this promotion track.

The most significant aspect of these developments has been the clinic director's transition from following a research center model to a law clinic model where students, instead of acting as research assistants, assume the responsibilities of professionals, supervised by a legal skills professor. In addition, the somewhat unique nature of the clinic's practice demands the formation of a distinct pedagogy, something that continues to be developed.

Conservation Clinic Methodology and Pedagogy

Universities run on semesters; the real world does not. This poses a fundamental methodological dilemma for all live client clinics, particularly in environmental litigation, which often is complex and driven by events and dockets that are out of the clinician's control. While courts and even opposing parties are frequently willing to work within the parameters of clinics, cases can lie dormant, explode in the middle of final exams, and otherwise frustrate the efforts of clinicians to assure quality experience.

The nature of the Conservation Clinic projects and clients obviates some of these difficulties, while providing opportunities to develop diverse legal and policy planning skills, as well as skills that are shared among all professions. The clinic's director usually assumes responsibility for initial project identification and assigns students to projects based on their interest and experience.[3] In this way, the clinic has greater control over its project portfolio and can help to shape projects to fit within the academic calendar. Of course, this is an idealized scenario, as factors out of the clinician's, and sometimes the client's, control militate the actual course of events. Students can enroll for one semester or one year and this, too, becomes a significant factor in the project development.

All clinic projects share a common set of requirements. Students must interview the client and prepare a "scope of work" based on the needs of the project. Usually the scope of work takes the form of a signed, contractually binding letter of agreement between the clinic and the client, often negotiated by the student. Ordinarily the project has a significant substantive applied legal and policy research component, and generally includes interdisciplinary research as well. For example, in the case of the heritage highway project, law students teamed up with a landscape architecture studio to prepare an elaborate application packet that included a detailed review of local land use codes as well as a visual quality assessment and historical research. In addition, a project will typically have a policy product of some sort. These vary from a draft of comprehensive plan policies and local ordinances, as in the community wetlands regulation project and green building program, to policy recommendations, as in a statewide study of the impact of locally sanctioned feral cat colonies, predating protected wildlife, and the community watershed planning initiative. Finally, most clinic projects include a formal public or private forum in which students must present their work to the public, the clients, or both. For the heritage highway project, students tested their public facilitation skills at four community meetings and presented the project to the governing bodies of two cities and two counties. For the green building program, two students presented the program they had designed and implementing ordinance they had drafted to the Gainesville City Commission.

In addition to hands-on professional practice, legal education clinics must respond to pedagogical requirements that stem from their nature as centers for professional-skills development. Thus, clinicians must employ educational techniques that are tailored to the skills students are expected to use after graduation. In a traditional litigation clinic this is often done through a short "boot camp" offered at the beginning of the semester, accompanied by practice manuals and courtroom simulations. Guest practitioners may supplement this by offering insights and practice tips. In an interdisciplinary, nonlitigation practice environment like the UF Conservation Clinic, a different set of skills is emphasized, including some that require students to leave behind the bulldog litigator image many have been taught to believe is at the center of their legal education.

The Conservation Clinic has evolved a flexible format that dovetails its pedagogy with its diverse client and project base, and supplements skills training offered elsewhere in the curriculum. Skills taught in class include public facilitation, regulatory and transactional negotiation, legislative drafting and negotiation (e.g., simulated hearings), local government and public agency hearing processes, opinion letter drafting and the provision of rapid professional advice. Multiauthor professional report preparation that integrates text and graphics is another feature of the clinic's skills training. Students often use their clinic reports as writing samples in seeking employment. In addition to teaching these skills, the clinic has experimented with other professional skills activities, including drafting press releases and funding proposals, which are considered extremely important in the nonprofit world. For example, a press release written by a student on the impact of feral cats on the environment yielded statewide media attention, and her report contributed to a significant shift in state policy.

A major reason that the clinic has been successful in developing a smart growth project portfolio is the interdisciplinary nature of many of its project teams. Interdisciplinary practice is a necessary component of creative problem solving, which is crucial for lawyers to meet client needs adequately (Weinstein 1999, 319). Weinstein contends that law schools, due to the attitudes and values of the students the discipline attracts, compounded by pedagogy aimed at emphasizing certain skills, have poorly prepared students whose careers may extend beyond the traditional institutions of the law. The clinic's project teams have included students in landscape architecture, urban and regional planning, business administration, ecology, and economics, who were drawn to the clinic because of its interdisciplinary nature and its effort to integrate science, public policy, and the law. Several graduate students who enrolled in the clinic have gone on to law school.

In order for interdisciplinary teams to function effectively, members must have good communication skills, be able to function in a group setting, and display respect and understanding for members from other disciplines (Weinstein 1999, 327). The Conservation Clinic seeks to prepare students for this practical environment, which is especially important in the context of environmental and land use law.

Some Clinic Smart Growth Projects and Their Legal Context

One of the more striking developments in contemporary environmental law has been the national trend toward local environmental law, a movement that has caught the attention of several leading scholars (Nolan 2002; Tarlock 2003). Local governments are either seizing the initiative to fill gaps in state and federal law, or being enabled by states through the delegation of programs and responsibility. This trend has been complemented by the increasing importance of land use law as the policy basis for environmental protection efforts. Land use has always been the primary province of local government. The confluence of these developments provides a portfolio rich in clinical opportunities at the local level, where university students can take advantage of proximity and access to offer services where they are needed, while at the same time deriving educational benefit. This section describes several clinic projects where local government, land use law, and smart growth tools converge.

Local Government Comprehensive Planning

Florida has one of the most comprehensive growth management programs in the United States. Since 1967 Florida has been a home-rule state, which means the state has delegated broad powers to local governments, including the power to make land use decisions and enact environmental protection ordinances (Sorensen 2002, 7). In the 1970s, however, concern that local governments were not making good development decisions led the state legislature to develop a multitiered growth management system rooted in land use planning (Carter 1976). A series of legislative acts restricted local government home-rule authority over land use planning, creating a growth management system based on state and regional oversight. Each local government is required to have a comprehensive plan, which the courts have interpreted as the community's "land use constitution" (*Machado v. Musgrove*, 519 S0.2d 629, 632 [Fla. 3d DCA 1987]).

The contents of the comprehensive plan are dictated by statute, elaborated through administrative regulations, and enforced by the Florida Department of Community Affairs. The plan must include requirements such as future land use, capital improvements, transportation, conservation, recreation and open space, and utilities (Fla. Stat. ch. 163.3177, 2002). All comprehensive plan elements must incorporate goals, objectives, and policies that are backed up by data and analysis. These two requirements offer an especially fertile opportunity to integrate law and policy planning with other disciplines whose methodologies provide the basis for developing data and analysis.

A local government comprehensive plan may also include optional elements, which offers a unique but seldom used opportunity for Florida communities to pursue smart growth initiatives. For example, the Conservation Clinic assisted the town of Marineland with the preparation of an optional sustainable tourism element to its comprehensive plan. Marineland hosts Florida's oldest tourist attraction and is seeking to market itself as a new science, education, and heritage tourism model based on principles of sustainability. Marineland's new optional element offers a way of demonstrating this commitment.

Once a local government has adopted an approved comprehensive plan, it must implement the plan through land development regulations. According to Florida statute ch.163 (2003), all land use regulations must be consistent with the comprehensive plan (Brown 1991, 17). The plan may be amended only twice a year and must be reviewed and updated periodically. Each step in these processes requires the involvement of citizens and provides opportunities for administrative and judicial challenge. Originally any local government land use decision was treated as a legislative action, entitled to great deference by the courts. This all changed with the Florida Supreme Court case, *Board of County Commissioners of Brevard County v. Snyder,* 627 S0.2d 469 (Fla. 1993), in which the court determined that most rezoning actions were "quasi judicial" and subject to greater judicial scrutiny. A quasi-judicial rezoning hearing looks more like a judicial hearing than a legislative process, and local government commissions engaged in such hearings have effectively become a new judicial branch. Such hearings demand an entirely distinct set of professional skills for lawyers and nonlawyers alike. Politicians in the public eye do not view traditional courtroom tactics favorably, yet individuals' property rights can be significantly affected and a record must be protected. Quasi-judicial hearings provide a rich source of material for clinic simulations, involving the use of planning, economics, and conservation science students as expert witnesses, often based on the clinic's own projects.

Urban Wetland Mitigation and Small Basin Watershed Planning

The unique nature of the comprehensive plan as both a regulatory and a planning document makes it ideal for pursuing interdisciplinary clinic projects rooted in smart growth. In fall 2002 the clinic began working with the city of Gainesville's ad hoc advisory committee on creeks and wetlands in a politically divisive effort to draft new comprehensive plan policies for local wetland regulation. Essentially, the clinic served as staff counsel to the appointed committee of the city commission that was charged with reviewing the current policies and drafting new ones as well as land development regulations. Two law students participated in a semester-long, extremely contentious public regulatory negotiation that finally yielded new plan and ordinance language, which the committee forwarded to the city commission. The clinic's recommended plan policies were adopted. On the clinic's advice, the committee included language that mandated that the city adopt local basin plans for each of the town's four watersheds.

The following semester the clinic teamed up with the university's Center for Wetlands in a self-initiated interdisciplinary project to develop a methodology for small-basin watershed planning in Gainesville (see Box 4.1). The project team included a landscape architect in the graduate interdisciplinary ecology program, a wetland science graduate student, and two law students. The report included a basin-by-basin ecological characterization of the city's creeks and wetlands, a spatial analysis of the status of wetlands in the city and county, and an assessment of legal and policy obstacles and opportunities for basin management in a multijurisdictional political milieu. The team presented its report in the context of a divisive debate over a citizen charter initiative to ban all development in wetlands, a policy that would effectively end the practice of wetland mitigation within the city. The local environmental community was divided between those who viewed locally based wetland mitigation as a smart growth strategy and those who believed it would contribute to the deterioration of the city's wetland resources and inner-city neighborhoods. The initiative failed at the ballot box, largely on the strength of the ad hoc committee's environmental credibility and novel approach to community-based wetland management, but all sides agreed that the mandate for local basin planning policy should be pursued at once.

The clinic's small-watershed planning project illuminates the problems and possibilities inherent in interdisciplinary applied education, especially the reconciliation of different approaches. The wetland science student, charged with providing an ecological characterization of the basin, began by proposing a rigorous study that would be years in development. The landscape architecture ecology student proposed a series of maps that would require new field data. One law student was faced with the daunting prospect of inventorying the city's property records to establish ownership patterns along urban streams. Clearly, students could accomplish none of these activities in an academic semester or year. What became apparent instead is that the absence of information is itself a significant policy fact. For example, after a random search revealed that some creek sections were privately owned, it became evident that property records would have to be inventoried to determine who actually owned the creek bottom before urban stream restoration could occur. City planners had been assuming that all creeks were in public ownership, or at least subject to easements.

For this project, two policy tools served as integrating forces across the disciplinary divide: geographic information systems (GIS) technology and a final report with conclusions and recommendations. Land use maps and resource overlays provide the spatial representation for a set of written policies and policy distortions. Report conclusions represent the sort of "ultimate facts" that lawyers traditionally utilize to make their case. A factual conclusion tested against a written policy yields a legal conclusion. A final report with conclusions and policy recommendations based on spatial data analysis completed the disciplinary integration. To accomplish this, the law students were forced to draft defensible conclusions that the science students and their professors at the Center for Wetlands could accept. This occurred through lengthy and intense team negotiation where each draft conclusion was discussed, debated, and then couched in language that satisfied the scientists. In the end, however, the team would agree on the powerful, and potentially controversial, ultimate policy conclusion: under all existing and proposed conservation and land use policies in Gainesville, wetlands would continue to degrade and, hence, become subject to consideration for mitigation under the policy adopted by the city. This mitigation policy had been recommended by the clinic the previous year.

Downtown Redevelopment

In addition to framing growth management legislation, the state has created a number of specific opportunities for local pursuit of smart growth initiatives. The 1969 Florida Community Redevelopment Act (CRA) was established to attract investment in blighted downtowns (Fla. Stat. ch. 163.330–463 [2002]).

Box 4.1

Getting Out in the Field

The wetlands start where the lawyer stops walking and starts talking.

The Gainesville basin planning project revealed the importance of "getting out in the field," something not usually emphasized in the law school curriculum. For the better part of a semester students had been poring over land use maps and identifying areas set aside for conservation and those slated for development. Eventually, the project team came to realize the significance of a large wetland complex that straddled city and county in northern Alachua County. A satellite image revealed that these wet pine fatwoods were the headwaters of most of the region's creeks, therefore, an area of watershed-wide concern. Land use maps showed this region as a swath of green space, protected by conservation easements designed to protect the city's well fields. Clinic students ventured into the field, by land and air (with the help of a clinic student pilot), and discovered that the policy maps were misleading at best.

Figure 4.1 **Satellite photo of area basin concern**

Source: U.S. Geological Survey Digital Line Graph (DLG) data for 1:24,000 Hydrography.

(*continued*)

Box 4.1 (*continued*)

Closer inspection revealed that the supposed conservation area had been ditched, drained, and logged by forestry operations, activities specifically authorized by the conservation easements, but not adequately reflected in the land use plan or maps. The conservation value of these lands as a regional headwater had been seriously compromised.

Figure 4.2 **Students in front of single-engine plane prior to the aerial overflight**

Figure 4.3 **Aerial photo showing actual condition of wetlands (ditched, drained, and deforested)**

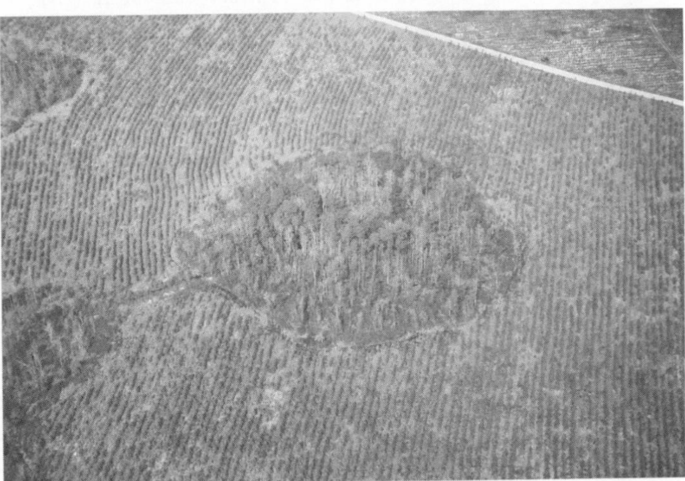

The CRA has enjoyed a renaissance since urban infill has become a watchword of the smart growth movement. This act allows communities to employ tax increment financing to revitalize downtowns, preserve historic areas, and otherwise enhance their surroundings. In fall 1999 clinic law students coauthored "City Beautiful: Creating a Community Redevelopment Area in Your Community,"[4] a paper that outlined the steps a community must take under the act to designate a community redevelopment area, create a redevelopment plan, and establish a trust fund. The following semester clinic law and planning students were able to take advantage of this research when the city of Cedar Key retained the clinic. Cedar Key is a small fishing village on the Florida gulf coast rapidly transitioning to a tourism economy. The clinic worked with the city commission and attorney to designate a community redevelopment area aimed at retaining the city's traditional working waterfront, in the face of gentrification from the tourism sector of the town's economy.

In fall 2000 the historic town of Marineland, Florida's smallest incorporated municipality and host to the state's oldest tourism theme park, retained the clinic. Located on Florida's northeast coast, about one and a half hours from the University of Florida, Marineland has been designated a Remarkable Coastal Place by the State of Florida Department of Community Affairs. The clinic worked with the town council and attorney through the citizen-based Marineland Revitalization Working Group to define a community redevelopment area and prepare a redevelopment plan. The clinic also drafted the state's first sustainable tourism policy for Marineland as an optional element to its comprehensive plan. In 2001 the city of Flagler Beach, immediately south of Marineland, retained the clinic to assist it with its own redevelopment plan.

In the 1998 Brownfields Redevelopment Act, the Florida legislature recognized that the reuse of industrial land could assist the state in a number of ways, including the preservation of open space, and could efficiently use existing infrastructure while incorporating environmental justice concerns (Fla. Stat. ch. 376.77–875 [2003]). Financial and regulatory incentives were created to encourage voluntary cleanup and redevelopment of brownfields. In 2001 the clinic teamed up with the university's Center for Construction and the Environment to undertake a land use and zoning analysis and make policy recommendations concerning redevelopment of neighborhoods surrounding an EPA-funded brownfields site in downtown Gainesville. The clinic offered recommendations for implementing the project team's redevelopment vision, including redrawing the existing Community Redevelopment District to include the brownfield and its contiguous neighborhoods, and to make appropriate land use and zoning changes.

Green Building

Green building programs encompass energy efficiency, good materials use and recycling, water conservation, landscape considerations, and indoor air quality. Local governments have begun to embrace policies designed to encourage green building through incentives, regulations, and certification programs of the U.S. Green Building Council and Florida Green Building Coalition.

In spring 2001 a clinic team of joint MBA-law students initiated a project with Gainesville's Department of Community Development to create a green building program for the city. The clinic team ran a stakeholder workshop that brought together more than forty representatives from the construction and real estate sector, green building advocacy entities, local utilities, and city government. The workshop suggested there was ample interest in incentive-based green building to justify moving forward with a program. The clinic drafted a Green Building Program and Ordinance, enacted in October 2002. The Gainesville program is the first such program in Florida and is now being promoted as a model by the University of Florida's Energy Extension Unit.

Problems of Interdisciplinary Collaboration

These case studies depict a few of the many projects the University of Florida Conservation Clinic has undertaken to assist local communities seeking to pursue smart growth policies. All clinic projects are listed on the clinic's Web site, and substantive research is hosted there where permissible.[5] Of course, as is the case with all professional practice, not every project yields successful outcomes or results in smart growth law and policy.

The Conservation Clinic model provides useful lessons in the difficulties inherent in interdisciplinary collaboration between law and other graduate students and their professors. These lessons include mundane, but not inconsequential, problems such as that posed by the spatial and temporal isolation of the law school from the main campus. The University of Florida Levin College of Law is located on a remote corner of the campus, separated from the main academic complex by massive sports facilities and student housing. Not only is it physically separated from the rest of the university, it operates on a different calendar. Academically the law school is viewed as a separate professional school rather than as a part of the graduate school. Graduate students must, therefore, receive course-specific approval to enroll in law school classes they wish counted toward their degree, a largely symbolic disincentive to interdisciplinary collaboration. Law schools throughout the nation face similar difficulties.

Once the framework and logistics for interdisciplinary collaboration have been settled, the actual collaboration must be developed over an artificially short time frame that is based on the academic calendar. This requires integrating disciplinary approaches, methodologies, presentation styles, personalities, and even citation formats for generating the report. Law students eager to test their advocacy skills sometimes do so at the expense of their colleagues. They are taught to "think like a lawyer" and "get to the issue," which can be frustrated by the deliberate methodological ethos and reluctance to draw policy conclusions based on limited data that their colleagues in the sciences characteristically demonstrate. Like all good scripted events, public policy presentations do not reveal the often difficult and sometimes acrimonious internal decision-making processes that precede them. A greater emphasis on conflict resolution in law schools and an expanded view of the role of the lawyer in society have improved this dynamic.

Clinic-Client Relationships

In general, communities are tolerant of the difficulties inherent in pursuing skills training in a professional environment and are appreciative of the students' efforts to juggle their sometimes-daunting course loads with their professional obligations at the clinic. In most cases, the clinic's smart growth projects are those a community might not otherwise have taken on due to lack of resources to retain professionals. Even so, once the political commitment and accompanying representation decision have been made, the fact that students are at the center of smart growth policy development does not provide a basis for excuses. The inadequate performance of one student or student group can wreak havoc on scheduling and damage carefully cultivated clinic-client relationships. The clinic director must assume full responsibility for the work product of the student professionals. For programs having the resources, it is beneficial to have faculty or affiliated researchers willing to step in and help. The Conservation Clinic's relationship with law faculty and colleagues at the public policy research center has been instrumental when such circumstances arise. At the same time, clinical professors must exercise caution and avoid the temptation of taking on too much, especially in an interdisciplinary policy practice arena where the clinician is often outside of his or her acknowledged field of expertise.

Working in the sometimes politically charged town-and-gown atmosphere of a major university can also impose problems. In terms of comprehensive planning, the University of Florida is the "elephant in the room," largely exempt from local comprehensive planning policies, yet wielding the single greatest effect on growth in the community. University administration policies frequently diverge from local wishes (and sometimes good smart growth policy), creating the potential for interinstitutional and even employer-employee conflicts.

Conclusion

Despite these challenges, representing communities in the pursuit of interdisciplinary smart growth policies provides a rich mix of practice and pedagogy. In the context of legal education, such clinics as the Conservation Clinic cannot replace the traditional litigation clinic, especially for those students seeking to pursue a career in environmental and land use litigation. A robust legal education curriculum, however, should provide both forms of service learning.

Notes

1. *Service education* is a term used to describe the broader commitment of universities to bring pedagogy and practice together to provide community service. Clinical legal education represents just one manifestation of this larger commitment, which extends to all disciplines. A 1999 report from the presidents of one hundred prominent state universities and land grant colleges commissioned by the Kellogg Foundation concluded that public universities were not doing enough to support their communities and, as a consequence, were losing a significant opportunity to train the next generation of professionals and leaders (Kellogg Commission on the Future of State Universities and Land Grant Colleges, 1999).

2. These statistics are maintained by an ad hoc group of environmental law clinicians affiliated with the American Association of Law Schools.

3. In some cases, however, students themselves bring projects to the clinic, often as a result of their own interests and contacts. This is especially the case with graduate students, whose research is frequently driven by grants and contracts from external entities that can benefit from a policy component to the project.

4. See http://conservation.law.ufl.edu/pdf/CRAfinalreport99.pdf.

5. See http://conservation.law.ufl.edu.

References

Brown, James Jay. 1991. Land use planning and zoning in Florida: An overview. *Florida Environmental and Land Use Law Treatise,* ch. 25.

Carter, Luther. 1976. *The Florida experience: Land and water policy in a growth state.* Baltimore: Johns Hopkins University Press.

Carter, Terry. 2002. Law clinics face critics: Business interests fire up challenges to schools' environmental law projects. *The American Bar Association Journal* 88:24–26.

Esty, Dan. 1999. Rethinking environmental clinical education. Unpublished paper presented at the annual meeting of environmental law clinicians (January).

Gorovitz-Robertson, Heidi. 1998. Methods for teaching environmental law: Some thoughts on providing access to the environmental law system. *Columbia Journal of Environmental Law* 23:237.

Joy, Peter A. 1994. The MacCrate Report: Moving toward integrated learning experiences. *Clinical Law Review* 1:401.

Kuehn, Robert R., and Peter A. Joy. 2003. An ethics critique of interference in law school clinics. *Fordham Law Review* 71:1971–2050.

Nolan, John R. 2002. In praise of parochialism: The advent of local environmental law. *Harvard Environmental Law Review* 26:419.

Sorensen, Ken. 2002. *The local government formation manual.* Florida House of Representatives, Local Government and Veterans Affairs Committee. http://www.leg.state.fl.us/publications/2003/house/reports/local_bills/LGFM.pdf.

Tarlock, A. Dan. 2003. The potential role of local governments in watershed management. In *New ground: The advent of local environmental law,* John R. Nolon, ed. Washington DC: Environmental Law Institute.

Weinstein, Janet. 1999. Coming of age: Recognizing the importance of interdisciplinary education in law practice. *Washington Law Review* 74:319–66.

Part 2

SMART GROWTH AT RESEARCH CENTERS

5

Using a Geographic Information System (GIS) to Help Shape Redevelopment of Small Urban Centers

Christine Danis, Laura Solitare, Michael Greenberg, and Henry Mayer

This chapter is about the involvement of the National Center for Neighborhood and Brownfields Redevelopment (the Center) in a two-year university-based effort to assist six small towns in New Jersey plan for their collective redevelopment in concert with smart growth principles. In the first year of the project, the Center worked in partnership with a steering committee of regional, county, and local municipal officials to collect data; identify specific areas or neighborhoods that might accommodate growth; develop a baseline geographic information system (GIS) build-out model; examine such economic implications of added growth as vehicle trips and employment opportunities; and measure potential impacts of such growth on local educational systems. In the second year of the project, the Center helped the six communities build their decision-making capacity in order to plan for smart growth on a regional scale.

Overview of the National Center for Neighborhood and Brownfields Redevelopment

Established in 1998 at the Edward J. Bloustein School of Planning and Public Policy, the Center was designated by the Rutgers Board of Governors as a strategic planning initiative of the university. It is one of six major research centers at the Bloustein School and is funded primarily through project-based grants from private foundations and federal, state, and county governments. The university funds the Center director's salary and the facilities; the remaining salaries, hardware/software, and expenses are funded by grants. The Center operates in the belief that restoration and revitalization of urban neighborhoods will improve job opportunities, the local quality of life, and public health. Through educational and outreach programs, and especially applied community-level research, the Center is committed to the betterment and long-term vitality of neighborhoods and the health of the public.

The Center's staff includes a mix of Rutgers faculty, full- and part-time researchers, postdoctoral associates, and students. The Center employs doctoral, masters, and undergraduate students to work on a range of projects. Several doctoral students in Rutgers's Urban Planning and Policy Development program have completed their dissertations as part of the Center's research; the masters and undergraduate students working with the Center gain valuable experience in environmental planning and community development, while working in a professional environment.

The Center's mission focuses on two complementary areas: (1) the control of sprawl, with concentration on its related adverse environmental impacts on our natural resources; and (2) the revitalization of our cities and old industrial suburbs, with special consideration given to areas in need of redeveloping contaminated, abandoned, or underutilized properties. A goal of the Center is to be active in smart growth urban redevelopment in New Jersey.

New Jersey's Smart Growth Strategy

New Jersey is one of several states, including Colorado, Maryland, and Wisconsin, that actively focus on smart growth from the state level. New Jersey's approach stems from its state plan (New Jersey State Planning Commission 2001), which depicts the growth management strategies needed for the most densely populated state in the nation. New Jersey initiated the state plan in response to the declining economy and quality of life in urban centers, sprawling development, increased traffic, degradation of natural resources, and loss of open space. The state plan is in essence a statewide smart growth initiative that urges communities to develop more compact, mixed-use designs that protect the environment and provide for more efficient infrastructure systems, while at the same time permitting expected growth to occur. One of the key elements in designing the state plan was to assign *designated centers:* places that will accommodate the state's projected growth. The state offers incentives to these centers, in the form of technical assistance and funding, to plan for and accommodate the growth.

The study area represents three New Jersey state plan-designated centers, consisting of six towns in Somerset County: the entire town limits of Bound Brook, Manville, Raritan, Somerville, and South Bound Brook, and a small portion of Bridgewater Township. As part of a designated center, the towns in the study area are willing to accommodate further growth and have sought assistance in planning for it.

The Center joined this project to provide the designated centers with the technical resources needed for smart growth. It formed a partnership with Somerset County and each of the six towns to develop a strategic planning initiative. One of the main steps in the process was to pull together the existing but scattered players and pieces. The Somerset County Planning Board, as do other statewide county planning boards, has the responsibility for countywide and regional planning, but does not have the authority to legislate or directly make local land use decisions. The state planning agency serves as a technical and funding resource with the power only to influence local land use decisions through statutory or permit-driven regulations. The state plan serves as a template document that, when applied, brings with it technical resources, priority funding, and recognition of compliance with statewide initiatives.

Study Area: Somerset County and Designated Centers

Somerset County, one of twenty-one counties in the state, occupies 305 square miles of central New Jersey and consists of twenty-one individual municipalities (see Map 5.1).

Based on data from the 2000 U.S. Census of Population and Housing, Somerset County's population was 297,490, and it had a land density of 975.4 persons per square mile (less than the New Jersey average density of 1,134.5 persons per square mile). From 1990 to 2000 the county population increased 24 percent compared with 9 percent for New Jersey as a whole. During this period Somerset County grew more rapidly than any other county in the state (Census Bureau 2000), which makes the need for smart growth planning urgent.

As can be seen in Table 5.1, the study area has a population of 43,809. It has a lower percentage of nonwhite persons (17 percent) compared with the county as a whole, as well as the state and the nation; it has a relatively large percentage of Hispanic or Latino persons (18 percent). While the study area's median household income is higher than the national average, it is lower than both the New Jersey and the Somerset County averages (it is 64 percent of the county's median household income). The study area has the lowest public transit user rate (3 percent) compared with the other areas. In terms of education, as measured by the percent of the population with college and advanced degrees, the study area has fewer educated persons (21 percent with associate's or bachelor's degree; 8 percent with an advanced degree) than the comparison area. As in Somerset County as a whole, there is a low rate (4 percent) of vacant housing

Map 5.1 **Project study area, Somerset County, New Jersey**

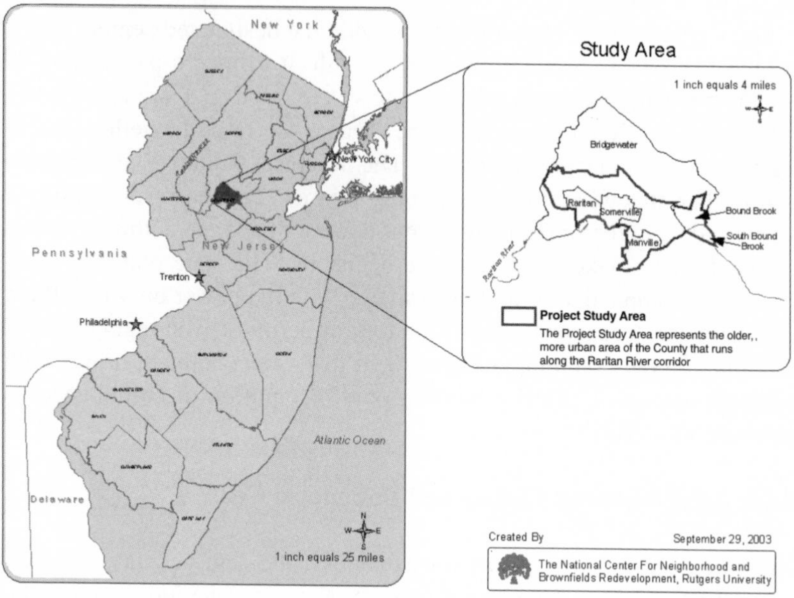

Source: The National Center for Neighborhood and Brownfields Redevelopment, Rutgers University (September 29, 2003).

in the study area, and while the county has a higher-than-average rate of owner occupancy than both the nation and New Jersey, the study area has a lower rate. Housing rentals in the study area cost more than the New Jersey and the national averages, but less than the average for the county. Fewer people on average in the study area purchase their homes than in the state and county, but the rate is higher than the national average.

The more affluent communities in the county, widely known for large houses, equestrian activities, and golf courses, are located in the rolling foothills. This is in strong contrast to the communities in our study area, which lie in the Raritan River valley, once the home of such large industrial facilities as Johns Manville in Manville, GAF in South Bound Brook, American Cyanamid in Bridgewater, and Woolen Mills in Raritan (Mayer, Danis, and Greenberg 2002, 353). Industrialization left an estimated 435 known contaminated sites in the county, of which 104 are located in the study cities (Somerset Coalition for Smart Growth 2000, 4). These sites were once the employment and economic centers of the county, but now they are defiled community eyesores. The loss of jobs and resulting idle land have also translated into higher tax rates on the remaining residences and businesses in the municipalities (Rutgers 2000, 73–77; Somerset County Board of Taxation 2000).

Table 5.1

Quick profile of the study area and surrounding regions

	United States	New Jersey	Somerset County	Study Area Towns
Total population	281,421,906	8,414,350	297,490	43,809
Nonwhite population	25%	28%	21%	17%
Hispanic or Latino	13%	13%	9%	18%
Journey to work: use public transportation	5%	10%	4%	3%
Education: associates or bachelors degree	22%	24%	33%	21%
Education: advanced degree	9%	11%	19%	8%
Median household income in 1999	$41,994	$55,146	$76,933	$49,892
Poverty rate	12%	8%	4%	7%
Vacant housing	9%	7%	3%	4%
Owner occupancy	66%	66%	77%	58%
Median rent asked	$469	$660	$900	$752
Median housing value	$111,80	$167,900	$222,400	$156,200

Source: The National Center for Neighborhood and Brownfields Redevelopment, Rutgers University.

The towns in the study area have much in common: they share many transportation and other infrastructure facilities; they are relatively small; and they have limited resources. Leaders in each of the towns believed that the best strategy for their future was for the towns to cooperate and collaborate for regional smart growth.

Project Implementation

The project was the result of a partnership between the Center; the county's planning director; the Regional Planning Partnership (RPP), a local nonprofit organization that had developed a GIS build-out model; and several local officials who were serving on an EPA brownfields pilot project. The Center served as the university resource and conduit for knowledge and technology to communities unable to staff a full-time planner and/or had limited local resources. It worked alongside the County Planning Board staff and local officials to develop the project's steering committees and establish its smart growth principles by applying a combination of technical resources, local knowledge, and collaborative decision making.

The project focused on two key elements: (1) bringing stakeholders together through a steering committee and individual community meetings, and (2) using GIS models to evaluate redevelopment alternatives. The Center staff and graduate urban planning students worked with mayors and other town representatives to gather individual redevelopment plans and ideas and to examine both the localized and regional impacts of the associated projected growth in population and jobs. Land use decisions in New Jersey are largely in the domain of local governments; it was thought that a bottom-up planning process involving all the towns would have a greater chance of success in building a regional perspective than more traditional top-down efforts from the county or state. It was important, therefore, to design a project that reflected input from local officials, because they ultimately are responsible for the redevelopment decisions in their towns. Toward this end, the Center was careful to include on the project's steering committee the director of planning for Somerset County, several other county staff members, the mayor, and at least one other representative of local government from each of the six municipalities.

The Center's interaction with the steering committee followed four phases. First, the Center collected data about existing land use and infrastructure in the study area. Preliminary meetings with the committee showed that local governments lacked the resources necessary to provide information to the Center; they were also unsure of how to share data with others. As a result, the Center gathered the information and sent it to the local governments to check for accuracy and completeness. The Center then met and shared data with each town and gathered feedback at a steering committee meeting. Although towns were reluctant to perform data collection, they were willing to comment on whether or not the information that the Center put together was representative and up-to-date.

Second, the Center worked with local governments to identify areas or neighborhoods with vacant or underutilized properties that could accommodate new development. The partnership discussed the property details and considered redevelopment alternatives, which were based on existing or proposed plans and local stakeholder input. In these discussions, the county and each town talked about their redevelopment challenges, hopes, and dreams for their community; they shared thoughts on their joint and individual needs and difficulties or obstacles for making them a reality. The discussions revealed that each town has similar needs and challenges. The participants began to focus on appropriate land use options, enhancing their transit options, building on the local downtown economy, and, finally, increasing the downtown residential population.

Third, the Center used a GIS model to evaluate redevelopment or rezoning impacts. As they planned for redevelopment, the communities found themselves routinely stalled by concerns about the limitations in existing infrastructure. They identified wastewater and water supply systems as a major concern.

To address this issue, the Center invited the operators of such systems to participate in discussions with the steering committee to determine the impact of alternative land uses on local infrastructure. But confirming the condition and capacity of existing systems in these communities and the region was difficult, if not impossible. It became apparent that for many communities and service providers, sharing data or planning information was not part of their operating practices. As a result, one of the project recommendations is for Somerset County to develop a technical task force to evaluate thoroughly existing infrastructure conditions, particularly water and wastewater systems.

The Center, working with the RPP and the county, took the lead in redevelopment modeling. In order to keep on task, the Center needed the communities to move forward with their ideas, not to get caught up on impediments to planning for revitalization. Each town presented a redevelopment option, and the steering committee meetings offered an opportunity to view a live-model demonstration of the potential impact of these options and to ask questions and discuss the implications. It was important that these meetings were action-based and that they kept the officials updated on the agenda for the next meeting. It was important, too, that each town had representation at the meetings. As a result, they were well attended; officials who have busy schedules and are not full-time mayors or planners found the meetings productive and an opportunity to gain insights about their towns as well as their neighbors.

Fourth, the Center examined those redevelopment projects that required intermunicipal and county cooperation. It facilitated discussions with the local officials that focused on building partnerships. As this project came to an end, the steering committee was concerned that, after two years of working together, all the knowledge and new relationships would just disappear. Because the County Planning Board was an active partner, however, there was an opportunity to use the county's master plan–update initiative as a way of continuing the work. These six towns, which serve as the growth centers for the county, were already on board, informed and able to continue collaborating as part of a subarea for the countywide initiative. Such continuity was critical to these communities, and concerns began to surface about what the next steps might be. Once the towns realized that the project was not just an academic study, the partnership could move forward and tie into other planning projects within the communities and the county.

The Impacts and Effects of Zoning and Planning: The Role of GIS

Instead of continuing to talk in abstract terms about development and impacts, the Center decided to use GIS-based tools to help local officials visualize existing and proposed land uses in relation to their neighboring communities. The Center used the Goal Oriented Zoning (GOZ™) model, which RPP developed, to work with the towns on residential and commercial build-out scenarios based on existing or proposed zoning. The results of the build-out data were then used to compute associated impacts on the community, such as increases in population, number of schoolchildren, local jobs, vehicle trips and miles traveled, water and sewer demand, and air and water pollution. By making refinements to the model, the Center was able to take already developed land and run "what if" redevelopment or rezoning scenarios, and compare them with current conditions. In short, the Center gave local officials a hands-on planning tool that was reflective of their town and useful for evaluating alternative situations for revitalization and planning for future growth. This was of particular value to these communities, which have large brownfield sites that are pivotal to the redevelopment of their downtown areas and critical to their economic sustainability. Such a tool also provided them, for the first time, an opportunity to work side by side with neighboring towns in visualizing and examining the cumulative environmental and infrastructure impacts of their individual plans.

Many GIS planning support systems enable users to evaluate different development or redevelopment scenarios. The Center found that this ability to model alternatives quickly was of great interest to the communities. Most local officials, planners, and stakeholders want to see rather speedily what a change in residential density or land use will mean for their communities in terms of people and traffic, for example. The fiscal, environmental, or infrastructural impacts that the GOZ™ model developed, however, was less understood by the general audience; those impacts were best comprehended if they were compared with existing conditions. For example, how much additional potable water would a town need as a result of a build-out scenario? The communities also responded to GIS as a local planning support system because it provided a quick picture of where redevelopment was occurring and the direct impacts that changes in density or floor area ratio would impose on population size, schoolchildren, and traffic.

The modeling and ensuing discussions led the mayors and other town officials to think beyond the day-to-day problems and issues associated with managing a local government, and to raise questions about how they would like to see their communities develop over the next ten to twenty years. Their initial focus was on whether the model could provide better impact information on a handful of areas that they were promoting for redevelopment. But they have begun to rethink how these properties could be best used to meet the community's needs, and to consider them in the context of similar redevelopment plans within their miniregion. The use of a GIS model did not obfuscate the planning discussion; instead, it served as a powerful visual and learning tool that empowered the communities to expand their thinking about how redevelopment could look.

One of the challenges in working with GIS is the frequent lack of current and representative data to build the database. The New Jersey Department of Environmental Protection (NJDEP) land use data were from 1995 to 1997; in a county that grew by 24 percent between 1990 and 2000, the existing baseline conditions did not represent the county's current land use conditions. Thus, the data gave a false starting point for any build-out projections. This outdated GIS baseline condition would be true of any GIS model analysis. Responding to this concern, the Center developed an approach for updating the NJDEP data to 2002 conditions using orthophotographic images and ARCGIS, a software program used for geospatial analysis.

Examples of Using GIS

The town of South Bound Brook, which was 0.9 square miles in size, realized that the traditional approach for stimulating economic growth in their main street area was based on the idea that dense commercial zoning would spur economic development. In the words of the mayor during one of the planning meetings, the thinking was that "if the town zoned for economic development, the businesses would come." When the existing zoning conditions were modeled, the build-out based on floor area ratio values indicated that approximately four thousand jobs could be available in this small area. Nevertheless, in reality, there are about nine hundred jobs available in the entire town, which currently includes a twelve-acre brownfield site along the river and low-density strip mall centers. The use of GIS permitted this town to better understand the implications of zoning and local land use ordinances and to recognize the mismatch between zoning and existing conditions. The zoning at the time also did not allow for mixed-use development and limited professional office opportunities. As a result of the build-out analysis, the mayor and town officials rethought the redevelopment stance for the brownfield site and looked again at existing zoning for the commercial area and the overall community. The county helped the town in applying for state funding to plan for redevelopment of the main street area and brownfield site as a mixed-use community that linked commercial and residential growth to the surrounding transit opportunities while preserving the beauty and integrity of the river. As a result, both the state and national brownfields community saluted the town as a leader in innovative redevelopment.

The town of Raritan, which continued to be overshadowed by Somerville, the county seat, decided that it needed to rethink the main street linkage to its neighbor, while maintaining the quaint residential character and generating tax ratables. The existing zoning for this area, however, limited commercial growth and did not permit professional office development. As a result of collaborative planning discussions, town officials decided to present several alternative zoning and land use ordinance changes for the area. The Center performed a GIS build-out analysis of these alternative floor area ratio and density values for that zone, and also discussed and evaluated the impacts of alternatives. As a result, the town moved forward with rezoning to promote professional office use and light commercial development. This also prompted the town to rethink their streetscape and architectural design guidelines to ensure that they maintained the character of the community. They, too, benefited from state and county planning grants to support their planning initiatives.

Reflections on the Project

The process of working collaboratively through a steering committee, with the Center serving as a neutral partner, was well received by all involved in the project. In fact, this project was the first time that the towns had sat down together to plan for their future. They listened to their peers, local officials, consultant planners, state regulatory representatives, and academics as a united group working for a better future for themselves and their stakeholders. They learned that they could achieve more for their respective communities as a group than as competitors for limited business and residential properties. For years they had competed for economic development initiatives and municipal service contracts; they are now aware that they need to collaborate and find a unified voice.

The Center met individually with each town to review its existing information on the town's land use, demographics, economics, and infrastructure. After these meetings, the Center created for each town a unique inventory of its existing resources (land use, infrastructure, and so forth) and planning data that were required in evaluating future growth and redevelopment plans. Most of the local officials found their inventory to be invaluable—they did not have the capacity (trained planning staff and funding) to create one on their own, yet it yielded the crucial information they needed for smart growth planning. As a university partner, the towns welcomed the Center as a source of information and research capacity, and for bringing an objective perspective to the table regarding information and redevelopment.

The use of GIS was essential to developing the big-picture perspective of what local decisions mean to the region. The technology was particularly valuable in enabling the Center to present the idea of creating a mixed-use downtown environment to support the communities' economic, transit, and quality of life concerns. At the beginning of the project, most of the communities did not understand how they might implement smart growth in their downtowns and large brownfield sites. In the end, however, the communities realized that they can create a more vibrant pedestrian-friendly downtown by evaluating zoning, parking, and land use policies. They also understood that there is a need for continued collaboration in addressing economic and infrastructure concerns as they plan for regional smart growth.

The Somerset County Planning Board is developing the Strategic Smart Growth Plan for the county with a $250,000 grant from the New Jersey Economic Development Authority. According to the director of the planning board, the project served as an opportunity for the board and the six towns to test the effectiveness of GIS and modeling in facilitating master plan activities. Building on the information collected from this project, the planning board has contracted with the Center to continue compiling the GIS modeling data for the entire county and to have the university serve in support of the smart growth strategic planning effort. This continuing work for the county, which was widely supported by the municipal governments, shows the potential worth of university-based centers to impact urban redevelopment and smart growth projects.

Lessons for Future Smart Growth

The project served as a practical application of grassroots regional planning. It inspired the county and the towns to think differently about their existing zoning, ordinances, and redevelopment plans. For example, the town of South Bound Brook reevaluated its existing redevelopment plan for a large brownfield in their central business district. Because of participation in this project, the town updated their existing redevelopment plan to incorporate more housing and design guidelines. In another example, Somerville, the county seat, was concerned about whether parking availability in the downtown area could support increased residential development. The Center performed a GIS evaluation of the downtown to consider several mixed-use options and parking requirements. The findings suggested that if the town were to rethink its approach to on-street parking and implement a permit system, there would be parking sufficient to support denser housing than their current zoning permits.

The final conference for the project brought together the communities, county, state, and private agencies, planning consultants, local business owners, academics, and graduate students to refine and discuss the needs of small urban centers. The conclusion spotlighted partnerships, the need for better data and more technical resources at the local level, and, most of all, the greater power they command as a group than as individuals. At the meeting, the partnership developed a set of recommendations specifically for New Jersey; however, these suggestions would be valid for communities across the country as they plan for smart growth:

1. Develop legislation that will empower counties as planning agencies to provide oversight to municipal planning approvals;
2. Provide more opportunities for municipalities to have access to planning support systems;
3. Improve the infrastructure knowledge of local, county, and state entities regarding the capacity and condition of wastewater systems in particular;
4. Confront critical transportation needs;
5. Encourage state agencies to address small-scale local issues, instead of focusing solely on larger regional issues, and to examine the concerns of older bedroom communities; and
6. Tackle issues about enhancing the downtown economy, and creating a twenty-four-hour/seven-day-a-week residential population to support it.

This partnership exemplifies how university-based centers can serve as resources to towns and counties and demonstrates the power of GIS as a planning support system. As the design and implementation of policies to address development concerns move forward in the most densely populated state in the nation, the Center should serve as a valuable asset in developing a clear-eyed grassroots vision for the state.

References

Census Bureau, U.S. Department of Commerce. 2000. Census of population and housing summary file 3. Washington, DC. http://www.census.gov.

Mayer, H., C.M. Danis, and M. Greenberg. 2002. Smart growth in a small urban setting: The challenges of building an acceptable solution. *Local Environment* 7(4): 349–62.

New Jersey State Planning Commission. 2001. *The New Jersey State Development and Redevelopment Plan.* Trenton: New Jersey Department of Community Affairs.

Rutgers University. 2000. *New Jersey legislative data book, 2000.* Center for Government Services, Edward J. Bloustein School of Planning and Public Policy. New Brunswick: Rutgers University.

Somerset Coalition for Smart Growth, Inc. 2000. *Somerset County's center-based EPA brownfields assessment demonstration pilot.* Somerville: EPA Brownfields Assessment Demonstration Pilot Grant Report, February 16:1–13.

Somerset County Board of Taxation. 2000. *General tax rate table.* Somerville, NJ: Somerset County.

6

Encouraging Smart Growth in a Skeptical State: University-Stakeholder Collaboration in Central Indiana

Greg Lindsey, John Ottensmann, Jamie Palmer, Jeffrey Wilson, and Joseph Tutterrow

In 1981 the Indiana General Assembly eliminated the State Planning Services Agency, thus effectively ending the state's role in encouraging land use planning and developing a capacity for planning at the local level. In the mid-1990s county commissioners in suburban Morgan County, near the Indianapolis International Airport, abruptly ended a comprehensive planning process and dismissed its planner because of citizen complaints about the erosion of property rights, confiscation of property, and intrusion of government into private affairs.

These two incidents reflect historical and, to a large degree, prevailing attitudes toward planning and growth management in the state. Indiana has been and remains conservative and deeply suspicious of the reach and scope of government. Hence, the fervor and debate over smart growth that have preoccupied planners and policy makers in Maryland, Oregon, Florida, and elsewhere across the nation have scarcely surfaced here. In Indiana the debate instead has focused more on the merits of planning and whether it offers benefits to the residents of local communities. It has emerged not because of concern over sprawl, but because of the loss of farmland—policy makers believe that the agricultural basis of their rural, rustic lifestyles and Hoosier culture are at risk.

University-stakeholder collaborations on land use issues in Central Indiana both are shaped by this culture and represent attempts to expand policy discussions to address a broader range of issues related to land use and growth.

Since the late 1990s, university faculty and staff at the Center for Urban Policy and the Environment (the Center) in the School of Public and Environmental Affairs (SPEA) at Indiana University–Purdue University, Indianapolis (IUPUI), have collaborated with the Indiana Land Use Consortium (ILUC), a loose-knit stakeholder organization, and the Indiana Land Resources Council (ILRC), a state commission headed by the lieutenant governor, to facilitate discussions about planning and growth management, to educate people about the principles of smart growth, and to provide information and tools for planners to work more effectively in their communities. This chapter describes such collaborations and considers their outcomes. It then concludes with a discussion of lessons for future collaborations both in Indiana and beyond.

Program Activity Planning and Collaboration

University collaborations with policy makers and stakeholders on land use and smart growth have evolved over time in both planned and unforeseen ways. The process perhaps best matches the conceptual models of adaptive and incremental planning. That is, collaborators generally have not established particular goals related to smart growth or pursued a specific approach. Rather, collaborators have worked together in an organic process, using their expertise to respond to and shape external forces and events, and to initiate and revise particular projects according to perceived needs. Although the three projects on which this chapter concentrates have been pursued systematically and rigorously within specified time periods, they have occurred in a dynamic environment and been shaped by fortuitous events. Like any evolutionary or adaptive process, the origins of these collaborations on land use and growth issues are difficult to pinpoint.

Focused on here are collaborations between January 2000 and May 2003, although the association predates this time period (Table 6.1, pp. 98–99). From the university perspective, the rationale for the partnership is rooted in the IUPUI mission of civic engagement and the SPEA commitment to "making a world of difference." IUPUI and SPEA created the Center in 1992 with a large award ($8.5 million) of general support from a major foundation to undertake research and service related to their public service directives. The Center's mission is to produce information that will help inform policy decisions related to quality of life in the region and state.

IUPUI and SPEA have provided additional financial support for the Center, including the director's salary and funds for a senior scholar. Professional staff employees, faculty from both SPEA and other units in the university, and graduate research assistants carry out the Center's work. Activities include policy-oriented, community-based research supported by major foundations and other sources as well as contract research and service undertaken for clients in the public, nonprofit, and private sectors.

Although the Center does not have an explicit educational mission, it has worked to support SPEA's educational goals in a number of ways. Annually it supports between five and ten graduate students as research assistants in SPEA's master of planning and master of public affairs programs. These students participate in nearly all Center activities, gaining valuable hands-on experience in community-based research and service. Many have been coauthors of Center publications. In addition, students in the master of planning workshop course and other SPEA classes have worked on planning projects for community clients through the auspices of the Center. SPEA students also have participated in many other Center research projects, especially ongoing studies of the use of greenways in Indianapolis and in Indiana as a whole.

Subsequent foundation awards ($3.4 million in 1999; $4 million in 2002) have enabled the Center to initiate a broad program of research in Central Indiana focused on community investments. It then extended particular projects statewide and across selected regions in other states. The primary objectives of this program have been to build relationships with key organizations and leaders in a region and to study investment strategies used by governments, businesses, nonprofit organizations, and households. As one element of this broader program, the Center financially supported collaborative projects on land use. The rationale for addressing planning and smart growth issues as part of a research program focused on investment is that planned, coordinated investments across sectors are likely to be more efficient and to lead to improvements in regional performance and quality of life. Like other Center initiatives, this research was designed to provide graduate research assistants with opportunities that complement their formal classroom instruction.

From the perspective of the state government, the ILUC, and stakeholders concerned with land use issues, the collaborations are outgrowths of statewide agricultural policy initiatives in the 1990s, including the Hoosier Farmland Preservation Task Force (1997–1999) and its predecessor, the Ag and Natural Resources Working Group, which produced a report for the legislature in 1997, *Indiana Land Use on the Edge.* The Indiana Land Use Consortium was founded in 1997 by a group of stakeholders that included the Indiana Farm Bureau, Indiana Planning Association, Indiana Association of Realtors, Indiana Association of Cities and Towns, and a number of state agencies and entities within several universities, including the Center. The mission of the ILUC is to serve "as a catalyst for education and a forum for discussion

Table 6.1

Evolution of university-stakeholder collaborations on land use issues in Indiana

Collaborators	Pre-1999	1999	2000	2001	2002	2003
Indiana Land Use Consortium (ILUC)	1997, founded 1998, 1st conference	2nd conference	3rd conference Land use principles adopted	4th conference Elkhart County pilot project	5th conference Data catalog published. Putnam County pilot project	6th conference Putnam County pilot project continues
Indiana Land Resources Council (ILRC)	1997–1999, Governor's Hoosier Farmland Preservation Task Force	General Assembly passes enabling legislation (no sunset), mission defined	Members appointed Director hired Educational programs initiated	ILUC conference ILUC project sponsor. Funds Center to extend inventory and land use change project statewide. Land use forum created	White papers issued. ILUC conference. ILUC project sponsor. Educational programs continue	Forms Rural Waste-water Task Force. Farmland Task Force. ILUC conference. ILUC project sponsor. Educational programs continue
Center for Urban Policy and the Environment (the Center)	1992, founded 1992–1998, planning and land use projects	Foundation award through 2001. Staff is ILUC vice chair. Research aligned with ILRC mission	Work on land use and planning projects. Regional outreach forums	Work on land use and planning projects	Foundation award thru 2004. Staff is ILUC chair. Staff is Indiana Planning Assn. president. Research linked with Indiana Advisory Commission on Intergovernmental Relations	Work on land use and planning projects continues

Land cover change project	Project conceptualized	Mapping of land use change in central Indiana initiated	Central Indiana mapping finished Complete Indiana mapping initiated	Indiana mapping finished. Results in ILRC newsletter	Land use change issue brief. Academic talks and journal submittals
Planning inventory and smart growth audit	Project conceptualized	Planning inventory issue brief Stakeholder design of audit template	Planning tools issue briefs Conference talks	Conference talks Low-density issue brief	Audit summary report
Land Use in Central Indiana (LUCI) model	Project conceptualized	Prototype developed and conceptual model refined Date assembled	Satellite imagery incorporated Model estimated Programming and beta version developed Stakeholder input	Program demonstrations and debugging Conference talks	LUCI released LUCI issue brief. Regional seminars *Public Works and Management Policy* article LUCI used in contract research

to foster responsible land use decisions and practices in Indiana."[1] The ILUC holds an annual conference, "Communities at the Crossroads," and has adopted a set of guiding principles for land use that embraces some elements of smart growth. It supports work by state and local agencies to educate people about alternative strategies for managing land use. The ILUC followed the work of the Farmland Preservation Task Force and joined hands with it in recommending that the legislature create a permanent state body to address issues relating to land use, which it did in 1999.

The Indiana General Assembly created the Indiana Land Resources Council to "(1) collect information; and (2) provide: (a) educational assistance; (b) technical assistance; and (c) advice; to local governments regarding land use strategies and issues across the state."[2] The ILRC, headed by the lieutenant governor and including nine members representing diverse interests, is authorized to facilitate collaboration, compile data on land resources, coordinate educational programs, give technical assistance, write and publish model ordinances, and help communities to obtain grants. Formation of the ILRC in some respects signifies a reversal of the legislature's previous decision to eliminate the State Planning Services Agency, but the ILRC has been given few resources and has funding only for a director and a part-time assistant. Since its inception, the ILRC has supported ongoing activities such as the ILUC conferences, begun development of information resources to enhance its educational initiatives, and developed a number of policy documents and papers on land resources issues.

Collaborative efforts between the university and land use stakeholders solidified in 2000 following the creation of the ILRC, the Center's receipt of the second foundation award for work in Central Indiana, and an explicit decision by the Center's leadership to align some of its research initiatives with the mission of the ILRC (Table 6.1). Specifically, the Center committed funding to document historic and current land cover and land cover change, to describe the scope of local planning, and to provide tools for stakeholders to understand the consequences of land use policy choices. Collaboration among Center researchers, ILRC staff, and ILUC members was thereby intensified. Members implemented projects designed to provide neutral, credible information, to build trust among stakeholders, and to increase understanding of the strengths and weaknesses of planning.

Program Activity Implementation

The Center's work on each of the three Central Indiana projects was started more or less simultaneously in spring 2000 (Table 6.1). The land cover change project and the planning inventory and smart growth audit were completed for Central Indiana in 2001; the ILRC then provided financial support to extend the projects statewide. Data and insights from these two projects provided the technical foundation for development of the Land Use in Central Indiana model (LUCI) and shaped the types of policy options and scenarios for users of the model to explore. Key elements of each project are summarized in Table 6.2.

The level of collaboration across projects varied, with greater stakeholder input on the research design for the smart growth audit and on development of the LUCI model than on the methodology for the land cover change project. The ILRC and the ILUC focused the research by identifying policy issues and research needs, reviewing research design and templates for data collection and analysis, evaluating model output, testing and debugging the LUCI model, and deciding how to disseminate and use the findings. This collaboration was especially important in the early phases of implementation because it led to a sense of shared understanding of the problems and, more important, of trust that collaborators were committed to common efforts. As stakeholders contributed to the research design, for example, their suspicions that the work was being done to advance a particular point of view diminished, and they became more accepting of the idea that the research would produce information useful for all stakeholders.

Land Cover Change Project

Concern about the preservation of agricultural land in Indiana manifested in 1997 with the formation, by executive order, of the Hoosier Farmland Preservation Task Force (see Table 6.1). Although the task force described the loss of farmland in its 1999 report to the governor, questions remained about the rate and spatial distribution of lost farmland and about the role of urban development in contributing to such loss. The ILRC was authorized to collect additional information about Indiana's land resources. Center faculty and staff recognized that the conversion of agricultural land to other uses could be best understood in the broader context of urban development and other land use changes, and that satellite imagery could track land cover changes. Hence, internal resources were allocated from general foundation support to develop a time-series database of changes in land cover/land use in Central Indiana, which also supported development of the LUCI model.

The Center discussed these plans with ILRC members to illustrate how the database would provide information helpful to the ILRC, particularly in their compiling data on land resources. Hot-button issues in the state concerned the rate of agricultural land loss and the extent to which urban development caused it. It became clear that this research could help inform the debate over these issues, and ILRC members voiced support for the initiative.

Table 6.2

Three major collaborative projects on land use in Central Indiana

	Land cover change project	Planning inventory and smart growth audit	Land Use in Central Indiana (LUCI) model
Objective	Document land cover change between 1985 and 2000 in Central Indiana and balance of state. Create data foundation for LUCI model	Inventory county and municipal plan commissions in Central Indiana and balance of state. Assess comprehensive plans. Assess subdivision regulations	Develop model for predicting effects of policy choices on regional land use patterns
Collaborators	ILRC: Funded balance of state analyses ILUC: Supported project to document loss of farmland	ILRC: Funded balance of state inventory ILUC: Helped develop smart growth template	ILRC: Input on structure of model and policy scenarios ILUC: Input on structure of model and policy scenarios
Scope	Central Indiana and state. Scalable, spatial database for analyzing change in 16 categories of land cover	Central Indiana and state inventory: all counties and municipalities over 2,500. Audit: 35 counties and 50 municipalities	Central Indiana Bureau of Economic Analysis region: 44 counties,17,369 square miles. 18 policy options
Data	Landsat Thematic Mapper and Enhanced Thematic Mapper Plus satellite imagery for 1985, 1993, and 2000, 30 meter^2 resolution	Comprehensive plans. Subdivision regulations. Smart growth templates	Satellite imagery, census data, farmland, wetlands, riparian buffers, slopes, sewer and water, tax rates, school test scores, and employment
Technical methods	Computer-based, unsupervised classification of imagery with manual checking; GIS integration of databases	Professional judgment. Intercoder reliability assessments	GIS to integrate databases. Logistic regression to estimate aggregate discrete choice model. Programming in Visual Basic

(*continued*)

	Land cover change project	Planning inventory and smart growth audit	Land Use in Central Indiana (LUCI) model
People	Faculty: 1 @ 0.25 FTE for 1.25 years. Students: 2 @ 20 hours/week for 10 weeks	Faculty guidance Staff supervision: 1 @ 0.5 FTE for one year; 1 @ 0.3 FTE for one year. Students: 3.5 @ 20 hours/week for one year. Staff support (clerical, editing)	Faculty: 1 @ 0.5 FTE for four years. Students: 1 @ 20 hours/week for ten months; 1 @ 20 hours/week for five months. Staff support
Resources	Center: $20,000 ILRC: $30,000	Center: $90,000 ILRC grant: $9,900	Center: $200,000
Outcomes	Land cover change database. Center issue brief. ILRC newsletter articles. AAG and Indiana GIS conferences. Journal article submittals. Student gained experience in GIS and remote sensing. Better understanding of rates of urbanization and loss of agricultural land	Three Center issue briefs. ILRC newsletter articles. ACSP, APA, IPA conference presentations. Local use of templates. Students gained research experience, coauthored issue briefs, and gave talks at IPA conference. Better understanding of scope of planning in Indiana and obstacles to implementing smart growth	LUCI model and Web site. Center issue brief; ACSP, IPA conference talks. 17 regional seminars. Students gained GIS experience. Metropolitan Planning Organization evaluation of census urbanized areas. Two sponsored applications: watershed land use change ($27,000), and transportation planning ($48,000). *Public Works Management and Policy* article

Note: FTE = full-time equivalent.

The primary objectives of the project were to produce a scalable, spatial database that would permit planners to query for data on land cover change at local to regional scales; to provide a series of visual images of land cover change that would enable the ILRC, the Center, ILUC, and others to inform the public about patterns and processes of land cover change; and to provide data for development of LUCI (Table 6.2). Analytic work began in fall 2000 with the acquisition of sixteen satellite images of the forty-four-county study region from the Landsat Thematic Mapper (TM) and Enhanced Thematic Mapper Plus (ETM+) remote sensing system, in the mid-1980s, early 1990s, and 2000–2001. Modeling approaches using the geographic information system (GIS) were applied to categorize image pixels into one of sixteen land cover classes. These categories then were collapsed into eight more general categories for purposes of analysis, and the resulting maps were compared with one another to produce estimates of land use conversion. After seeing the initial results in spring 2001 and discussing their implications, the ILRC commissioned the Center to extend the analyses statewide.

The Central Indiana results show that rates of conversion from agricultural and forested land to developed cover are substantial (Figure 6.1) and are greater than rates of population change. Agricultural and herbaceous land (e.g., grassland) accounted for approximately 80 percent of all land converted to urban use between 1985 and 2000. Most of the remaining converted land had at one time been forested. In general, more land was changed to urban use in counties that already had higher proportions of urban use. While the analyses show clearly that substantial areas of agricultural land have been transformed, it is difficult to determine exact amounts because cover in the categories of agricultural and herbaceous land can change over time, depending on cropping practices.

Developing the land cover change database required about sixteen months of effort by a faculty member and two graduate student assistants from the IUPUI Department of Geography, who gained valuable experience in the interpretation of remotely sensed data. The total cost of the work for Central Indiana was approximately $20,000, while the costs for the balance of the state were $30,000, bringing the total to about $50,000. The greatest challenge in this research was interpreting results and relating findings to those of other studies and databases on lost agricultural land. Some stakeholders have found it difficult to understand and accept that there may be many reasons for a rate of agricultural land loss. It is possible also that a rate amount depends on how it is measured. Few technical challenges were encountered in this research because standard techniques were used in the analyses.

Inventory and Assessment of Planning Practices

Indiana has 92 counties and more than 550 municipalities. Planning is not required at the local level, and since the demise of the State Planning Services Agency, no state organization has had responsibility for tracking or monitoring local planning activity. Hence, at the time the ILRC was established, no centralized source of information about the scope of planning in Indiana existed in state government, although the Indiana Planning Association did maintain a list of plan commissions. The Center realized that information about planning methods would be helpful for the ILRC in meeting its statutory mandate. Basic data from an inventory of planning institutions were a prerequisite to undertaking more detailed investigations into planning prac-

Figure 6.1 **Simplified land use change map of Central Indiana study region (1985–2000)**

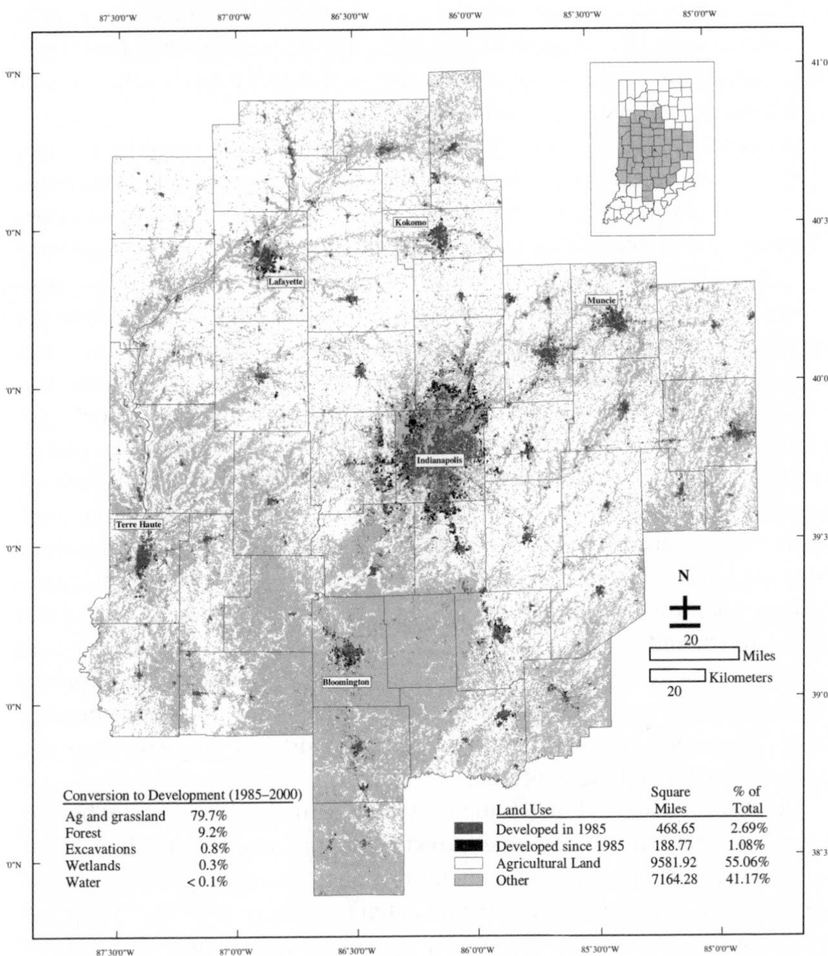

tices. First inventoried were the planning practices in the 44-county Central Indiana region, which determined that 35 counties and 47 of 51 municipalities with populations of more than 2,500 that do not participate in a county plan commission had adopted comprehensive plans and had in place zoning ordinances and subdivision regulations.

Following this inventory, the Center met frequently with stakeholders from ILUC, ILRC, and other organizations to develop templates to guide audits of comprehensive plans, zoning ordinances, and subdivision regulations. Although the explicit purpose of the meetings was to fine tool the templates, an implicit objective was to build trust among stakeholders with different views on land use issues. Some stakeholders representing development interests were suspicious of smart growth and considered it a euphemism for regulation; they doubted the objectivity of smart growth research. Over time, however, participants came to realize that the proposed research could inform local choices, not justify preordained political positions.

The final templates, which were comparable with those used in a similar project in Illinois, addressed six principles of sustainable development (Berke and Conroy 2000, 21), eleven principles of smart growth, and other issues important to Indiana policy makers. For example, the audit of comprehensive plans addressed such smart growth tenets as compact urban form, maximizing use of existing infrastructure, providing variety and choice in housing, establishing a balanced multimodal transportation system, improving development review processes by increasing flexibility, and creating mixed-use, walkable neighborhoods—and other smart growth features. The audit of regulatory tools included a review of such innovative development and infrastructure standards as shorter setbacks, maximum lot sizes/minimum densities, reduced parking requirements, narrower street widths and pedestrian easements; restrictions on use of agricultural land and sensitive environmental areas such as wetlands, floodplains, and steep slopes; and provisions to encourage traditional neighborhood design. The templates were used to guide smart growth audits of planning tools used by Central Indiana counties and municipalities. To complete the audits, research assistants read, interpreted, and coded each comprehensive plan, zoning ordinance, and subdivision regulation. The students coauthored the Center reports on this work and presented them at planning conferences.

The research showed that counties and municipalities cooperate, but few jurisdictions have integrated smart growth principles into their planning documents. Most Indiana local governments rely on traditional regulatory requirements that, in many cases, have the potential to actually contribute to sprawl. For example, county governments, on average, adopted only 16 percent of the seventy-five specific development controls that were assessed, and only 22 percent of the counties adopted 20 percent or more of these controls. And, despite the state's focus on farmland preservation throughout the 1990s, only two counties use agricultural zoning for farmland protection. Following completion of the inventory, the ILRC commissioned the Center to extend the inventory statewide.

The inventory and smart growth audit took about three months for two Center researchers and required about fifteen months of work by four graduate students, who shared responsibility for reading and assessing the planning tools. A faculty member helped conceptualize and supervise the work, the costs of which totaled about $90,000. The costs for the inventory of the balance of the state were $9,900, bringing the total to more than $100,000, since this estimate does not include costs for faculty supervision or clerical and editorial staff assistance.

Challenges in completing the audit included convincing stakeholders that results were not predetermined, developing the templates used to assess the planning tools, obtaining the planning documents, and ensuring consistency in evaluation. As stakeholders' understanding of the research grew, their trust in the process also increased, and, by critiquing drafts, they played a critical role in developing the templates. Obtaining documents for their review was a problem because several communities had only single original copies and were unable or unwilling to duplicate them. Several community visits were required to complete the audits. Finally, to ensure consistency in evaluation and minimize error associated with interpreting by analysis, a subset of each type of document was read and coded twice. Potential variation associated with coding decisions was documented, and it was determined that differences stemming from interpretation were minimal.

The Land Use in Central Indiana Model

In fall 1999, as the Center developed its research agenda on investment in Central Indiana and continued conversations with members of ILUC, it became clear that there was substantial interest in developing a model to predict changes in land use (Tables 6.1, 6.2). The Center leaders decided to support development of the model, and intensive work on it commenced in early 2000. Version 1.0 was released in May of 2003.

The LUCI model predicts the probability of conversion of nondeveloped land to residential use in 17,369 one-square-mile grid cells in Central Indiana. It uses aggregated logistic regression to estimate a discrete choice model for the conversion of land from nonurban to urban use. Data from the land cover change project provide the foundation for the LUCI model. Independent variables in predicting development include proximity to existing development; accessibility to employment by zip code; the location of transportation, water, and sewer infrastructure; and school district standardized test scores.

The LUCI model was designed to be utilized by policy makers and citizens, not just planners and other experts with training in modeling. In addition, as part of a strategy to maximize use, the model was planned from the outset to be freely available to potential users, who can manipulate eighteen policy variables to construct different scenarios. Because the purpose of the model is to illustrate the effects of policy choices on development patterns, results from any given scenario always are juxtaposed and compared with a current-trends or a user-specified scenario. Output is available in both map and tabular format; the latter includes dozens of statistics ranging from acres of agricultural land and wetlands that were developed, to increases in the average commuting time. The current-trends scenario indicates that substantial amounts of land will be converted to urban use by 2040 (Figure 6.2).

From conception to completion, the development of LUCI took more than two years for its creator and required the support of two research assistants who helped build databases necessary for estimation of the model. One graduate student of planning collected and digitized information on the areas provided with water and sewer service from all of the utilities in Central Indiana. A geography graduate student was responsible for assembling many of the layers of GIS data required for the model. Both gained valuable experience in the application and use of GIS. Costs for the project are difficult to estimate because LUCI's creator devoted much of his discretionary research time to the project. Direct labor costs to the Center, which account for a substantial portion of total costs, have been more than $200,000.

Development of the LUCI model presented a number of challenges, ranging from data assembly to explanation of the structure of the model to stakeholders who had no background or basis for conceptualizing it. For example, since there is no centralized source in Indiana for information about the availability of water and sewer service, all utility providers in the region had to be contacted, then service regions were digitized. The model and its potential value in informing policy decisions was explained to stakeholders. Although participants generally indicated support for efforts to develop the model, they did not always understand it or thought that it might have little practical value. Their support clearly increased after working versions of the tool became available and its capacity to inform policy debates became evident.

The Nature of Collaboration

Community-based research at academic institutions is closely related to the paradigm of action research and related approaches that aim both to contribute to social science and to develop solutions to practical problems in ways consistent with community and academic values (Rappaport 1970; see also Stringer 1999). Community-based research is informed by and initiated in response to priorities and needs identified by people within the communities that are served (Bringle and Hatcher 2002; Strand 2000). It is, therefore, collaborative and action-oriented, with an explicit objective of social change. An inherent challenge in community-based research is the need to build trust and effective working relationships among collaborators.

Figure 6.2 **LUCI forecasts of conversion of land to urban uses, 2000–2040**

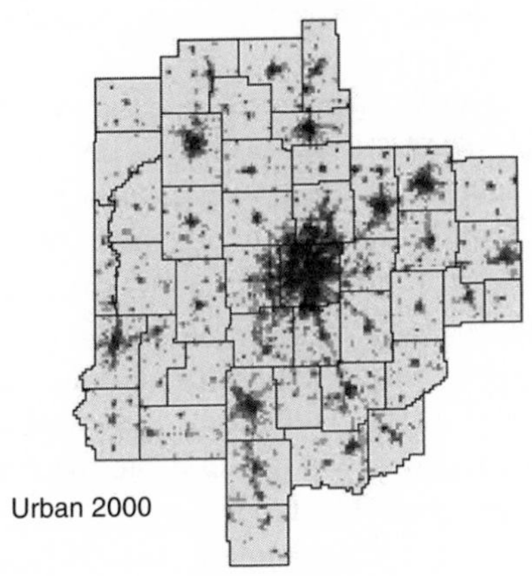

The Land Use in Central Indiana model (LUCI) allows users to explore the patterns of urbanization associated with a variety of assumptions and policy choices through 2040. The map to the left shows urbanization in 2000. The two maps below show the results of differing population projections. The map on the bottom left reflects the pattern associated with using the official census projections that are produced by the Indiana Business Research Center. The map on the bottom right reflects the pattern if the population growth from 1990–2000 were to continue.

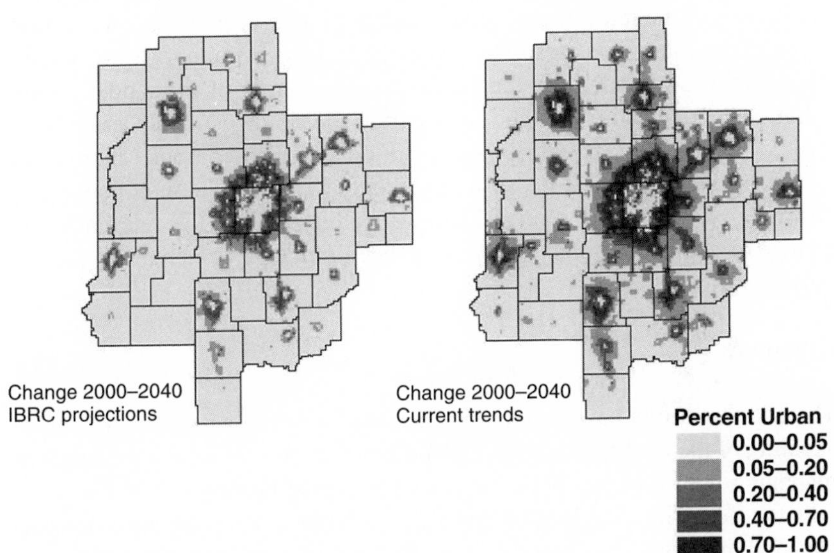

From the perspective of social science, this collaboration has tackled the broad academic problems of describing and explaining land use change, assessing local use of planning tools to encourage smart growth, and forecasting regional patterns of development. As an example of community-based research, this collaboration has attempted to address the practical problems of managing land resources in Central Indiana and of educating planning practitioners and decision makers in the region. This collaboration has been successful primarily because all partners have come to believe that the research is designed to inform the policy-making process, not to dictate or prescribe particular solutions.

In general, practitioners are skilled at identifying problems, but they sometimes need assistance in conceptualizing solutions or specifying the information required to solve a problem. Conversely, researchers at universities excel at producing knowledge, but sometimes they fail to ask questions of greatest relevance to practitioners responsible for solving problems. This collaboration has built on the participants' respective strengths and has overcome these potential weaknesses through joint problem definition and research design. In the case of the smart growth audit, Center researchers worked with the ILRC, ILUC, and other stakeholders to refine the templates used to assess planning tools prior to the audit. Because stakeholders agreed on the items in the templates, they subsequently did not complain that different items should have been assessed, and they generally interpreted results in the same way. In addition, researchers learned of nuances in local planning tools and increased the relevance of their work. Similarly, during the construction of the LUCI model, its creator periodically asked practitioners to work with iterations of the model and then revised the structure of the model to pay attention to their concerns and incorporate their suggestions. Certain features of the model, including policy options used to construct alternative scenarios, were included because of stakeholder input. These collaborative efforts have resulted in mutual learning, increased both the relevance and quality of the social science, and have been essential to achieving project outcomes.

Outcomes

The collaborations have resulted in increased knowledge and better understanding of the land resources in Central Indiana, current local approaches to managing land use, and policy options for managing future land use. Specific outcomes have included databases, conference presentations and seminars, publications (see Central Indiana Bibliography, below), a computerized planning tool, new contract research, and continuing dialogue among a broader set of stakeholders (Table 6.2). Students have gained valuable professional experience in the use of GIS and remote sensing technologies, and in the design, conduct, publication, and presentation of evaluative research.

This project to understand the dynamics of land use change has produced a scalable spatial database in the region that, with financial support from the ILRC, has been extended statewide. The ILRC's willingness to fund the expansion of the work is evidence of its practical value. Among other applications, a work group comprised of representatives from state agencies and stakeholder organizations is using this database to deepen understanding of the rate of agricultural land loss in Indiana. Members of the work group now have a better understanding of the strengths and weaknesses of different databases and why they produce varying estimates of land use change; they have learned that complementary measures provide greater insight into the scope and patterns of the problem.

The smart growth audit provides a factual basis for debates over the merits of current planning practice and an approach that local planners can adapt for updating and modernizing existing planning tools. Planners from several communities responsible for updating zoning ordinances and subdivision regulations have used the template to guide discussions with local planning commissions about proposed regulation changes. Legislators and interest groups have used the planning inventory to inform proposals for changes to state enabling legislation. Graduate students, who shared responsibility for reviewing documents, made especially important contributions to the audit.

The LUCI model, which is built upon a generalized version of the land use change database, perhaps has yielded the most tangible outcomes. Activities associated with the release of the LUCI model included a set of seminars for planners and academics in universities in each of the six metropolitan areas in Central Indiana as well as a number of demonstrations for other agencies and stakeholders. The *Indianapolis Star* carried a feature article about the release of the LUCI model in May 2003, and more than eighty people downloaded the model from the LUCI Web site on the day the article was published. The Metropolitan Planning Organization in Indianapolis used output from a beta version of LUCI to assess preliminary U.S. Census designations of urbanized areas, and the Center has been contracted to use the LUCI model in two projects in the region. A Center project for USFilter, the firm that manages water utility services in Indianapolis, and IUPUI's Center for Earth and Environmental Science involves forecasting land use change in the watersheds of three reservoirs that provide drinking water for the city and its suburbs. A project for the Indiana Department of Transportation involves development of a customized, nine-county version of the model (LUCI-T) that will be used to generate population and employment forecasts for use in transportation models. These applications are evidence of the model's practical value, which was enhanced in large part by input from practitioners. The collaborative efforts have paid off with a tool that people are using to inform themselves of land use decisions.

The three primary products of the collaboration—the land cover change database, the smart growth audit, and the LUCI model—were not produced to meet specific goals established by the Center when it received support for its initiative on investment in Central Indiana. Nor were these products commissioned by a community client. Instead, they are the result of decisions made during the collaborative process to address explicit needs for information and tools to improve management of land resources in the state, and they illustrate the incremental and adaptive nature of such a process.

The key challenges in the process were to develop a shared understanding of the need for new information and tools and to overcome skepticism that academic research can lead to better policy and practice. For example, the members of the ILRC knew they needed information about land resources and planning practices to fulfill their statutory mandates to educate and provide technical assistance, but they had few resources and were uncertain how to collect data. Similarly, members of the ILUC knew that information about the likely consequences of alternative planning policies could inform debates over planning at the local level, but none envisioned a GIS-based computer model that could illustrate graphically and statistically the implications of policy choices. Center researchers understood how these databases and computerized models could be developed, but needed better understanding of the policy context in order to develop the most relevant products. These challenges were met through communication and an ongoing dialogue about the rationale for alternative strategies for meeting needs. This dialogue led to trust and a shared understanding of priorities that, in turn, resulted in tangible products and a deeper commitment to continue collaborating.

Conclusion

This work on land use in Central Indiana reflects IUPUI's mission of civic engagement and SPEA's and the Center's commitments to applied research that addresses problems facing the people of the region and state. The work can be distinguished from other initiatives by its scope and longevity. The projects included both the assessment of a resource base and the development of tools for evaluating alternative approaches to manage the resource. It has required application of sophisticated knowledge of remote sensing and GIS technologies, statistical modeling, and policy analysis. The work also has been enduring, continuing for more than four years, which has been possible because of the commitment of key individuals willing to invest substantial time and resources in anticipation of potential outcomes.

The general process used to accomplish this work could be replicated elsewhere, depending on the availability of financial resources. The crucial element of the collaboration has been commitment: the willingness of people from the Center, ILRC, and ILUC to invest in a process based on simple faith that shared efforts will result in social change. Researchers and stakeholders elsewhere can replicate this process by incorporating stakeholder input in research design, accepting that problems typically are more complex than they appear, and accepting that time is required to build trust. Such a collaborative process can provide many meaningful opportunities for students to learn about both research and practice.

The Center's projects have required substantial resources that were not available in the public sector in Indiana. Total estimated costs for Center personnel's time exceeds $400,000. The Center has been able to undertake these initiatives only because of a generous award from a private foundation. Depending on the availability of funds from either public or philanthropic sectors elsewhere, university-community partners may have to adjust initiatives.

This collaboration has resulted in a number of related projects and will continue in the future as people work together to improve management of land resources in the state. As initiatives evolve to make Indiana a more hospitable place for planning, university-community partnership will be a necessary, although not a sufficient, condition for success.

Notes

1. See www.indianalanduse.org.
2. See www.in.gov/legislative.

References

Berke, P.R., and M.M. Conroy. 2000. Are we planning for sustainable development? An evaluation of 30 comprehensive plans. *Journal of the American Planning Association* 66(1):21–33.

Bringle, R.G., and J.A. Hatcher. 2002. University-community partnerships: The terms of engagement. *Journal of Social Issues* 58:503–16.

Rappaport, R.N. 1970. Three dilemmas in action research. *Human Relations* 23:499–513.

Strand, K.J. 2000. Community-based research as pedagogy. *Michigan Journal of Community Service Learning* (Fall):85–96.

Stringer, E.T. 1999. *Action research,* 2nd ed. Thousand Oaks, CA: SAGE Publications.

Central Indiana Bibliography

Hirsch, S. 2003. Public can get free forecast of area's growth from LUCI. *Indianapolis Star,* May 21, www.indystar.com.

Indiana Land Resources Council Web site. 2003. www.in.gov/oca/ilrc/.

Indiana Land Resources Council. 2002. *2001 annual report.* Indianapolis: State of Indiana.

Indiana Land Use Consortium Web site. 2003. www.indianalanduse.org/.

Land Use in Central Indiana Model Web site. 2003. http://luci.urbancenter.iupui.edu.

Lindsey, G., and J. Palmer. 2000. *Planning in Central Indiana.* Indianapolis: Indiana University–Purdue University Indianapolis, School of Public and Environmental Affairs, Center for Urban Policy and the Environment.

Ottensmann, J. 2003. Land Use in Central Indiana model and the relationships of public infrastructure to urban development. *Public Works Management and Policy* 8(1):62–76.

Ottensmann, J., and G. Lindsey. 2002. *Low density development increasing in Central Indiana.* Indianapolis: Indiana University–Purdue University Indianapolis, School of Public and Environmental Affairs, Center for Urban Policy and the Environment.

Owen, R., K. Dickson, G. Lindsey, and J. Palmer. 2001. *Central Indiana counties rely on conventional development controls.* Indianapolis: Indiana University–Purdue University Indianapolis, School of Public and Environmental Affairs, Center for Urban Policy and the Environment.

Palmer, J., and J. Ottensmann. 2003. *New model predicts growth patterns in Central Indiana.* Indianapolis: Indiana University–Purdue University Indianapolis, School of Public and Environmental Affairs, Center for Urban Policy and the Environment.

Palmer, J., and J. Wilson. Unpublished manuscript. *Land cover in Indiana 1985, 1993, and 2001.* Indianapolis: Indiana University–Purdue University Indianapolis, School of Public and Environmental Affairs, Center for Urban Policy and the Environment.

Sapp, D., S. Payton, G. Lindsey, and J. Kirlin. 2000. *Central Indiana: Visions of a region.* Indianapolis: Center for Urban Policy and the Environment (00-C09).

Wilson, J., and G. Lindsey. Forthcoming. Socioeconomic correlates and environmental impacts of urban development in a Central Indiana landscape. *Journal of Urban Planning and Development.*

Worgan, A., J. Harbourn, G. Lindsey, and J. Palmer. 2001. *Traditional planning prevails in Central Indiana.* Indianapolis: Indiana University–Purdue University Indianapolis, School of Public and Environmental Affairs, Center for Urban Policy and the Environment.

Part 3

SMART GROWTH BY COLLABORATION

7

Smart Growth and Community Preservation: One Citizen at a Time

Priscilla Geigis, Elisabeth Hamin, and Linda Silka

In states like the Commonwealth of Massachusetts, with strong home-rule traditions and little political support for state-imposed planning directions, moving toward the goals of smart growth has been challenging. Local control, legislatively organized in Massachusetts and many other states as home rule, is fiercely defended here, making state-mandated smart growth a political chimera. Instead, implementing smart growth will have to occur town-by-town, city-by-city. For that to happen, the citizens who make many of the planning decisions—town planning board members, conservation commissioners, housing nonprofit groups, town meeting members—must understand smart growth principles and have a sense of how they can be implemented.

It is to this end that the University of Massachusetts (UMass) and the commonwealth's Executive Office of Environmental Affairs (EOEA) entered into a partnership designed to provide smart growth education to current and future local leaders. In Massachusetts smart growth is also known as community preservation, and the citizen training is acquired through the Community Preservation Institute (CPI). This chapter describes the implementation of the institute and its outcomes, the design of the university-state collaboration, and the lessons learned from the effort.

Designing the Community Preservation Institute

The Community Preservation Institute is one of the most successful results of a collaborative effort between UMass and EOEA, as each partner seeks coordinated mechanisms to leverage what each does best, while benefiting the citizens of the commonwealth and their own institutions. In January 2000, after preliminary discussions, the Commonwealth Partnership (CP) was officially formed, with the goal of developing opportunities for collaboration in teaching, research, and community-based outreach between EOEA and the university. EOEA previously had been preparing a smart growth policy called Community Preservation, which included several efforts: to increase geographic information system (GIS) capacities in all municipalities across the state and provide data and maps describing likely futures for all towns and cities, given their current zoning; to provide funding for community development plans; and to increase investments in land protection and adaptive reuse of historic buildings.

While the partnership did explore collaboration in a variety of environmental disciplines, community preservation seemed to be a natural connection between the university and state entities; they formed the Community Preservation Working Group composed of a diverse mixture of state managers from the environmental agencies and professors and administrators from the university. They quickly recognized that the university and EOEA had similar missions—to use their resources and expertise to serve a wider community. Both groups are centralized organizations composed of several component, self-sustaining entities, with five UMass campuses and four units under EOEA. One of the challenges—that ultimately became a key to the success of the partnership—was recognizing the need for representation on the Commonwealth Partnership organizing committee and the need for input from each of the five campuses and each of the four agencies, instead of from just a few representatives from UMass or Environmental Affairs as a whole. Such inclusion established "buy in" to ideas early on, allowing for quicker, easier, and more lasting consensus on basic issues.

The working group developed a list of programs, community outreach opportunities, and departments within the university and the state that were related to smart growth. The list revealed a wealth of experience embedded in both programs and people that, once combined, could be a powerful educational tool for local leaders. Thus was the Community Preservation Institute born. The goal of the CPI is to promote a point of view that challenges sprawl development and replaces such an approach with smart growth principles, at the same time expanding the constituency of leaders who will make bold smart growth choices at the local level. As described below, each partner—EOEA and UMass—had a somewhat different perspective on smart growth. Through the development of the CPI, the Working Group was able to ensure that those perspectives were integrated into an effective program for community leaders.

EOEA was very committed to changing land use patterns across the state and believed that the best way to achieve such change would be to provide tools and information to local leaders to enable them to make informed, balanced decisions about growth in their communities. After exposing local leaders to GIS-based tools, thereby graphically illustrating potential growth scenarios, it was important that leaders be informed about practical ways to establish the principles of community preservation in their growth decisions. To have the widest impact on the landscape, where land use is controlled locally, local decision makers needed to be empowered, and EOEA knew that a bottom-up approach would work best. For that, citizens would need to be engaged and active. The Working Group was a way to produce such engagement by, in effect, starting a conversation about community preservation across a spectrum of policy and opinion makers.

Working with UMass also gave EOEA an opportunity to influence research and teaching agendas while at the same time helping the administration and faculty to become more aware of EOEA's issues and perspectives. And, finally, the administration knew that there is strength in coalitions; individual agency administrations and agendas may come and go, but developing long-term coalitions among powerful groups can make real policy implementation easier and more lasting. For the CPI, EOEA's hope has been that the initial evening course devoted to citizens might become a fuller curriculum for regular university students. EOEA has taken steps in that direction, but this slow-growing idea remains long-term.

Just as EOEA had agency-specific goals for the partnership, UMass did too. The memorandum of agreement (MOA) under which the Commonwealth Partnership was established is filled with language about what each of the partners—EOEA and the UMass system—hopes would be achieved by entering into this relationship. The MOA indicated that each partner intended to move together beyond the arm's-length, short-term contacts that had characterized past efforts and find ways to deepen those collaborations so that each partner would be better prepared to tap the other's resources as new opportunities such as the CPI emerged.

The goals of the university in undertaking the partnership were varied. First, the CPI was seen as providing an opportunity for UMass to increase its impact through close connection with a relevant and successful agency initiative. The collaboration required the individual campuses of UMass, which often act entirely independently, to develop innovative, nimble ways to work together as a system. The UMass leaders hoped to uncover hidden talent on the individual campuses and to see if such new talent could be "grown" by challenging faculty to engage in interesting integrative tasks. In many ways UMass is trying to create a new kind of lean, distributed state university system, and the CPI offers opportunities to test out some of these ideas. UMass will always be an underresourced system within an otherwise wealthy state.

Therefore, all of the needed expertise will never be available on any one campus. The system must find ways to work across the campuses and to be nontraditional in its approach to collaboration with groups such as Environmental Affairs.

The characteristics of smart growth make it an excellent arena for this sort of institutional development and experimentation. Addressing smart growth requires interdisciplinary efforts. Campuses all over the United States have begun to confront thorny questions about how to increase communication among disciplines that traditionally have gone their separate ways and, therefore, have not been effective in working with outside partners. For example, faculty in engineering who focus on transportation would typically have little contact with faculty in economics who analyze the costs of development. Smart growth discussions cannot progress, however, without faculty from very different disciplines finding ways to integrate their areas of expertise. UMass faculty need to bring their research into the CPI training and find ways to change this research so that it will provide resource materials for smart growth initiatives. In other words, the CPI, if done well, can be seen as an intervention that will in subtle ways change the faculty and the institution while it informs the participants who are taking the CPI courses.

Program Design and Implementation

In spring 2001 UMass and Environmental Affairs launched the first Community Preservation Institute in Westborough, Massachusetts; through 2003, the program has had 252 graduates from 136 communities. The CPI attracts a wide and diverse array of participants, ranging from teachers and elected officials to lawyers, developers, activists in the environmental, housing, or historic preservation communities, state employees, nonprofit representatives, and concerned citizens. CPI is a nine-evening course designed to introduce twenty-five local leaders per class to innovative planning concepts and practices; the core classes are described in Table 7.1.

All of the courses were derived from key smart growth insights interpreted for the New England landscape. First, all planning begins with environmental realities so that important lands and ecological processes are protected. Each program includes initial sessions on water resources and land preservation, and many devote an entire evening to biodiversity. Second, smart growth supports existing town centers. New Englanders are fortunate that smart growth corresponds well with the traditional land use form; for this reason, community preservation can be discussed when advancing a smart growth agenda.

The classes recognize the functionality of the traditional regional landscape, with its compact towns featuring a mix of uses and a variety of housing types

Table 7.1

CPI core curriculum

1. Introduction, including a role-play to get participants thinking about the actors in a development project and their various motivations.
2. Land Preservation and Natural Communities, which includes information on how developers value land, along with conservation easements, conservation subdivision design, and so forth.
3. Water: Managing a Finite Resource, which demonstrates how to develop a municipal water budget and calculate the impacts of new development on water resources, as well as ways to mitigate the negative consequences of development.
4. Creative Housing, which describes how to undertake a simple housing-needs analysis as well as the various programs the state and feds have to support affordable housing.
5. Breathing Life into Old Places: How Historic Roots Can Help Revitalize a Community, which explores how elements of a historic and cultural landscape can assist a community in defining a theme that will drive its future in terms of economic development, downtown revitalization, and historic preservation.
6. Adaptive Reuse, which describes how to undertake projects to reuse existing buildings, especially those with historic or community value.
7. Creative Zoning: A Blueprint for Development, which provides an overview of both tried-and-true zoning approaches and also emerging techniques for smart growth.
8. Tying It All Together: Where Do We Go From Here?, in which students review the course and present their projects.

9. **Curriculum added to particular sites to address regional issues:**

- Natural Resources as an Economic Catalyst: Farms, Forests, and Recreation
- Downtown Revitalization
- Transportation: Connecting People and Places
- Community-Based Biodiversity Conservation
- Green Development
- Green Neighborhoods
- Environmental Justice
- Brownfields and Community Revitalization
- Diversity in Community Preservation

and prices, all set in a walkable neighborhood design context. Major challenges to this traditional urban form include changing technological needs (obsolete mill buildings, for example) and difficulties in providing housing for moderate-income families. Therefore, sessions on adaptive reuse and providing affordable housing are featured in the curriculum. Another challenge is that existing zoning in Massachusetts towns often does not support the desired smart growth/traditional form. Sessions are included, therefore, that describe alternative approaches to zoning so citizens would be savvy enough to press the town meetings, planning boards, or city councils to consider alternatives to the widely prevalent 1950s suburban zoning codes. Achieving change, however, always requires political support from the community and its decisions makers. Almost every session considers which groups one could turn to for coalition building on that topic, and how to combine agendas to maximize political support in town meetings or city council hearings.

While the curriculum is designed to highlight a different community preservation theme each week, smart growth is also about making connections among all the challenges to good planning. For example, the class entitled Breathing Life into Old Places: How Historic Roots Can Help Revitalize a Community focuses on adaptive reuse of buildings, using case studies of historic mill buildings converted to affordable and market-rate housing, thus reemphasizing concepts learned in the Creative Housing class. The class entitled Water: Managing a Finite Resource illustrates the importance of conducting water analyses and negotiating budgets to ensure that high water quality and quantity are safeguarded as communities continue to grow. As examples of practical applications, instructors discuss creating water-district zoning as well as other measures to protect the water supply, again touching upon the material covered in Creative Zoning: A Blueprint for Development and in Land Preservation and Natural Communities. These connections across sessions are vital in helping students see the realistic complexities of smart growth and how necessary it is to consider many components while still taking action where possible.

Participants also needed to recognize that each campus and its surroundings were unique, so specialty classes were created that respond to particular needs in certain regions. For example, Diversity in Community Preservation was offered at UMass Lowell, located in a historic industrial city with the highest Cambodian population in the nation as well as other immigrant communities. This course was designed to show both how cultures and traditions reflect perceptions about growth and development and how important it is to be inclusive of diverse interests when making decisions. At UMass Dartmouth, located in a southeast coastal community near the busy fishing port of New Bedford, a course was offered that described such natural resources as agriculture and aquaculture as catalysts for economic development. In Westborough, along the I-495 high-technology corridor that has experienced unprecedented growth in recent years, a course on zoning was held. The class showed students that the automobile-dependent, big-box retail outlets that they did not like was the very development that fit the community's zoning scheme, and that the mixed-use downtown villages, a traditional growth pattern in the commonwealth, were deprived of development because of current zoning. In Amherst, a course on the preservation of working farms complemented the town's longstanding commitment to agriculture. Finally, in Boston a course on brownfields and environmental justice assisted urban leaders.

Almost all evening sessions include a lecture component followed by an exercise that students undertake in class to make the lecture more meaningful. An example is the role-play exercise used jointly by professor Robert Ryan and attorney Arthur Bergeron. They describe a piece of valuable farmland that would be sold for development unless it could be purchased. They gave the purchase price of the land and likely sale price of the new homes, and then assigned roles to each of the students (developer, landowners, conservation commissioners, etc.). It was up to the students to use the principles explained in class for determining profits and costs, and then finding community coalitions that could raise the money needed to save the property and negotiate with the landowners. Other instructors ran similar exercises, asking students to think through the potential connections of affordable housing and adaptive reuse, or to calculate storm levels and aquifer recharge and then imagine zoning solutions to storm-water problems.

A second way individual sessions are made more meaningful is through the inclusion of a project component in the curriculum. Participants are divided into teams before the first night class, based on their interests regarding smart growth—housing, historic preservation, land protection, and so forth. The teams are asked to select a project, preferably addressing a growth issue facing their own town, where they could really make a difference. Students research the issue, find smart growth solutions, and then make a presentation to the class on the last evening of the institute. These presentations are intended to serve as dry runs for presenting their projects to town meetings for actual funding or support, and in several cases, students did exactly that. Completing these projects is the most ambivalent part of the course for students. Many are very busy professionals, and, since no significant class time is allowed, out-of-class meetings for the teams are difficult and sometimes almost impossible. For others, however, the project is the best part of the class, and, in the end, via e-mail, phone, and limited outside meetings, all teams have produced excellent projects that provide a good class summary of topics discussed throughout the CPI sessions.

A team of an academic and a policy maker teach most evening sessions. Team teaching is important for two reasons: it provides academic background about any given issue along with a practical and/or political application, while also giving two different viewpoints. Both academics and practitioners become resource people for students to consult when addressing community growth issues in the future. These "people tools" are some of the best tools provided to local leaders grappling with land use issues. A point was made of bringing in such key people, as university or state department heads to teach at the institute and thereby become its champions. To keep courses running smoothly, a project coordinator from the university's Donahue Institute attends each class to organize and distribute materials, pass out the next week's reading or explain its location on the Internet, and in general handle administrative tasks.

Feedback, Evaluation, and Changes

The institute is still evolving, incorporating changes with each offering based on participants' responses gained through official feedback sessions. Class and course assessments are repeatedly sought from students, and their critiques are considered carefully. With each new offering, UMass and EOEA adjust the format of CPI to meet the needs of the constituency. One issue that became apparent was that while students enjoyed the team teaching, they were frustrated by the lack of continuity in instructors, since no one except the project coordinator was there each evening. For the most recent offerings of CPI at the Amherst campus, an alternative structure was explored for the course: a lead instructor with knowledge of smart growth and only one guest instructor for each evening. As expected, there were gains in continuity over the different course sessions but some loss of multiple perspectives on a particular topic. Both structures are viewed as successful, and the choice for future classes probably will relate to ease of administration and costs, rather than reflecting a clear pedagogic preference. As the program developed, the Internet was relied upon more for delivering reading materials and extending discussions among students. This resulted in creation of a Web page (http://commpres.env.state.ma.us), with access to a wide range of documents and articles available to students and alumni long after graduation.

Since its initial offering at one UMass location, the institute has expanded to all five UMass campuses, allowing greater access for local leaders throughout the state. Participants requested longer classes and more of them, so the institute added thirty minutes to each class and ran two-and-a-half-hour classes for nine weeks instead of two-hour classes for seven weeks. Participants requested that there be more interaction with classmates, so team projects were established. They wanted to "experience" their course work, so field trips were organized to explore farms, housing developments, and city sidewalks. Responding to student requests, the CPI now offers alumni classes in GIS, coalition building, and public participation, and a pollution prevention and advanced water policy course. The continuous distribution and assessment of student evaluations are basic to the program's success, along with actually implementing changes when student opinions clearly point to the need of such changes.

A major challenge that all such programs face is that the time commitment for this training deters some leaders from attending. Since the goal is to expand the constituency for smart growth and good planning, the partnership is exploring the possibility of offering the nine-week program on a limited basis and presenting the community preservation curriculum in an abbreviated weekend format in order to reach a larger audience. An important initial step was to determine which nights most local towns held their commission and town meetings, and thus schedule the CPI on a different night, as many students already serve in some town capacity.

When creating the institute, EOEA and UMass decided to provide full scholarships to local leaders to attend CPI and to limit classes to twenty-five at each location. The entities reasoned that scholarships were investments in communities since the local leaders whom the institute was designed to attract were already the most active in their communities and in the best positions to affect land use change. Further, CPI served essentially as a reward for their taking additional evening time from already overloaded schedules. The small class size was the most conducive to an interactive format; however, the cost per pupil was high, especially at a time of tight budget constraints. It started at $5,600 in the first year, including significant curriculum design and startup costs, and fell to $1,400 per student in the most recent year. It may be necessary to either charge a nominal tuition or seek foundation support to help subsidize the nine-week institute, and perhaps to increase class size.

The initial evaluations of the CPI focused on assessing the extent to which this high-quality, innovative set of courses had met the needs of diverse adult leaders; increasingly, attention is turning to assessing the long-term impacts of the training. The intent is to understand how the training is being used to address smart growth issues. Graduates are reporting that as a consequence of the training, they are running for local- and state-level elected office, presenting their team project findings at local forums, and using the team projects to actually preserve land and to lobby for affordable housing projects. An example of the connections between the institute training and the realization of smart growth outcomes highlights the power of educating citizenry on this key topic, as reported by Environmental Affairs in the January 2003 issue of *Community Preservation Press E-Letter*:

> Marc Connelly and Jane Sears Pierce from Holliston, and Tammy Gilchrist from Westborough decided to go beyond the classroom when they selected their team project as part of the Community Preservation Institute. When student teams were asked to explore solutions to current issues taking place in their home cities and towns, the three decided to develop

> their project around a land purchase that was rising to the top of the Town's agenda and to use their work as the foundation for a presentation before a future Town Meeting.
>
> The group examined the purchase of a 210–acre parcel in Holliston known as the Fairbanks property. The unique property, included in the state's BioMap of critical biological resource areas, contains vernal pools with several rare species including yellow and blue spotted salamanders and spotted turtles. The parcel additionally abuts a large piece of Milford conservation land on one side and 172 acres of Holliston Town Forest on the other. The group presented their land acquisition strategy to classmates and received constructive feedback that helped them finalize their presentation to the Town.
>
> Using knowledge and skills gained through the Institute, Connolly and Pierce, also Holliston Open Space Committee members, found coalition stakeholders in the community and examined and worked out the final details of the land purchase. "Many of the town boards had to be notified, advised, etc. to get everyone on board and in agreement. That was the hardest of all tasks. It was a real eye-opener for all of us," remarks Marc Connelly about this exploratory and support building process. At a Special Town Meeting on December 17 [2002], the Town voted unanimously to purchase the property using a combination of funds from an EOEA Urban Self-Help Grant, the Conservation Commission, the Trustees of Reservation, Community Preservation Act, and private donations. This parcel and the abutting conservation and town forestland is now considered the largest piece of open space inside the I-495 belt, with a total area of about 2,500 acres. (http://commpres.env.state.ma.us/Newsletter/e-letter.asp)

Yet another important way that feedback has been gathered about the CPI was by having a faculty member with expertise in planning (Dr. Elisabeth Hamin, the second author of this chapter) oversee the CPI offerings at UMass Amherst; as a part of that role, she sought to identify possible benefits for traditional and nontraditional students of incorporating CPI courses and approaches into the regular UMass curriculum.

It is not often in academia that faculty has the opportunity to hear other faculty as well as practitioners present not only their research but course content, too. As the lead instructor for the Amherst fall 2001 Institute, Dr. Hamin had the chance to learn from the guest presenters as well as from the students, who were highly motivated and brought to classes the sorts of questions that can only come from real-life experience: Why did agency XYZ do that when they said they would do this? How can I reach out to my Conservation Commission? What are the possible funding sources for this housing project? Surprisingly, even planners from a local regional planning association attended, which suggests that holistic training in new approaches will be welcomed by a wide range of audiences.

The institute is not directly connected with the university's undergraduate or graduate curricula, being instead centered on the adult nondegree learner. Discussions are under way on how the institute could become a part of the regular course offerings, and to test this, a planning graduate student and a landscape architecture graduate student were invited to participate in the curriculum for course credit. One nondegree student and one student in an unrelated discipline also ended up in the course by their own initiative. Conversations with these students suggested that they found it remarkably worthwhile, in that it presented topics in a holistic fashion, allowing them to make connections across topics in a way that is more difficult in discrete courses. In addition, they found the other students—the citizen planners and activists—to be marvelous role models for future activism, and they reported that they developed increased respect for the knowledge of the residents with whom they would be planning. Upon reflection, it seems that the CPI course as it has been constructed would be a very valuable general education course, particularly appropriate for those entering professions that affect land use and communities, such as transportation engineering, public policy, environmental design, sociology, and other disciplines. Even as a general-education offering, courses should retain a majority of nondegree students in each class, thus providing a valuable alternative learning experience for full-time students while keeping the core mission of the curriculum intact.

Overall, the sessions included in the CPI curriculum worked well. The curriculum started with some grounding in science through the biodiversity and water management classes. As might be expected, the sessions led by academics tended to center on lectures that provided significant background but perhaps less policy than might be useful, while the classes led by policy makers tended to skip some baseline knowledge that students may have needed. Student course evaluations suggested that the most successful sessions were ones that struck a balance between basic learning and current policy, providing them with a sense of deeper learning on the topic as well as concrete ideas about how to apply that learning—a constant challenge in a brief session. Additionally, students really wanted to participate in each session. This is not surprising, in that many students brought a great deal of both practical and scholarly knowledge to the classes, were investing their own free evenings, and thus felt empowered in their knowledge and their right to ask questions.

From the perspective of a faculty member in planning, the central role of the CPI is in developing future social capacity. Conversations and results to date suggest that the students who take this course are more likely to feel enabled and qualified to participate in local government. It helps move the planning profession toward its goals of working with the public rather than for them, as it helps create a knowledgeable and engaged public and a potent lobbying and coalition-building force for smart growth at the local level. The CPI's long-term impact will have been in sensitizing a wide range of citizens and future professionals to the connections between natural and social systems, finances and land use, regulation and incentives, and the value structure (which often brings them to the course in the first place) of vibrant, livable communities with clear urban/rural divides. In this way it makes smart growth a normal way of thinking for a wide variety of people, rather than exotic or added-on rhetoric in civic policy.

Institutional Challenges and Outcomes

The development of the CPI did not come without some frustration. EOEA and UMass had to overcome significant barriers, both internally and between institutions. No doubt the biggest challenge has been political, as administrations have changed both in Environmental Affairs and UMass. Because EOEA provides funding for the CPI and the state is facing fiscal challenges, it is difficult to assess the stability of the full nine-week course. It may be time for the working group to aggressively pursue additional partners or grants that can provide the necessary operational financial support. A major impediment of the working group is each player's differing perspective of timelines and political responsiveness. Environmental Affairs, as a cabinet-level state agency, operates in a short time frame consonant with its political nature. With administration turnover every four years on average, it is necessary to develop and implement cooperative ventures within a short time span. Environmental Affairs operates on a day-to-day schedule with meetings that reflect the ever-evolving priorities of the administration, and personnel are expected to be responsive to administration agendas. In contrast, UMass operates on a longer and more protracted timeline shaped by an academic calendar set a year in advance. Faculty exhibit a certain ambivalence about political agendas, as well as very little free time to devote to outreach projects when they must carry a full-time teaching and research load. In addition, the value assigned to outreach activities varies department-by-department and administration-by-administration.

The process of working together to overcome these barriers and differences has solidified the tie between UMass and EOEA in the Commonwealth Partnership to a point where collaboration is common with respect to smart growth. Concrete examples include the three authors of this article collaborating on a citizen-oriented book on smart growth; discussions on coordinating GIS software purchase and skills training between Environmental Affairs and the university's Department of Landscape Architecture and Regional Planning and related centers dealing with GIS; and preliminary development of high school workshops in smart growth and community preservation delivered by the university's Extension to Communities program.

Within UMass the collaboration has yielded outcomes often subtle but still quite real. There has been an increase in resources directed to land use and smart growth amid a university-wide period of resource scarcity. Faculty can more easily identify others outside their own discipline who have related interests, again increasing the viability of research on specific topics. There is also a certain recharge of faculty interest that comes from the challenge of teaching experienced community members, discussing issues with policy makers, and gaining greater awareness of their policy agendas. In the state government, results have also been nuanced but are real. Upper-level department managers from environmental, housing, and transportation agencies are now meeting regularly as a working group to develop a smart growth agenda for the commonwealth. This has the potential to significantly change the way the state does business over the long term. The partnership has vaulted smart growth and community preservation to the top of political agendas in ways that would have been difficult for the agency alone.

Even outside of official partnership activities, this strong relationship opens doors for new opportunities. One of the institute's professors took his landscape design studio class to an UrbanRiver Visions charette sponsored by EOEA in Easthampton, Massachusetts, to help community leaders redesign the downtown riverfront as a catalyst for economic development. This program was recognized with a 2003 Charter Award from the National Congress for the New Urbanism, and students benefited from interacting with local leaders grappling with real community issues.

Conclusion

At times the partnership has seemed to move very much against the tide—that is, the swift currents of local control, political change, the policy-making enactment process, and the expectations of universities for how their faculty will be promoted and rewarded. The group has had to recognize and work with many paradoxes, including: (1) in Massachusetts smart growth can be accomplished only through local actions, yet it requires state-level leadership to encourage this to happen; (2) community preservation is focused on retaining the positive characteristics of towns and cities, yet, by its very nature, community preservation often entails radical changes in how cities and towns must act if they are to preserve community characteristics;

and (3) universities often undervalue community outreach at the same time that students call for courses to be relevant to real-life issues and administrators push faculty to generate funding for projects.

The partnership has prospered through individual relationships, though it increasingly needs to transcend them if it is to sustain itself through leadership and personnel changes. Everyone involved remains convinced of the value of this collaboration, which joins pressing political views with longer time frames, and knowledge of day-to-day needs and resources with bigger-picture connections. The surprise has been that the slow, often unwieldy process by which universities adopt new elements also serves as a stabilizing force. Whereas Environmental Affairs is buffeted by sharp political winds, the university is much less affected by political change. UMass can continue to act as a repository for the partnership's ideas well into the future, testing out the viability and coherence of different approaches for pursuing community preservation and suggesting which ones hold promise and which ones do not. This ability to build on the strengths of each institution is a model that promises wide replicability in many states.

8

Smart Growth and Landscape Conservation in Rural Pennsylvania

David W. Gross and Edward W. LeClear

This case study describes a collaboration between Cornell University's Department of Natural Resources and the Edward L. Rose Conservancy, a local land trust in Susquehanna County, Pennsylvania. The objective of the study is to inform community leaders, land trust volunteers and staff, and academic faculty about the promise of partnerships between universities and land trusts as an approach to helping communities address various landscape conservation and smart growth planning issues. Two basic goals of smart growth are demonstrated in this study: (1) preserving open space, farmland, natural beauty, and critical environmental areas; and (2) encouraging community and stakeholder collaboration in planning and development decisions.

Program Planning and Collaboration

The Place

Susquehanna County is located in the Endless Mountains region of the Commonwealth of Pennsylvania, on the northeastern border with New York State. The primary area of interest for our purposes is the northwestern corner of the county (see Figure 8.1).

As did much of Pennsylvania, this once forested landscape underwent dramatic change during the eighteenth and nineteenth centuries as forests were cleared for timber, which opened up pastures and cropland and led to the establishment of farmsteads, mills, and small businesses (see Figure 8.2). Today, farming is in decline and the forest is returning. Timber production, quarrying, and recreation have become important economic uses of the land.

Figure 8.1 **Project area in Susquehanna County, Pennsylvania**

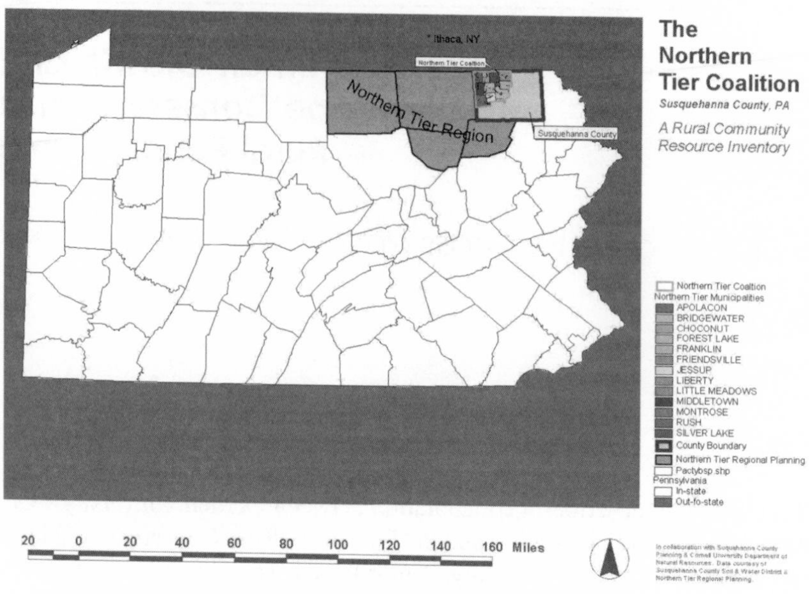

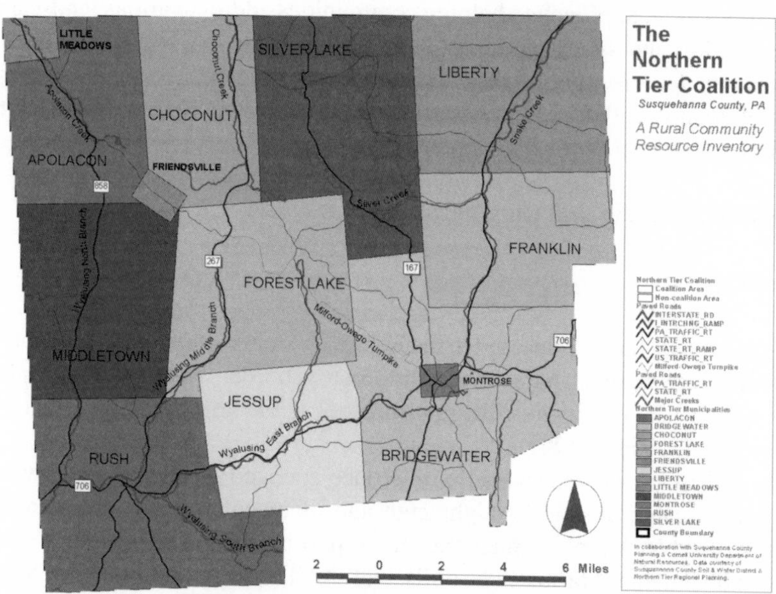

Source: Barney, Gross, and LeClear, 2002. *A resource inventory and report for the Northern Tier Coalition of Susquehanna County, PA*. Ithaca, NY.

Figure 8.2 **Various locations in the Susquehanna County project area**

Source: Gross, D. 2002. Susquehanna County partnership assessment, stake holder interview survey. Unpublished. Ithaca, NY.

Rural hamlet development has been replaced by commuter, retiree, and second-home amenity development (Barney, Gross, LeClear 2002, 2).

Preservation of its rural character is a major concern for this area as it faces outside development pressures from commuters working in New York State (primarily in Binghamton) who seek the amenities of the region as well as Pennsylvania's lower tax rates. Slow, steady growth, coupled with the increasing conversion of seasonal vacation homes to year-round residences, has led to rising concern about "rural sprawl": very low-density residential development around small villages, suburbs, and natural attributes such as lakes, and strip-style commercial development along rural arterial roads. The natural elements—rolling, tree-covered hills and green pasturelands—must be protected to preserve the rural character of the area. In addition, the health of the farm economy rises to the forefront of any discussion of land use protection.

Organizing Process and Goals

In 1999 the chairman of Cornell's Department of Natural Resources (DNR) received an inquiry from an alumnus seeking technical assistance for a small land trust, the Edward L. Rose Conservancy (ELRC), in Susquehanna County. The ELRC was established in 1987 as a nonprofit, 501(C)3 organization, whose bylaws call for pursuing natural resource conservation, providing sanctuary for wildlife, and preserving scenic beauty throughout Susquehanna County. The alumnus, an active ELRC board member, welcomed an infusion of fresh ideas to advance the organization's conservation planning and resource management interests.

A partnership soon developed between the ELRC and DNR, through the generous support of a small foundation headed by the alumnus and his family. Early in the collaboration, the Cornell team observed that attention to the ELRC's organizational development needs was essential for it to fully capitalize on new information and potential for expansion. Thus, research aims that the team identified for the group required a better understanding of the organization's long-range goals. A full-day retreat for board members helped the ELRC refine its direction: to more specifically map out its geographic area of concern (i.e., lakes, watershed, and highlands); to identify pressing issues potentially impacting the area; to define key goals that respond to conservation concerns; and to explore collaboration options. The retreat confirmed the ELRC's primary conservation goals for the area: (1) to retain the rural character, including scenic quality; (2) to preserve the cultural heritage; and (3) to enhance and protect surface and groundwater resources. The most immediate research need identified for the ELRC was to make an inventory of the area's natural and cultural resources.

As the partnership with the ELRC evolved, participants came in contact with an ever-widening set of community-based organizations, since developing a resource inventory required networking with numerous local agencies. As such involvement in the community became better known, more people reached out with information as well as requests for assistance in their own ongoing planning and resource protection interests. By the second year the Cornell team was invited to help the newly formed Northern Tier Coalition of Townships (NTC) to develop a multimunicipal comprehensive plan for much of the geographic area in which the team was working. The information collected and the community relationships established in the collaboration thus far would provide the basis for the subsequent spin-off effort between Cornell and the NTC, which became the ideal community-public policy companion to the continuing collaboration between the DNR and the ELRC.

Each of the three partners (the private foundation, the ELRC, and the DNR) had its unique vantage point and goals for the collaboration. As the projects progressed, the team realized that understanding each other's perspectives was essential to developing and sustaining a productive partnership. The family administering the foundation sought to provide resources that will support the growth and development of the ELRC; will sustain the conservation and cultural heritage protection efforts in Susquehanna County; and will enhance the DNR's ability to teach students about the conservation of rural areas. Cornell saw the collaboration as an opportunity for professional development of faculty, staff, and students through specific land conservation planning and management projects, in partnership with a land trust. Clarification of the ELRC's goals evolved only gradually as it adjusted to the idea of having new resources available and as the team better understood how to align expertise to its needs. Each workshop, consultation, and site visit resulted in a fuller appreciation of the range of possibilities. A convergence of ELRC needs and Cornell resources evolved after many meetings.

Program Activity Implementation

Community and University Resources and Roles

Resources committed to the effort are diverse, but core support for the collaboration comes from the family foundation, which negotiates with the chair its annual contribution to the department at the end of each year. In advance of that meeting, faculty and staff discuss with ELRC leadership annual work proposals. The foundation grants have met a range of expenses, from direct graduate student support, student internships, staff salaries, and travel expenses to lesser costs for publications and events. Many class contributions to the area used grant resources only for travel or publication costs.

Community resources directed at the effort are substantial, but largely not financial. The principal direct cost borne by local partners was the NTC contribution to cover the expense of producing a report and accompanying maps. Although a modest amount, this represented an important commitment to planning by townships that lack discretionary resources. Impossible to measure is the vast investment of time that community hosts have generously given to Cornell staff and students.

Whereas community stakeholder and university roles in this collaboration might at first seem to be those of client and resource provider, respectively, the relationship is far more nuanced. The collaboration is a three-way relationship: the foundation provides funding; the university commits staff and students; and local organizations (principally the ELRC and the NTC) are the beneficiaries. This is not the typical relationship between an organization securing assistance from a contracted technical provider, for the university and the benefiting organizations have independent relationships with the foundation. Consequently, communication occurs in many directions, and coordination among the three participants is sometimes difficult. This unique arrangement gave the Cornell team the impetus to view itself as a *full* partner rather than solely as a resource for a client. The level of trust and confidence needed to assume this full partnership role is substantial.

Deployment of University Resources

As an initial investment in the partnership, the DNR dedicated a portion of one faculty member's time to serving as team leader; he sustained local relationships, brokered resources, and guided many projects. The department also used a part of the grant to acquire necessary staff, including a half-time employee who worked for more than two years on several projects. More recently, a portion of another faculty member's time has been devoted to overseeing student summer interns.

Students participated in a number of ways in addition to their course contributions. Three students have been summer interns in the project area. The first intern developed a trail plan for an ELRC preserve, and more recent interns have conducted biological assessments for important properties identified through collaborative conservation planning with the ELRC. A graduate student, also supported through the partnership, developed a greenway planning strategy for the borough of Montrose, the Susquehanna County seat.

Four classes have been placed in projects in the county. The first was the department's senior practicum course, in which students visited the area to conduct a rapid, one-day threat assessment of several upland lakes. Local watershed groups, the County Soil Conservation District, and the ELRC hosted the event. Aware that Cornell's Department of Landscape Architecture welcomed engaging new communities in its studio classes, the team arranged to have portions of two courses held in Susquehanna County. One studio assessed the promise of a Montrose Heritage Greenway, and the other developed designs for a memorial park on a local family's farmstead as a tribute to their son (and all the other victims) lost on September 11, 2001. Finally, a class on conservation planning taught by Cornell team members developed a natural resource inventory of the coalition area and did research on conservation concerns raised by the township supervisors. The course examined issues relevant to current conservation planning, and lecture topics included bioreserve system planning, private conservation and the land trust movement, public planning for conservation, and the social implications of the conservation movement.

Planning Techniques

Initially, the ELRC focused on developing a resource guide and an inventory as the core items needed to launch the conservation planning collaboration. As information was collected, the Cornell team introduced board members to GIS maps and other landscape and cultural resource information. Much of the data was later utilized in developing a companion document for the NTC.

Landscape architecture studio presentations also were utilized. Numerous community organizations participated in the Montrose Heritage Greenway studio. At a public meeting students introduced their planning and design ideas needed to protect an area farm, to revitalize a community park, and to more fully recognize the community's black heritage as part of the Underground Railroad. Students in the other studio course presented their individual designs for a memorial at the end of the semester to a family member, a local volunteer leader, and members of the Cornell team.

Planning workshops and field trips were important elements as well. ELRC board members participated in several workshops, helping to build capacity in identifying conservation issues and strategies and facilitating critical decision making in the conservation planning process. The Cornell team took numerous field trips to the area, and both landscape architecture courses had one-day on-site visits. The conservation planning course had two field visits, one for an overview and the other for students to work with individual township leaders on specific planning issues. Another field trip was organized for the lake assessment effort.

Each course resulted in documentation, varying according to the scope of the student projects as well as the amount of faculty and staff follow-up. The landscape architecture classes created maps and design schemes; the conservation planning students contributed to the *Resource Inventory and Report* for the NTC and developed team reports for small groups of townships. Students in this class also produced individual reports on such topics as the Clean and Green property tax-relief program, forestry issues, intensification in animal agriculture, water quality, intermunicipal cooperation, development planning, and wildlife management. The class presented its findings at a well-attended public session at a local school.

The Cornell team has participated in several planning processes established with both the ELRC and the NTC. In a series of meetings, a special Conservation Planning committee of ELRC volunteers appointed by their president worked with the Cornell team to produce the ELRC *Conservation Plan* as a companion document to the *Natural Resource Guide and Inventory.*

Barriers and Challenges

At times the three-way relationship of the foundation, department, and ELRC led to confusion about program direction, expectations about use of departmental resources, communication channels, situational control, and accountability. The Cornell team sensed, particularly at the beginning, that ELRC leadership thought the multiple agendas hindered their attempts to direct the organization. Furthermore, the rapid flow of new ideas and the additional demands on volunteers and staff often outstripped the ELRC's capacity to capitalize fully on the partnership. On occasion ELRC members have been frustrated by maintaining less control of products and outcomes than they might have had with a consultant. A candid discussion of these issues at a meeting of the three partners at the beginning of the second year resulted in a strengthened partnership, renewed commitment, better understanding of roles, and improved communication.

Introducing Conservation Planning and Smart Growth Concepts

In the collaboration with the ELRC, the Cornell team focused mainly on applying landscape ecology analytical tools to conserve the scenic surroundings. Landscape conservation was described as maintaining and enhancing the functional elements critical to a community's sense of place (e.g., landscape diversity and water quality) and blending such interests as farmland protection, biodiversity conservation, historic preservation, sustainable development, and community building. The landscape conservation process introduced was threefold: mapping and inventorying all important natural and cultural elements, developing conservation plans, and taking action to conserve landscape diversity through partnerships and projects. The team also focused on strengthening the ability of the ELRC to be more strategic in selecting target conservation opportunities.

Several key principles of smart growth—including natural resource and working lands protection and stakeholder involvement—drove our attempts at helping community leaders and decision makers to preserve the rural character of the community and protect significant environmental resources. To achieve these two objectives, the team used innovative technologies and participatory planning processes. As the collaboration expanded to include other community partners, a variety of smart growth strategies were utilized: (1) developing a system of greenways and trails, (2) building collaborations among local government officials to focus on a regional perspective toward land use and open space protection, (3) collecting data on natural resources, biodiversity, agriculture, cultural heritage, and development trends through a systematic inventory, and (4) encouraging the NTC to design and implement zoning and other regulatory and programmatic tools to protect natural resources and working lands.

The participatory strategies utilized by the Cornell partnership also urged citizen and stakeholder involvement in developing the various products and the subsequent drive by the NTC to generate a multimunicipal comprehensive plan. For instance, the GIS-driven data analysis conducted by Cornell students was based on interviews with local stakeholders and yielded information that would have been difficult to obtain through traditional sources.

The team realized, however, that while many of the smart growth strategies were conceptually sound, the unique aspects of the NTC area required innovation. A distinction lay between the broader smart growth tools and the more specific "Smart Growth Toolbox" of ordinances, design overlays, and other regulatory practices. Once the NTC process began, the team soon found that many of the tools of smart growth did not appeal to rural stakeholders as effective solutions for preserving rural character. Similarly, a number of the smart growth options discussed in the conservation planning course required significant adaptation to the rural setting. As only one community in the study area had dense residential development and its land prices were low, density bonuses for development and conservation design options were poorly suited. Transfer of Development Rights (TDR) programs were also difficult to promote because of the quantity of open and inexpensive land, the small market for dense development, and the increased rate of farm loss. Unlike in areas such as southeastern Pennsylvania, prime agricultural land was removed from production in Susquehanna County not for development, but by poor commodity prices and lack of interest among family members in keeping up the family farm.

Finally, one smart growth tool—differential tax assessment for agricultural properties (known as the Clean and Green program in Pennsylvania)—appeared to work against the stated objective of protecting farm- and forestland and instead encouraged purchases of land for subdivision. Because Clean and Green requires a ten-acre parcel or larger for admission to the program, and subsequent assessment of land at agricultural/forest value instead of best use value, many property owners in Susquehanna County have subdivided larger parcels while simultaneously discontinuing production. The result is a landscape riddled with ghost subdivisions, increased fragmentation of rural land, and a reduced tax base for local government services. Hence, a smart growth tool helpful in a high-growth area proved a hindrance for sound land use and planned development in a rural setting (Berger 2002, 14).

What Was Learned in the Process?

The collaboration made it clear that open and frequent communication among all partners is essential. Throughout the process, the Cornell team sought to better understand the roles played by the foundation, the department, and the ELRC. Clarifying the specific contribution of each player has led to more precise detailing of product and process expectations.

The team also learned that utilizing contemporary GIS technologies is essential to engaging local partners. The ELRC's *Natural Resource Guide and Inventory and Conservation Plan* and the *Resource Inventory and Report* for the NTC all made extensive use of GIS technology to portray resource information. Each inventory identified, mapped, and quantified areas of conservation significance, cultural heritage, water quality, and other functions. GIS may also be employed to overcome resistance to zoning by focusing on potential development outcomes on the landscape. As in many other rural counties, when the partnership began, none of the local governments that constituted the NTC had passed a zoning ordinance, and land use regulation through zoning was a contentious topic. Through a community-based GIS approach, which emphasized local knowledge of resources and resulted in a broad array of information layers and maps, the compatibility of zoning with resource and landscape protection became evident to many NTC participants. Resistance to zoning abated as local leaders could envision which resources might potentially be lost or protected by a zoning classification system.

But not all smart growth tools work as designed in rural areas; sometimes they require adaptation to the landscape, development patterns, and economy of the region. Smart growth for a rural setting is different from those for other environments, and university curricula do not always illustrate the differences. Students enrolled in the conservation planning course noticed that the growth management and agricultural preservation techniques taught in class and in other courses in the university did not accurately reflect these differences.

Multimunicipal thinking, a shared understanding of issues, overall receptivity to fresh ideas, and a willingness to take political risk are all key elements of the NTC's planning endeavors. A combination of these four characteristics in the leadership team that created the NTC guaranteed its success and provided a foundation for a workable multimunicipal comprehensive plan. Another lesson learned was that revisions to state planning enabling law and program funds dedicated to emphasizing those revisions can have a direct and profound effect on innovation at the local government level. In recent years the Commonwealth of Pennsylvania has been at the forefront of progressive land use legislation to protect thousands of acres of agricultural lands, open space, and natural resources, while encouraging regional planning and maintaining local authority over land use. The revisions to the Pennsylvania Municipalities Planning Code (MPC) in 2000, known as Growing Smarter acts 67 and 68, provided a number of innovative land-use tools and paved the way for a legally recognized multimunicipal planning process. Municipalities thus gained relief from the "any and all land uses" rule requiring each community to provide for all land uses within its borders. Growing Smarter allowed communities to spread land uses among all municipalities *within* the multimunicipal comprehensive plan. This change was significant, because fear of specific land uses was a strong catalyst for NTC cooperation, and the ability to designate undesirable zones across a wider geographic area was viewed favorably. In addition, grant money set aside by the Pennsylvania Department of Community and Economic Development (DCED) for contracting outside consultant services to develop the NTC's multimunicipal comprehensive plan spurred the NTC's smart growth innovations. By securing outside funding for the comprehensive plan, the NTC ensured that the resource data collected by the Cornell team would be used systematically as part of a broader land use plan.

Operational Issues: Opportunities and Challenges

The volunteer organizational leaders with whom the Cornell team worked in Susquehanna County are an exceptional group of advocates committed to protecting the quality of life in this rural area. They have astounded the team on many occasions by their generosity, thoughtfulness, and determination. But as these projects evolved, their limitations were recognized, particularly of time, and the team made special efforts to sustain communication and to focus on administrative and logistical details.

Land trusts have been criticized by some as elitist groups seeking to protect their own conservation interests without regard to other environmental and social justice issues (Raymond and Fairfax 2002, 638). The ELRC has received this criticism from local residents who considered their initial focus to be too narrowly related to their own property concerns. As the focus of the ELRC has expanded both geographically and conceptually during this project, the organization is now seen as a valued resource to other conservation efforts, both private and public. The Cornell collaboration helped the conservancy enhance its credibility, but its presence and participation in community-based efforts were the primary catalyst for change.

With limited resources, the question always remains, how can a land trust get the biggest conservation payoff? One reason the Cornell team sought to bridge private conservation efforts (ELRC) with public planning efforts (NTC) was to make fuller use of the resource information and conservation planning ideas. The team realized that it could achieve a greater conservation payoff by enlarging the discussion about resource issues.

Outcomes

Local Impacts

The ELRC is now at the threshold of achieving its goal to help "preserve the area's rural character and natural environment" (Edward L. Rose Conservancy 2001, 1). Since 1999, the partnership between ELRC and Cornell has resulted in a greater understanding of the area's natural and cultural resources. All participants in the process recognize that the ELRC's aim to protect area rural attributes depends on responsive local planning, sustaining working landscapes, and paying attention to specific conservation opportunities. Considerable progress was made in organizational development during this period, including the establishment of an executive director position. Additionally, the graduate student supported through the ELRC partnership completed a master's project titled *The Montrose Heritage Greenway: A Planning Guide and Summary of Recommendations*. The ELRC subsequently received a state planning grant to contract with a consultant to further the effort.

The NTC initially regarded the Cornell collaboration as supportive, nonthreatening, and attractive because of Cornell's prestige (Gross 2002, 4). Some observers considered the collaboration to be a prime impetus to the formation of the NTC. Its teaming up with the university captured public attention and enabled the NTC leadership to more fully comprehend the issues. Further, the discussion of bylaws has led to specific follow-up actions. The NTC has recently been awarded a Pennsylvania Department of Community and Economic Development Grant to continue its comprehensive planning effort.

University Impacts

Faculty and staff characterized the partnership as a "conservation laboratory" linked to their ongoing resource management, landscape ecology, and public policy research interests. It allowed them to test and work through new conservation strategies and tools derived from natural resources research and to better appreciate issues faced by land trusts. Students in courses participating in this collaboration had a chance to apply their knowledge and skills in a real community situation. Individual trips to the area provided firsthand looks at community issues and rural life in Pennsylvania. Student interns learned how to organize community-based projects.

The greatest reward for Cornell faculty and students has come directly from the people with whom the team worked in Susquehanna County; local residents have made a special effort to express their gratitude. They characterized the Cornell group as "open, honest, professional, and practical" (Gross 2002, 4). Similarly, the Cornell team valued the sincerity, generosity, and dedication of their hosts. The Pennsylvania House of Representatives also recognized the Cornell team for its "unique planning and conservation partnership with the people of Susquehanna County" (Pennsylvania House of Representatives 2002).

Challenges in Producing Outcomes

The intensity of these projects, together with the logistical complexity of workshops and field trips, tested local sponsors' capacity to meet all their commitments. Although this was never a major problem, it did strain relationships at times and put an additional burden on the Cornell organizers. Maintaining oversight of multiple ongoing projects involving several different local organizations, courses, graduate students, and staff was also a formidable challenge.

Susquehanna County is at very least a ninety-minute car trip from the Cornell campus. Although maintaining direct contact with local sponsors was not easy, the team made at least two weekly trips to the area during the course of the most intense work. E-mail and phone communication proved essential and quite productive. Nonetheless, multiple projects called for careful attention to communication needs.

Conclusions

What the Cornell Team Would Do Differently

Using resources to provide for a graduate student scholarship proved to be the most challenging way to support the collaboration. Finding a balance between meeting the academic demands of a graduate program and attending to community organizing aspects of the project was difficult for all parties. In addition, the scope of the project was changed frequently, and the travel logistics proved complex. Nonetheless, the student successfully completed the project, and the participants in the process were pleased with the outcome. University–land trust collaborations present excellent opportunities to utilize graduate research, but the projects need to be carefully mapped out to meet all the expectations. If the team were to start this collaboration anew, a graduate student would be chosen who is at the research phase, having completed his or her coursework.

Perspective Changes at the University and Local Levels

Cornell's involvement has helped the ELRC become more science-based as it seeks land protection opportunities. The *Conservation Plan* considers a host of different natural and cultural resource protection criteria that result in a more defensible approach to project selection. The ELRC also has expanded its area of interest and engaged the community in conservation planning, including the launching of a greenway project. According to one NTC member, working with Cornell has helped them to start thinking positively about the area's future and how it can grow in smart ways (Gross 2002, 4). For the university, the DNR is now more comfortable in pursuing partnerships with community-based groups. Moreover, the experience has introduced it to the promise of more direct involvement with the land trust community.

The Cornell partnership with the ELRC continues. Another DNR faculty member has capitalized on the resource inventory and planning efforts to help the ELRC further understand the ecology of its current holdings as well as to identify specific conservation targets to add to its project portfolio. The Cornell team recently arranged a day-long exchange between NTC leaders and local officials in the Tug Hill region of New York, near Syracuse. The Tug Hill Cooperative Council has a twenty-five-year history of multimunicipal planning and has much to share with the NTC. Participants from New York and Pennsylvania state agencies, local officials, and land trust leaders spent the day learning about the Tug Hill experience. A similar exchange is planned in Susquehanna County.

Transferability

Most of the 1,300 land trusts in the United States are in close proximity to a university or college. The authors hope that this case study will inspire land trust leaders and college faculties to explore direct collaborations. Although an assessment of the current level of university involvement with land trusts has not been made, clearly the most frequent connection between local land trusts and area colleges centers on biologists and ecologists sharing their knowledge of a local area as board members or as technical advisers. A less common but major resource are faculty and students who may be enlisted through courses and applied research. This case study outlines a number of different contributions by these individuals, from basic resource inventory and assessment to more direct planning efforts.

The Cornell collaboration with the ELRC demonstrates the importance of identifying a local source of funding such as a community foundation of a mind to invest in the land trust–college partnership. As well, land trusts should expand their involvement with local planning agencies, because land trusts have much to offer in the way of resource information and conservation strategies. As communities seek to apply smart growth principles, land trusts can team up with college faculty to collect natural and cultural resource information, to analyze the current planning framework, and to apply special assessment tools like build-out analyses.

Important Issues for Replication

University collaborations with land trusts should be multidisciplinary. The Cornell-ELRC collaboration assembled faculty, staff, and students from natural resource disciplines, landscape architecture, and planning. The team leader had training in natural resources and a PhD in planning. The part-time staff member had degrees in landscape architecture, environmental management, and law. Their combined multidisciplinary perspectives were essential to the success of the effort. Universities need, as well, to introduce the best thinking about landscape science and planning practice that considers smart growth. Every land trust is organized differently and has its own particular fit in its community. University faculty, staff, and students can assist land trusts achieve more community-supportable outcomes through tighter accountabilities, enhanced scientific integrity, and with attention to social equity issues; in other words, they can help refresh objectivity and widen community contribution. The Cornell team can claim without hesitation that through its involvement, the ELRC has adapted to a much more community-based mandate, establishing its conservation voice in the area.

Acknowledgments

The authors give special recognition to their colleague John Barney, a key catalyst and contributor to much of the work described in this case study. He is now a consultant in Albuquerque, New Mexico, working in conservation planning and landscape design. We also express our appreciation to Edward L. Rose Conservancy administrators and the many other community leaders and volunteers without whom none of this would have happened.

References

Barney, J., and D. Gross. 2002. *A conservation plan for the Edward L. Rose Conservancy of Montrose, PA*. Ithaca, NY, and Harrisburg, PA: Center for Rural Pennsylvania.

Barney, J., D. Gross, and E. LeClear. 2002. *A resource inventory and report for the Northern Tier Coalition of Susquehanna County, PA*. Ithaca, NY.

Barney, J., D. Gross, and E. Minson. 2001. *A natural resource guide and inventory for the Edward L. Rose Conservancy*. Ithaca, NY.

Berger, B. 2002. The Pennsylvania farmland and forest land assessment act of 1974: Impacts on Susquehanna County. Unpublished course paper. Ithaca, NY.

Edward L. Rose Conservancy. 2001. *Comprehensive plan*. Brackney, PA.

Gross, D. 2002. Susquehanna County partnership assessment, stakeholder interview survey. Unpublished. Ithaca, NY.

Pennsylvania House of Representatives. 2002. Certificate of Recognition awarded to David W. Gross, PhD, Fairdale, PA.

Raymond, L., and S. Fairfax. 2002. The "shift to privatization" in land conservation: A cautionary essay. *Natural Resources Journal* 42(Summer):599–639.

9

United Growth: Michigan State University's Rural and Urban Land Use Strategy in West Michigan

Richard W. Jelier, Carol L. Townsend, and Kendra C. Wills

Recognizing the need for a united coalition to address sprawl issues in West Michigan, Michigan State University (MSU) in 1999 developed United Growth, an organization that unifies urban and rural interests. United Growth's mission is to contribute to the development of a vibrant and sustainable West Michigan region by forming a stable, citizen-based coalition of rural, urban, and suburban residents focused on promoting positive land use. From the beginning the project has concentrated smart growth efforts at the county level, despite the blurred lines of the metropolitan region that extend beyond county borders.

Two citizen committees guide the project. The rural committee primarily educates landowners, developers, and township officials on the tools and techniques to preserve farmland and natural resources, promotes agricultural productivity, and provides alternatives to low-density development. The urban committee addresses the disinvestment and abandonment associated with urban sprawl by assisting community-based organizations in mitigating specific manifestations of sprawl in their central city neighborhoods. In addition to the standing committees, more than eighty-five organizations have joined United Growth as project partners, extending the networking function and stakeholder participation of the program.

United Growth demonstrates that rural and urban residents have enough in common to significantly impact land use decisions. Three primary goals have driven the joint coalition: (1) promoting public education around land use issues, (2) building the capacity of organizations that impact land use decisions, and (3) pursuing applied community leadership and policy development. Dozens of individual projects and activities have been created around these goals. In its sixth year of operation, United Growth has become a model organization for grassroots engagement around land use. The program is comprehensive in incorporating the community and fostering strong relationships between interests that likely never would have met, unique in its special linkages between rural and urban constituencies, innovative in its approaches to combat sprawl, and inclusive in mobilizing not just MSU but other regional colleges and universities.

Urban Sprawl in West Michigan

Kent County, home to Michigan's second largest city, Grand Rapids, is a rapidly urbanizing area in one of the fastest sprawling metropolitan regions in the United States. It is the most urbanized county in West Michigan and yet the fifth most productive agricultural county in the state (Kleweno and Mathews 2002, 71). For the past twenty years, land in Kent County has been consumed by development four times faster than population growth (Kent County Land Cover 1997). In 1960 the Grand Rapids urbanized area (central city and contiguous suburbs) numbered 294,000 residents in 94 square miles of urbanized land; by 1990 the urbanized area included 436,000 residents in 223 square miles of urbanized land. The population grew by 48 percent, and the amount of land used to accommodate the increased population rose 137 percent (Rusk, Orfield, and Richmond 1997, 3). According to the latest U.S. Census of Agriculture data, Kent County lost 36,750 acres of farmland, 16.5 percent of total acreage, between 1982 and 1997. In February 2001 *USA Today* ranked the metropolitan Grand Rapids region as the sixth most sprawling area in the nation (of regions of 1 million or more people). Michigan land use projections portray a clear trend toward significant loss of agricultural land in West Michigan (see Figure 9.1).

It is estimated that between 1990 and 2020 there will be a 63 to 87 percent increase in Michigan's developed land, accompanied by only 11.8 percent population growth. Putting this into perspective, the amount of currently undeveloped land to be converted to residential and commercial use that will accompany the projected population increase of 1.1 million people will be roughly the same size as the land that served 9.2 million people during the entire state's history up to 1987 (Machemer, Kaplowitz, and Edens 1999, 6).

Kent County, in particular, is at a critical juncture. With a population of 574,335 in 2000, a 14.7 percent increase since the 1990 census, the county proved to be the appropriate physical setting for a partnership such as United Growth. In a population study, Nederveld Associates (2002) projected that

Figure 9.1 **Michigan land use, 1980 and 2040**

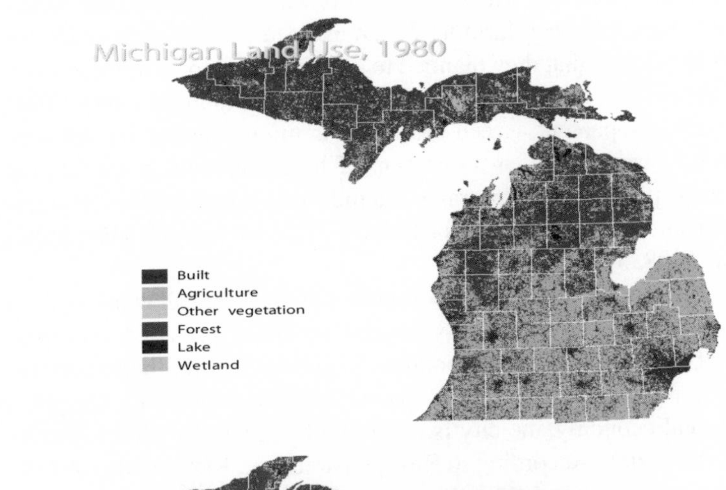

Source: Michigan Land Resource Project. Used by permission.

Kent County will grow another 197,864, or 34.5 percent, between 2000 and 2020, while the state of Michigan is expected to grow only about 5.2 percent during that same period. A more recent study by David Skole (2001) on Michigan land resources forecasts land use pattern changes in 2020 and 2040 based on current trends. The project demonstrates the need for immediate action to change current inefficient land use patterns before Michigan's land-based industries, which include agriculture, forestry, mining, and tourism, are dramatically weakened. Together, these resource-based industries account for $63.2 billion in Michigan's economy (Skole 2001, 2).

MSU Extension conducted its own comprehensive survey of 3,076 agricultural landowners in Kent County, which revealed alarming concerns. Over 75 percent of the more than 1,000 landowners who responded to the survey revealed that they had been farming for an average of fifty-eight years, yet 45 percent responded that they planned to sell their land for retirement. Furthermore, 67 percent reported that they were not able to make a profit from farming, while 74 percent agreed their land is more valuable for development than for farming. About 53 percent of landowners were not familiar with farmland preservation programs, including Purchase of Development Rights, Agriculture Security Zones, or Transfer of Development Rights (Bulten and Schaaf 1998, 3).

Central city Grand Rapids neighborhoods also had been showing signs of abandonment and disinvestments associated with urban sprawl. Most of these neighborhoods continued to lose population and several fell below 50 percent home ownership rate (Grand Rapids 1990 Census Profile). Despite a robust regional economy, the city is increasingly becoming poorer in comparison to the region. According to Rusk, Orfield, and Richmond (1997, 9), in 1970 the city of Grand Rapids commanded 88 percent of the average regional household income. By 1990 that share had slipped to 81 percent. Neighborhood commercial districts were also deteriorating and were no longer effectively serving the needs of their residents. Looking at the city of Detroit in the eastern part of the state, Grand Rapids could see clearly the negative consequences of unplanned growth in the region, resulting in disinvestment in the core city, overdevelopment on the rural edges of the metropolis, and pronounced racial and economic segregation.

Organizational History of United Growth and Role of MSU

In response to such trends, including urban core disinvestments, low-density land use patterns, loss of farmland, and deteriorating urban infrastructure, the United Growth project was born. Such a pioneering program is consistent with Michigan State University's status as the nation's first land grant university, which was instituted through the Morrill Act of 1862. An integral dimension of the act was public service, and a major feature of the land grant idea was that the work of scholars, particularly their research, could be directed toward serving utilitarian needs. MSU Extension was established in 1914 through the Smith-Lever Act, creating a longstanding affiliation for the university with farming and rural Michigan, with Extension agents operating in each of the state's eighty-three counties. Urban sprawl undermines both of these directives and provides an ideal opportunity for the engaged land grant university to advocate for positive land use planning, despite any controversy.

The seeds for United Growth were cultivated in large part by the Frey

Foundation, which formerly had directed resources to address urban sprawl in Grand Traverse County in northern Michigan. The foundation had invited regional government advocates and authors David Rusk (1993, 1999) and Myron Orfield (1997, 1999, 2003) to West Michigan to examine sprawling land use patterns. Local political and business leaders were already engaged in regional issues through the Grand Valley Metropolitan Council (GVMC), founded in 1988, and the West Michigan Strategic Alliance, launched in 2001. The Frey Foundation was interested in supporting a non-CEO approach that was more grassroots and representative of farmers, neighborhoods, religious organizations, and other community-based groups. The foundation awarded a grant of $176,400 for United Growth's startup efforts; support from other funders has grown throughout the project. From 1999 to 2003 United Growth was able to generate over $800,000 from more than twenty-five foundation and funding agencies, including the Americana Foundation, Comerica Bank, EPA's Environmental Education Grants Program, Grand Rapids Community Foundation, Steelcase Foundation, and People and Land (a project of the W.K. Kellogg Foundation).

Much of the early success of United Growth can be attributed to the direct involvement of MSU, which brought critical resources to the partnership, including financial backing, office space and supplies, utilities, salary and benefits, legal assistance, taxes and audits, and personnel administration. MSU also has provided a large share of funding; by 2003 it covered 32 percent of total operational costs (not including in-kind contributions). All told, this is a large investment, needed not only to adequately fund the project but also to demonstrate to the broader community MSU's support of United Growth.

MSU, through Kent/MSU Extension and the MSU Center for Urban Affairs-Grand Rapids (MSU/CUA), also served as the coordinating bodies for United Growth. United Growth invited full participation from other key area universities and schools, including Calvin College, Aquinas College, and Grand Valley State University. Faculty and students from MSU and other participating colleges have provided significant technical assistance on United Growth projects. United Growth then solicited project partners to help build the regional coalition, which would soon encompass more than eighty-five West Michigan organizations, touching every aspect of land use (see appendix to this chapter). Each organization formally commits to providing support and expertise to United Growth initiatives.

As with many university efforts, the success of United Growth has been dependent on grant funds. If the West Michigan funding environment had not been conducive to supporting projects like this, MSU never could have initiated United Growth. Due to this reliance on grants, United Growth generally plans only on twelve-month schedules, which has led to problems in creating comprehensive project goals and a long-term funding plan. Another weakness has been lack of a formal evaluation of the entire project.

United Growth's Three-Tier Approach

The partnership is geared to changing long-standing land use patterns. At the very beginning, United Growth established a three-pronged strategy for developing the coalition, based on its primary goals for land use: promoting public education, capacity building, and developing community leadership and policy. Project planners knew that focus on the public education phase was important because the issue of urban sprawl was not fully understood by many local actors at that time. United Growth started using a second strategy of capacity building by working with the Kent County townships on the rural side and with Grand Rapids neighborhood and community associations on the urban side. The third strategy of applied leadership and policy development saw committee members taking more active roles in legislative and policy matters.

Public Education

The first tier, public education, promotes grassroots awareness of current land use patterns and their implications for policy makers, educators, students, area practitioners, local citizens, and the media. United Growth's accomplishments in this area are especially noteworthy. As an educational tool, United Growth takes national trends and programs and from them articulates a local vision, adapting broad smart growth principles grounded in the West Michigan community.

United Growth has an annual project partners meeting, where participants listen to a keynote address and learn about all the partner projects related to the region's smart growth activities. United Growth also publishes a quarterly newsletter that is mailed to almost 10,000 households in Kent County and all the local, county, state, and federally elected officials as well as many statewide organizations. A comprehensive land use Web site (http://www.msue.msu.edu/unitedgrowth) links to most of the eighty-five project partner organizations and provides hundreds of resources and related links of interest to teachers, students, and practitioners in West Michigan. As part of its public education focus, United Growth publishes a list of current land use events, updates the activities of the urban and rural committees, and provides the online newsletter. The United Growth coalition has generated a database of more than 1,500 participants, which has become an important resource for information, mailings, upcoming meetings, and updates, and is used by a variety of organizations concerned with land use. The program provides frequent topical educational workshops on land use issues to a variety of organizations and has become a resource for the local media.

Capacity Building

The second tier, capacity building, equips community residents and organizations with skills and tools to implement both land preservation and urban redevelopment. The rural and urban committees have worked together to implement the Mini Grant program that provides assistance to small-scale community land use projects in both rural and urban settings.

The rural component of United Growth has pursued several strategies to assist townships in preparing for development and managing it when it does occur. It has:

- Identified prime and unique farmland and natural resource areas that should be considered for preservation, and created and implemented a survey measuring the public's estimation of the value of farmland preservation.
- Implemented a Citizen Planner Program that has trained more than sixty citizens, township planning commissioners, and zoning board of appeals members on key planning tools and methods. This noncredit course series leads to an optional certificate of competency awarded by MSU in land use and community planning with the successful completion of six core classes and a service project. United Growth has helped secure funding for thirty-two citizen planner scholarships. In northern Michigan, according to Wiesing (1996), the average planning commissioner term is two years. High turnover makes this training invaluable if not imperative.
- Played a significant role in the passage of a four-step conservation site planning process by Cannon township as a result of a United Growth–sponsored workshop. Indeed, classes on cluster development in Cannon township actually implemented a cluster development ordinance.
- Conducted an educational series designed on open-space conservation and compact design for sixteen townships (by national expert Randall Arendt and MSU faculty). As a result of the series, three townships in Kent County implemented open-space design ordinances. Arendt's concepts were incorporated into new state legislation in 2001, requiring about half of Michigan's local units of government (based on population) to adopt an open-space development ordinance.
- Assisted fruit growers on the "Fruit Ridge" in organizing and exploring

economic development opportunities, working to unify growers and townships. The Fruit Ridge is one of the most fertile fruit growing regions in the United States. The project has promoted its markets, historical sites, and attractions in an effort to increase profitability in farming, which will aid land preservation efforts. The project has helped the growers create Ridge Economic Agricultural Partners (REAP), a 501(C)3 organization, to formalize the partnership between Fruit Ridge growers and help ensure that its efforts will continue.

- Conducted four "Tours de Sprawl" of West Michigan for local leaders and created an educational Tour de Sprawl video for instructional use. The bus tour through inner-city neighborhoods, suburban congestion, and farming areas around Grand Rapids is narrated along a planned route. The local Catholic diocese, after participating in the United Growth Tour de Sprawl has made smart growth a key platform to engage parishioners, now incorporating Catholic pastoral positions to land use in eleven Michigan counties.
- Provided scholarships for twelve individuals to attend an Ultimate Farmland Preservation Tour to learn best practices in Pennsylvania, Maryland, and New Jersey over a four-year period.

The urban component of United Growth has pursued a variety of community-based strategies for the redevelopment and revitalization of central city neighborhoods. It has:

- Actively involved itself with the city of Grand Rapids Master Planning process, the first revision since 1963. In the new land use plan recently published, mixed use is a key strategy for central city redevelopment. United Growth held workshops with the city manager, planning director, and master plan community organizer for input and discussion.
- Partnered with South West Area Neighbors (SWAN) for two years in a neighborhood planning process. A leadership team of eight to ten residents was organized and led the neighborhood through the planning process. Three action teams helped to implement the action plan. Two "neighborhood summits" were organized by SWAN and the leadership team that involved more than 125 people. The housing action team and SWAN won a zoning victory with the city, downzoning part of the neighborhood to single-family, residential. A neighborhood-wide cleanup, with flower planting and other beautification measures, was held.
- Conducted a study of the SWAN business corridor. MSU urban and regional planning students recommended improvements and received the annual student award from the Michigan Society of Planners. The

planning process was written into a step-by-step manual entitled *Building Great Neighborhoods* so that other neighborhoods in Grand Rapids could follow this process. There is interest from a statewide urban initiative, the MSU Urban Collaborators, in making the manual available across the state. The Grand Rapids Planning Department has assured SWAN that the land use parts of their neighborhood plan will be incorporated into the city's master plan through an amendment process.

- Invited national expert Dan Burden of Walkable Communities to lead a walking tour in the Creston and Stockbridge business districts in Grand Rapids.
- Published a gentrification study on two target Grand Rapids neighborhoods, documenting the process of gentrification in one neighborhood and describing the potential in the other.
- Consulted on a redesign project of an urban pocket park that was experiencing problems with loitering and alcohol consumption and worked on crime prevention through physical design. MSU landscape architecture students prepared twenty-six designs for the park.
- Studied redevelopment along a key historic main street in Grand Rapids. Published the Wealthy Theatre District Historic Revitalization Plan, which mapped every commercial parcel, created visual maps, collaborated with other local organizations, including local neighborhood associations, business districts, schools, churches, and the city planning department.

Applied Community Leadership and Policy Development

The third tier, applied community leadership and policy development, works to advance change to promote better land use strategies. The joint urban and rural legislative committee strives to create important links with local and state policy makers. Michigan passed term-limit provisions in the state legislature in 1992 (three two-year terms in the house and two four-year terms in the senate), and this constant turnover is viewed by some as the major obstacle for land use reform. United Growth has met with each of the eleven house and senate representatives for Kent County and maintains important connections during the legislative session each year. The joint legislative committee meets monthly and tracks important state legislation, including monitoring and reviewing relevant bills to promote positive land use policies. They report their recommendations for action to the rural and urban committees, which must give approval. United Growth has become a vital resource on land use for elected officials at the city, county, and state levels.

United Growth's Key Projects

Of the dozens of United Growth initiatives, a select few will be illustrated here in greater depth. First, United Growth partnered with a Grand Rapids neighborhood to identify and consider the negative effects of sprawl on their community. Second, a youth land use learning series for Michigan's K-12 schools was developed. Third, United Growth joined forces with a township facing intense development pressure resulting in an open-space ordinance. Finally, the passage of a county-wide purchase of development rights program provided testament to the importance of the United Growth coalition.

Garfield Park Neighborhoods Association (GPNA) Project

The project undertaken in partnership with the Garfield Park Neighborhoods Association (GPNA) is an example of how United Growth's urban committee has implemented a citizen-based approach to urban land use planning. With limited funding, neighborhood associations usually do not have the resources to conduct research and technical work on their own; United Growth has provided assistance on a number of neighborhood revitalization projects.

The Garfield Park neighborhood is a diverse area in Grand Rapids and has one of the larger neighborhood associations with more than five thousand households. Since public education about sprawl is a principal strategy of the United Growth framework, several research and informational pieces were developed for GPNA. United Growth documented the decline in household income in the neighborhood, the decline in the white population, the decline in school test results, and how these specifics fit into the overall picture of resources leaving the city as a result of sprawl. The information was presented to the association's staff and board of directors. When asked to identify one issue related to urban sprawl, they instead named three:

- Negative perception of a local elementary school, Dickinson School, even though it has excellent test scores and is highly rated;
- Significantly lower than the city average home ownership rates in the Dickinson School area; and
- Crime/drug activity in the commercial area located one block from Dickinson School.

The neighborhood and United Growth worked together to identify strategies that would deal with these three issues. The project was able to acquire a $4,000 grant to develop marketing materials that highlight the positives of Dickinson School to the surrounding neighborhood. An MSU economic development class studied the small commercial corridor where drug activity occurred to consider what could be done to revitalize the business district. MSU conducted a survey of the houses in that part of the Garfield Park neighborhood, analyzing their condition, determining whether they are owned or rented, and gathering other baseline data; they then prepared a research report for the neighborhood.

In such a process, it is extremely important that community-based organizations gain the skills needed to properly put to use these tools and programs. Some of the specific activities undertaken to build the capacity of the GPNA to mobilize its residents and implement their revitalizing strategies include:

- Writing a proposal to a local foundation to financially support the project, especially staff time—$75,000 for three years was obtained;
- Surveying the Dickinson neighborhood to measure the attitudes of neighbors toward the school. A business class from Calvin College assisted the marketing committee in carrying out the survey. The information served as the basis for the development of a promotional brochure that was widely distributed within the neighborhood and elsewhere as well.
- Conducting multiple workshops on how to become a homeowner were held at GPNA's office, and participants were encouraged to buy in the Dickinson neighborhood;
- Encouraging neighborhood cleanup and beautification efforts; and
- Organizing residents into block clubs to fight crime as well as provide input on how the commercial area should be redeveloped.

Through partnership with United Growth, GPNA has become very proactive in attacking this multifaceted social and spatial phenomenon called urban sprawl.

"This Land Is Your Land" Learning Series

Land use has been named as the number one issue confronting Michigan's environment and yet was not a topic included in the K-12 curriculum. Without education, we cannot expect future leaders to be willing and able to change and improve current land use patterns. In summer 2000 the rural committee of United Growth embarked on creating a curriculum, "This Land Is Your Land: Lesson Plans for Land Use," designed to help students grow and develop into involved citizens who are literate in positive land use. Several grants were obtained to hire a curriculum consultant and pay for related project expenses.

The resulting curriculum, designed by United Growth members and the consultant, is linked to state testing standards and raises the students' consciousness about the importance of land use and growth management. Four primary units of emphases were established: community, geography, environment, and civics. After close examination of the standards, third, fourth, and fifth grades were identified as the levels where land use issues would best fit the state and local curriculum standards.

In fall 2001 "This Land Is Your Land" was reviewed and piloted in 15 classrooms, reaching approximately 375 students from several West Michigan area schools as well as one district near Lansing. In early spring 2001 and in 2002, the curriculum was featured at the Michigan Council for the Social Studies annual conference, which attracts social studies and civics teachers at all levels from around the state. The series was completed in winter 2002 and launched in early 2003. The Youth Land Use Curriculum also involves frequent teacher training. More than 75 teachers received in-service training for the curriculum. Starting in 2004, MSU Extension is developing a statewide youth land use educational program based on "This Land Is Your Land" curricular materials.

"This Land Is Your Land" will help young people contribute solutions to current and future land use issues. In an effort to make the learning series as accessible as possible, it was made available for downloading from the Kent/MSU Extension Web site (http://www.msue.msu.edu/kent/yourland). A brochure for marketing the curriculum was also printed to promote the materials in intermediate school districts, including every school in Kent County, professional teacher organizations, and others. The brochure includes a CD-ROM of the learning series. All MSU Extension offices in eighty-three counties have been informed of the series and encouraged to post the Web site link on their home page. "This Land Is Your Land" includes:

- Creative teaching strategies and learning methods with experiential and hands-on components;
- Lesson plans that meet the Michigan Curriculum Framework Content Standards and Benchmarks and prepare students for Michigan Educational Assessment Program (MEAP) testing;
- An introduction to controversial land use issues, presenting all sides of an issue in a fair and honest manner;
- Projects at the end of each unit that can be displayed; and
- Additional background information, data, facts, resources, and reference material for each lesson plan.

The series was also highlighted at the fall 2002 United Growth project partners meeting as a great success and example of how different land use interests can work together and create a useful public education tool. "This Land Is Your Land" was also featured in several member and partner newsletters, Web sites, and conferences, including the American Planning Society's national conference in 2003. Today the Web site receives approximately one thousand hits per month from educators all over the United States. In Michigan, more than fifty school districts have been directly informed of the series and have used the materials.

Open Space Preservation in Vergennes Township

Vergennes township in southeastern Kent County is a rural community of rolling hills, winding tree-lined roads, historical covered bridges, and family farms. Due to new highway construction, growth toward Lansing (the state capital) and excellent schools, Vergennes is experiencing development pressure. United Growth partnered with the township for three initiatives during a four-year period to respond to the township's desire to promote open space preservation.

Better Designs for Development in a Michigan Workshop

Randall Arendt, an internationally recognized expert on open-space conservation development, collaborated with MSU Extension land use experts to design a four-session, hands-on workshop on the four-step method to open-space conservation development design. The Better Designs workshop was offered to township officials and residents at no charge through a grant from United Growth.

Citizen Planner Program

To build upon the knowledge gained by the Better Designs workshop, United Growth brought MSU Extension's Citizen Planner Program to the community. Session topics include the basics of planning and zoning, legal foundations, subdivision regulations, open-space conservation techniques, running effective meetings, and managing conflict. United Growth secured grant funding to support scholarships for area residents to attend the ten-session training program. More than forty-five area residents participated in the program.[1]

Using the knowledge they had acquired, the Vergennes Township Planning Commission appointed an open-space preservation committee to promote citizen awareness of the issue and the techniques that can be implemented. The committee successfully sponsored two events targeted at large-parcel landowners and developers to encourage them to preserve valuable open space. The committee also conducted a township-wide survey to identify lands that residents thought should be preserved.

Mini Grants

The Vergennes open-space committee realized that in order for their goals to be achieved, the township must have an ordinance that encourages developers to preserve open space. United Growth awarded the committee a $1,100 grant to increase their capacity by hiring a planning consultant to work with them to develop an ordinance. The committee worked for more than six months on the ordinance, which was passed by the board in fall 2002.

United Growth also worked with the township and a private development firm to secure a $2,800 grant from the Frey Foundation to bring Randall Arendt back to the township to create a site plan for its first open space development. Since 2002, this site plan is still being used as the foundation for the development plan. The proposal is a likely candidate for the first development using the open space ordinance and will serve as a regional model.

Purchase of Development Rights Program in Kent County

A significant event in West Michigan since the inception of United Growth was the passage of Kent County's purchase of development rights (PDR) ordinance. In 2002 the county initiated a PDR program, a voluntary farmland preservation program that pays landowners the fair market value of their development rights in exchange for a permanent agricultural conservation easement on the land. After failing in committee by one vote, the board of commissioners' chairperson used his authority to bring the issue to a full vote of the board, where after heated public debate and intense lobbying it passed by a 14–5 vote. This was the first significant land use effort the county had undertaken since the mid-1970s, and the first policy issue directly acted upon by United Growth.

The rural and urban committees of United Growth passed resolutions to support the PDR program, and many United Growth members directly participated in writing the county ordinance. Staunch opposition was organized, which included the Home and Building Association of Greater Grand Rapids, the Grand Rapids Association of Realtors, and the Grand Rapids Area Chamber of Commerce. The Association of Realtors has subsequently withdrawn as a United Growth project partner. To implement the program, the county appointed an agricultural preservation board. Early on, six of the twenty-one townships in Kent County passed resolutions to allow farmers to participate in PDR, even before direct contacts and public relations had been fully employed. At this time, eighteen townships have passed resolutions in support of PDR. The immediate goal is to preserve 25,000 acres of farmland in the county.

The passage of the PDR ordinance is a good example of urban and rural interests working together to impact policy. The large support of urban committee members and their organizations demonstrated the urban-rural connections. When United Growth started, urban committee members did not even know what PDR was. Then they actively, on their own initiative, participated by testifying at the public hearing, contacting their county commissioner, and other advocacy. Urban committee members demonstrated that they understood how a rural issue is inextricably linked to urban revitalization.

Conclusion

United Growth is a successful model of bringing disparate interests together to form a rural and urban coalition, united around a common framework to promote better land use. The intensity of concerns about the loss of farmland, urban disinvestments, land fragmentation, social and economic polarization, and the general disengagement of community stakeholders around land use decisions, which led to the formation of United Growth, are not unique to West Michigan. Replication of the program's efforts to combine rural expertise and urban engagement is possible in other regions. In Michigan every county has an MSU Extension Service office that provides potential sites for replication across the state. MSU is currently in discussion with Muskegon County, Ottawa County, and Genesee County, which includes Flint. In addition, every state in the nation has an Extension Service through its land grant university, which could perform a similar outreach function if such activity is supported by the larger institution and the local funding community. The United Growth model is especially transferable to all states with a township structure.

At this writing United Growth is at a critical organizational juncture. Land use issues are intensifying in Michigan, with Governor Jennifer Granholm's appointment of the statewide Michigan Land Use Leadership Council, which developed a strategy to promote smart growth and planning coordination. The twenty-six-member bipartisan council was charged with addressing the trends, causes, and consequences of unmanaged growth and development in Michigan. It recently provided recommendations to the governor and the legislature designed to minimize the impact of current land use trends on the state's environment and economy.[2] United Growth could play an important role in implementing the recommendations developed by the Michigan Land Use Leadership Council in West Michigan.

United Growth is now attempting to transition from a solely MSU-managed project to a member-driven effort with a balance between staff and committee members leading the organization. During the transition the project management team has expanded to include more urban and rural committee members. The challenges include working on a sustainable funding strategy for United Growth to take the partnership into the future, which will likely include membership dues. United Growth has succeeded in achieving the first objective of bringing urban and rural together to promote a joint coalition. The litmus test for the future is whether urban and rural interests can together sustain an organization less dependent on MSU's stewardship.

Appendix. United Growth for Kent County Project Partners

Ada Township
AJS Realty
Algoma Township
Alpine Township
Americana Foundation
Aquinas College
Calvin College
Cannon Township
Center for Environmental Study at GRCC
City of Grand Rapids
Creston Neighborhood Association (CNA)
Diocese of Grand Rapids
Disability Advocates of Kent County
Dwelling Place of Grand Rapids
Dyer-Ives Foundation
East Hills Council of Neighbors (EHCN)
Fair Housing Center of Greater Grand Rapids
Frey Foundation
Gaines Charter Township
Garfield Park Neighborhoods Association (GPNA)
GRACE/Faith in Motion
GRACE/West Michigan Call to Renewal–Urban Sprawl Action Group
Grand Rapids Area Chamber of Commerce
Grand Rapids Community Foundation
Grand Rapids Dominicans
Grand Rapids REACH, Inc.
Grand Rapids Urban Cooperation Board
Grand Valley Metro Council
Grattan Township
Habitat for Humanity of Kent County
Heartside Mainstreet
Heffron Farms
Heritage Hill Association (HHA)

Home and Building Association of Greater Grand Rapids
Home Repair Services
Howard Christensen Nature Center/Kent ISD
Inner City Christian Federation
Interurban Transit Partnership
Kent County Board of Commissioners
Kent County Conservation District
Kent County Michigan Farm Bureau
Land Conservancy of West Michigan
Land Information Access Association
Langworthy Strader LeBlanc & Associates, Inc.
Lighthouse Communities Inc.
Local Initiatives Support Corporation
Lowell Area Chamber of Commerce
Madison Area Neighborhood Association (MANA)
Michigan Catholic Rural Life Coalition
Michigan Environmental Council
Michigan Farm Bureau
Michigan Farmers Union
Michigan Farmland and Community Alliance
Michigan Land Use Institute
Michigan State University
MSU Center for Urban Affairs CEDP
MSU Extension Services
Mountain Ridge Development LLC
Neighborhood Wetland Stewards
New England Financial, Agribusiness Unit
Office of Senator Ken Sikkema
Pettis & Associates Inc.
Pulte Homes
Robert B. Annis Water Resources Institute at GVSU
School of Public and Nonprofit Administration–Grand Valley State University
South East Community Association (SECA)
South West Area Neighbors (SWAN)
Sparta Township
Standard Federal Bank
Steelcase Foundation
The Delta Strategy
The Right Place Program, Inc.
Timberland Resource Conservation & Development
United Methodist Metropolitan Ministry of Greater Grand Rapids

USDA Farm Service Agency
Vergennes Township
Wege Foundation
West Grand Neighborhood Association (WGNA)
West Michigan Environmental Action Council
West Michigan Regional Planning Commission

Notes

1. For more information on MSU Extension's Citizen Planner Program, visit www.msue.msu.edu/cplanner.
2. See www.michiganlanduse.org.

References

Arendt, Randall G. 1996. *Conservation design for subdivision: A practical guide to creating open space networks*. Washington, DC: Island Press.
Bulten, Tom, and Kevin Schaaf. 1998. *Survey of Kent County agricultural landowners on farmland preservation issues*. East Lansing: Center for Urban Affairs.
Grand Rapids 1990 Census Profile. 1993. Grand Rapids: City of Grand Rapids Planning Department.
Kent County land cover change analysis: A study in urban growth patterns and loss of agricultural lands. 1997. East Lansing: Institute for Water Research. www.iwr.msu.edu/farmbureau/fbupdate.htm.
Kleweno, David, and Vince Mathews, eds. 2002. *Michigan agricultural statistics*. Lansing: Michigan Department of Agriculture 2001 Annual Report.
Machemer, Patricia, Michael Kaplowitz, and Thomas Edens. 1999. *Managing growth and addressing urban sprawl: An overview. Research report*. East Lansing: Michigan Agricultural Experiment Station.
Nederveld Associates. 2002. *Population growth report: Kent County, Michigan*. Hudsonville, MI: Nederveld, Inc.
Orfield, Myron. 1997. *Metropolitics*. Washington, DC: Brookings Institution Press.
———. 1999. *Grand Rapids area metropolitics: A West Michigan agenda for community and stability*. Grand Rapids: Grand Valley Metropolitan Council.
Orfield, Myron, and Thomas Luce. 2003. *Michigan metropatterns: A regional agenda for community and prosperity in Michigan*. Minneapolis: Ameregis Metropolitan Area Research Corporation.
Rusk, David. 1993. *Cities without suburbs*. Baltimore: Johns Hopkins University Press.
———. 1999. *Inside game/Outside game*. Washington DC: Brookings Institution Press.
Rusk, David, Myron Orfield, and Henry Richmond. 1997. *Today's winners—Tomorrow's losers: How urban, suburban and rural areas of greater Grand Rapids are being threatened by urban sprawl*. Grand Rapids: Frey Foundation.
Skole, David. 2001. *Michigan land resource project*. Lansing: Public Sector Consultants.
Wiesing, James J. 1996. *Attitudes of government officials in the Grand Traverse region on growth, development and the Grand Traverse Bay region development guidebook*. East Lansing: Michigan State University.

10

Promoting Smart Growth Through Participation and Partnership: The Community Design Team in Rural West Virginia

L. Christopher Plein and Jeremy Morris

In spring 1997 West Virginia University began a small-scale and tentative effort to develop teams of faculty, students, and professionals to assist rural communities in identifying challenges and opportunities for community and economic development. The project was called the West Virginia Community Design Team (CDT). Response to the initiative, by communities, academics, and professionals across the state, surpassed expectations. To date, twenty-four communities have participated in the program. The focus and tenor of the visits have varied according to need. Some communities face a loss of population and economic base, a few wrestle with sprawl and strip development as activity moves outside the town centers, and all face difficult choices regarding paths of community and economic development. The program has achieved a high degree of recognition and visibility across the state, not only as a community development approach, but also as a successful university outreach effort.

In addition to providing a case study in university outreach, this analysis illustrates the broad applicability of smart growth principles in the rural setting. Smart growth is primarily associated with urban and suburban contexts. It also has been pursued in some rural community planning and design efforts—especially in places facing pressures from suburban expansion or growth associated with resort and second-home development (Arendt et al. 1994, xix; Wells 2002, 3–4). West Virginia provides another perspective. Smart growth principles have been applied and promoted there in what some scholars (Stewart 1996; Lewis 1998; and Williams 2002) now call a postindustrial rural setting, made up of declining towns—once dependent on such extractive industries as coal and timber—that are experiencing population decline, infrastructure deterioration, and limited economic development prospects and are far from metropolitan growth areas. Through the CDT smart growth is encouraged as a proactive strategy for communities seeking to overcome economic decline and promote development.

Program Origins, Approaches, and Evolution

The West Virginia CDT is not without precedent. The program utilizes approaches from planning and design charettes, especially those developed by the Minnesota Design Team (Loveridge and Plein 2000, 11–12). Established in the early 1980s, the Minnesota Design Team focuses on community and economic development and is grounded primarily in the design of place and space through architecture, landscape architecture, and related disciplines (Mehrhoff 1999, xiv). University-based community design centers have also provided inspiration for the West Virginia effort. Over time, the CDT has emerged with its own distinct character and approach. For example, whereas the Minnesota team relies primarily on professionals in the field to organize and staff team visits, the West Virginia group depends mostly on faculty and students for this function (Loveridge 2002, 333–34). And although university-community design centers tend to be focused on one or a few disciplines, the CDT is multidisciplinary and more loosely structured than many of these centers. The CDT visits provide guidance on physical design issues for landscape, architecture, and transportation. They also encourage civic engagement and participation to build social capacity (Loveridge and Plein 2000, 12).

Each team consists of between twelve and twenty individuals, and is assembled after the program leader confers with the host community to ascertain the needs and interests to be addressed through the visit. Team participation is voluntary, and members are not compensated for their efforts. Participants represent fields as varied as civil engineering, public administration, sociology, landscape architecture, forestry, medicine, and public health. Visits are characterized by a deep immersion in the social, political, and economic affairs of the community and a concentrated effort to understand the landscape, infrastructure, and physical appearance of the locale. In less than forty-eight hours, the team learns about the community, identifies challenges and opportunities, prioritizes matters to be addressed, makes initial recommendations, plans, and renderings for design and strategy, and convenes the community to share suggested paths of action. The visits consist of information-gathering sessions that allow input from various stakeholders and the general public, community tours, and work sessions, and conclude with a town meeting where the team's initial recommendations are presented. After the visit, a written report is provided and a follow-up with the community is held approximately six months later (West Virginia CDT Manual 1998, 7–10; Loveridge and Plein 2000, 12; and Loveridge 2002, 338–39).

As a land grant institution, West Virginia University places an emphasis on community outreach and public service. Successful university outreach requires an appreciation of the challenges facing faculty and institutions in engaging in service, and the CDT program has been particularly sensitive to these challenges (Loveridge 2002, 332). Institutional outreach efforts necessitate a balance that provides a framework for service, but does not impose so much structure as to constrain or dictate the type and character of activity. Ideally, the institution should offer opportunities for outreach and blend faculty roles in teaching, research, and service. Thus, the CDT was designed to promote a flexible and integrative approach to faculty participation. A thorough review of the program's features aimed at facilitating participation in the CDT can be found in Loveridge, who identifies several keys to faculty engagement. In reviewing the initial phases of CDT program development and implementation, he notes a variety of factors crucial to success. For example, the time commitment for most faculty is limited to the short design team visit. In addition, faculty are recruited so that they can apply their expertise and engage in "scholarly public service," and they are provided the opportunity to further interact with the community after the visit (Loveridge 2002, 333–35).

Over time, other program features have further strengthened CDT. Initiated with a small seed grant from the university, the program is now sustained through nominal fees charged to participating communities, which help cover transportation and material costs, and through university support, which underwrites staff and overhead costs. The program has become institutionalized, with its own coordinator, office, and Web site. Initially, program operations were more or less ad hoc, with a few faculty members giving time not only to serve on teams but to provide administrative leadership as well. Now, with staff support and resources, the project is able to carry out and sustain multiple activities and visits. The CDT also has benefited from a close association with the West Virginia University Extension Service, which provides such material support as underwriting printing services and hosting the program's Web site. Technical specialists from the Extension, representing such fields as economic development, watershed management, and land use planning, are important members of CDT. County Extension agents help promote the program, act as liaisons between the community and team in some visits, and often serve as team members.

The CDT program has been very successful in recruiting faculty from across the academic spectrum. Perhaps most significant, a sizable core of faculty have become regular participants in the process, bringing knowledge and experience to each successive visit. By early 2003 more than thirty faculty members had participated in the program. Of these, about twenty-four had been on two or more CDT visits. The program has also offered a valuable learning opportunity for more than seventy students who have served as team members. The Extension Service has provided about twenty team members. In addition, approximately seventy-five have come from outside West Virginia University, including professional landscape architects, representatives of nonprofit community development organizations, state officials from various agencies, and faculty from other academic institutions.

Program Implementation: Positive Outcomes and Collaborative Activity

The West Virginia Community Design Team is notable for its longevity and breadth of activity. It has matured from an initiative led by a handful of faculty who gave time from otherwise busy teaching, research, and administrative duties to a program with its own staff and resources. Along the way, the capacity of the program has grown. Where once only a couple of visits could be carried out annually, it is now common for five or more visits to be conducted during the course of the year. A large roster of participants has grown to provide a recruitment base for team members. A steering committee, representing campus and community stakeholders, helps to provide guidance and review. The program has developed to a point where, in addition to regular CDT visits, the team approach has been applied to specific projects, such as health professional recruitment in small communities, helping to encourage a regional identity among communities connected with forest uses and assistance in recovery efforts in flood-ravaged communities in West Virginia.

But the true measure of program success comes from the participating communities. The CDT embraces a philosophy that change must be led by the community and that outside experts should play a consultative and facilitative role. This philosophy has deep roots in community planning and design and is one of the guiding principles of smart growth practice (Hoiberg 1955, 187; ICMA 2002, 79–81). Communities are encouraged to consider steps that have short-term, intermediate, and long-term objectives. In this regard, the CDT follows a smart growth practice that encourages communities to identify short-term action steps while planting the seeds for longer-term planning and development activities (ICMA 2002, 85).

Short-term goals and activities often center on improving the physical appearance of the community or correcting immediate concerns and problems. Communities frequently act on recommendations for making areas more pedestrian friendly and improving traffic patterns, with safety and access in mind. For example, suggestions for cross-walk placements and new parking arrangements have been adopted in communities as a means of improving access to services, sights, and surroundings. Other improvements, such as upgrading signage and installing attractive streetlights and planters on sidewalks, have also been adopted in response to CDT recommendations. One community on the banks of a popular white-water and fishing stream created river access points for boaters and anglers. Short-term activities tend to be clustered around projects that are considered doable with existing resources or that demand attention due to safety concerns.

Intermediate goals rely on community leadership but also require the cultivation of new resources and assistance from within or outside the community. The CDT often responds to citizen sentiments and longstanding concerns with suggestions on resources and programs that might be utilized to help achieve goals. The teams help communities visualize what the next steps might be. In this regard, the CDT helps promote efforts aimed at strengthening neighborhood-watch initiatives, accelerating planning and development for rails-to-trails and other recreational activities, and planning for the creation of community centers.

Longer-term goals recognize the importance of building and sustaining community capacity through collaboration, planning, and investment. Any long-term project requires sustained cooperation and effort by community stakeholders. Encouraging a shared sense of purpose can be particularly challenging in communities facing difficult economic circumstances, and the team addresses this in various ways. In its visits and reports, the team provides a baseline of not only community needs but assets as well. Building from an asset base is more encouraging than being presented solely with problems and challenges to be addressed. The team also promotes comparative analysis by helping communities understand their relation with state and national trends and by highlighting best practices and approaches used in other towns. Communities are also encouraged to set long-term goals by building on short- and intermediate-term successes. Finally, communities are urged to build long-term capacity by accessing resources and building partnerships with those outside the community, such as the university, various state agencies, and philanthropic organizations.

The CDT process reflects the essential smart growth practice of bringing together stakeholders to engage in networking and collaboration. For example, in one site, consisting of a string of old coal-camp communities, the team helped to bring together interests that did not regularly interact, such as coal companies, the local health clinic, and various community groups. Together, these stakeholders began to outline ideas to improve health care access in the area and initiated strategies for recruiting health care professionals and revitalizing the community's clinic. They have worked together to develop a community center; land for the facility has been acquired, and construction planning is under way. In another case, the team visit provided added energy and focus to an already rich base of civic organizations and community service organizations. Team activities helped to reinforce and forge partnerships between the local main street organization, the local hospital, and a nonprofit collaborative called the Family Resource Network.

An emphasis on continuing community collaboration and interaction with the university and others permeates the CDT process. On the last night of the visit, a town meeting is held where the team presents recommendations and offers visual depictions in the form of maps, posters, and architectural renderings. These materials are incorporated into a formal report that is provided to the community and helps lay the foundation for follow-up efforts. CDT program leaders originally envisioned the report as a simple collection of materials presented at the town meeting. However, the reports quickly evolved into lengthy, well-crafted products featuring color printouts, transcriptions of team members' presentations, elaborate drawings, graphs and maps, and contact information for faculty and resources to assist in follow-up efforts. Communities have used them to support grant applications and other funding efforts. The content of the reports has become the basis for various other civic projects. There is a sense of community ownership in these reports; as one local participant put it, "it was our plan, it wasn't done by outsiders, what we said is in there."[1]

Approximately six months after the CDT, a follow-up visit is made. This provides an opportunity for residents to report on community building activities and efforts undertaken since the team's visit. Some activities are directly related to team recommendations, others are not. What is important is that the community has the chance to articulate activities to an interested audience, gain feedback and advice, and reconnect with faculty and others who may assist in follow-up projects and efforts. In the beginning, the follow-up team was made up of a few CDT representatives from the original visit, usually team leaders and the program coordinator. Now, a general invitation is put out to all those who served on the community's design team. This allows for broader participation and more opportunities for collaboration and interaction between team members and communities. In short, follow-up visits can play an important role in sustaining community action and in improving community design outreach efforts (Mehrhoff 1999, 117; Loveridge 2002, 339).

Program Activities: Hard Lessons Along the Way

The purpose of a case study is to reveal success and review failure; lessons can be learned from both types of experiences. Although successful in many ways, the West Virginia Community Design Team has not been without its problems and difficulties. Conflict over land use issues and schisms between groups have been encountered in some visits. The CDT is usually adept at facing conflict head-on, encouraging communities to recognize shared interests and to break down differences between both sides of an issue. As is widely recognized, one of the purposes of community design is to help bridge these gaps by identifying common interests and complementary approaches to addressing opportunities and needs (Plein, Williams, and Green 1998; Mehrhoff 1999; and ICMA 2002). Despite best intentions, these efforts do not always work.

Divisions between groups, especially those who are new to a community and those who have been long-term residents, are not uncommon and have been recognized as a barrier to cooperation and planning (Hoiberg 1955, 58–59). The CDT found itself in the midst of such a conflict in the early days of the program when it was approached by a group of energetic and interested community members who saw the team visit as a means of leveraging capacity building efforts. While the host committee secured the support of some major interests in the region, such as the local district office of the U.S. Forest Service, other stakeholders, primarily long-term residents, did not buy in to the visit. In their eyes, those hosting the visit were newcomers interested in disrupting the status quo. As a result, the CDT was not able to reach all community stakeholders, was seen by some to be in league with the newcomers, and, unfortunately, had limited success in encouraging community development and change (Loveridge and Plein 2000, 15–19). This sobering lesson taught the CDT the importance of thoroughly probing the level of community representation as part of the screening process and that key institutional players, such as local officials, need to be involved or, at a minimum, kept apprised of CDT-related activities.

Sometimes issues, rather than social status, stand in the way of success. In one community, team members were aware of a longstanding disagreement over land use planning policy. A recent controversy over a countywide comprehensive plan had helped fan the flames of debate. Prior to the CDT visit, team leaders met with community representatives and local officials to clarify the purpose of the visit: to concentrate not on the county, but on a downtown business district and neighboring residential areas. There was plenty of work to be done downtown, and a focus here was seen as a viable strategy for illustrating how smart growth initiatives could be adopted in a piecemeal and productive fashion. While the visit proceeded smoothly—there was good representation from local officials, community service organizations, citizens groups, and the public at large—the team's report was given a cold reception by some. Despite the team's best efforts, the CDT visit was caught up in a larger, enduring debate over land use planning. According to a local press report, some local officials criticized the presence of outsiders offering design suggestions. A few community leaders unsuccessfully sought to suppress the team's final report. This led to a change in program policy that clearly states in the memorandum of understanding that final reports must be released to the public. The experience also served to remind the team that larger political issues can sometimes overwhelm best intentions and preparatory efforts.

The CDT and Smart Growth Principles: A Closer Look

By practice and design, the West Virginia Community Design Team process embraces various smart growth principles. The most fundamental of these is fostering "distinct, attractive communities with a strong sense of place" (ICMA 2002, ii). To achieve this, four other principles play a supporting role: "encourage community and stakeholder collaboration in development decisions"; "mix land uses"; "create walkable neighborhoods"; and "preserve open space, farmland, natural beauty and critical environmental areas" (ICMA 2002, ii). All CDT visits stress the importance of sustaining a strong sense of community identity. Communities are encouraged to explore and understand their heritage, to examine historic events and eras that shaped their development, and to appreciate the importance of imparting this knowledge to future generations through proactive planning and design efforts. Physical attributes and characteristics of the community, combined with a sense of culture, help create an identity. Because teams include specialists in historic preservation, landscape architects, and civil engineers, such matters as building design, historical identity, transportation and pedestrian flow, and physical appearance are emphasized in community visits. Establishing a sense of place is key to planning charrette approach in general, and is a defining characteristic of design team approaches (Mehrhoff 1999, 62; Loveridge 2002, 337).

Establishing a sense of place requires an appreciation of the community's context not only across time but across space. Understanding the community's relationship to other communities, to its geographic setting, and to its regional context is crucial to smart growth planning. It is well recognized that communities transcend political boundaries, especially in rural areas where there has often been a strong identification between a town and the surrounding countryside (Lancaster 1952; Hoiberg 1955; Toner 1979; Radin et al. 1996; and Wells 2002). West Virginia's CDT communities reveal the variety of spatial relationships that exist in the rural context. In some cases, they serve as hubs for a region; in others, they are small hamlets and towns that look to other communities for services and diversion. Much of the work of a CDT visit concentrates on how the community relates to its surroundings and how it can find a niche in regional markets, such as in tourism, and in regional service delivery areas, such as in medical care. A central theme is that a sense of identity and purpose need not be sacrificed when efforts are made to cooperate with others in the region.

Many towns have a rich history rooted in extractive industries such as coal mining and timber. With these industries in decline, several of the communities are in transition. Smart growth planning and action require the restoration and revitalization of activity and a sense of identity in the community. One way this has been addressed by CDT is through focusing on how buildings and spaces that once defined an area can be renovated to play a renewed role as a focal point for a community. For example, in one coal field community that is suffering from a loss of population and employment, the CDT helped to develop a community center in an abandoned school building. This center will provide both recreational and job training opportunities. In another coal town the CDT visualized a market square that would provide not only business opportunities, but also youth facilities, an arts-and-crafts cooperative, and other events. While still on the drawing board, this plan is helping to guide activities in the community and has become central in grant applications (see Figure 10.1). These are but two examples of how recognized features in community landscape can be revitalized to act as magnets for activity and interaction.

Smart growth success depends on achieving an inclusive approach to planning and development and the capacity to manage planning decisions and policies. Interaction can lead to mutual understanding, respect, and trust. Otherwise complex and complicated issues can be demystified and broken down into understandable pieces and components. This is particularly important for successful land use design, which requires cooperation in both planning and implementation. Of all community-based pursuits, deliberation over land use can be the most challenging. Suspicion of planning is well entrenched in American society, especially in rural areas. Overcoming this sentiment depends on generating trust and resolving conflict. Decades ago a sociologist noted, "In rural areas throughout the nation the zoning idea has not made much headway to date. With the present growing emphasis upon community improvement the idea is probably destined to take root, but the

Figure 10.1 **Plan of town center in West Virginia**

Source: Community Design Team Report—Spencer, West Virginia, ed. Elizabeth Messer-Diehl (West Virginia University, 1999): 11.

highly personalized relationships of the small community must be recognized as a major deterrent" (Hoiberg 1955, 145). In the late 1970s a manual for newly appointed planners in rural communities advised, "To be effective, a new rural planner must sell himself first and planning second" (Toner 1979, 13). Rural communities may lack the administrative capacity to engage in planning activities and manage their results (Wells 2002, 6), thus increasing the need for community-based collaboration between government and nongovernmental actors. The most successful CDT communities are those that have been able to use the team visit to further generate and encourage this type of interaction.

Ultimately, effective community design must be a collaborative process involving stakeholders with differing viewpoints (Bacow 1995, 150–52). The CDT encourages broad stakeholder participation in community deliberations and town meetings associated with the visit and follow-up efforts. By positioning itself as a neutral actor in the process, it advances specific recommendations that have practical utility and are obvious in their benefit, rather than becoming embroiled in abstract and rhetorical clashes over the relative merits of zoning and land use planning. The program stresses that its recommendations are advisory and not binding. In the short run, this helps community members see the possibilities of particular options and strategies—such as developing a historic district that will attract tourists and promote small business development.

In a number of CDT visits, initial team recommendations have catalyzed and inspired planning and action. Tangible visualizations of future land use and building design can help set into motion and guide efforts to revitalize a community. For example, working with a community long dependent on the timber industry, the CDT depicted renovated facades on the main downtown strip bordered by homes and neighborhoods (Figure 10.2). The community is thus engaged in an active effort to revitalize and develop the business district. In this and other cases, the CDT has acted as an intermediary between aspiration and action. This design provided a vision for the community, which then retained the services of professional designers who have further developed ideas and plans articulated and illustrated by the team and the community. In addition, inspired by team recommendations, the community was successful in gaining a historic district designation for this area. The community also responded to the CDT's encouragement to build capacity through collaboration and citizen participation. These efforts are being recognized by government agencies and philanthropies that are providing grant dollars to help sustain community planning and cooperation.

Smart growth has emerged as a means of remedying planning practices that have resulted in a homogeneous landscape of separate land use areas typical of much of the urban and suburban landscape. By emphasizing mixed land uses, planning mistakes can be corrected (ICMA 2002, 1–3). Mixed land use can also be promoted where there has not been a legacy of regulation and control. In West Virginia rural communities are characterized for their eclectic and accidental land use patterns. Business districts intertwine with neighborhoods in many locales, and schools and public services are often found in the community rather than in outlying areas. Land use in many towns is decidedly mixed. This is a product more of history and topography than of design. In West Virginia rugged terrain and the fact that so much land is held either by coal and timber companies or is in federal hands means that developable space is limited. As a result, many rural communities have tightly clustered, mixed land use patterns. While recognizing some jarring and unsettling results in terms of visual appearance and compatibility, these accidental patterns provide opportunities for smart growth development. Design team visits often focus on how communities should embrace and enhance these patterns in order to preserve quality of life and to attract visitors and new residents.

The mixed land use patterns found in many rural towns offer promising

Figure 10.2 **Renovated facades on downtown strip in West Virginia**

Source: Community Design Team Report—Spencer, West Virginia, ed. Elizabeth Messer-Diehl (West Virginia University, 1999): 11.

opportunities for walkability, which creates a better sense of place and helps make possible economic growth and social capacity building (ICMA 2002, 26). It is in this aspect of smart growth development that the CDT often has its most immediate impact. In many of the towns that the CDT is called on to visit, sidewalks and other pedestrian amenities have fallen into disrepair; teams often recommend immediate action to repair them and address pedestrian safety issues. Several communities have done so, securing resources to improve sidewalk and pedestrian access. Some proposals are imminently doable. In one town, a CDT suggestion to simply reroute traffic allowed an alternative option for transiting the town, thus easing pressure on an arterial road. A once-congested and dangerous thoroughfare has been returned to its original purposes of accommodating local traffic and pedestrian flow. Team members also have assisted with follow-up efforts aimed at addressing transportation and pedestrian issues. The CDT has a close relationship with the West Virginia University Transportation Technology Transfer Center, which has provided team members and expert assistance to communities.

The CDT offers walking tours and trails depicted through maps and designs. Various facets of the community are integrated in the walking tours, which guide visitors and residents through neighborhoods to places of historic and cultural interest and to downtown shops and restaurants. Some communities have been encouraged to capitalize on their logging and coal heritage by envisioning trail development, especially those situated on abandoned logging and coal railroads. The CDT has assisted various communities in offering plans for rails-to-trails development and use; one town acquired its old railroad depot to serve as a trail head on its rails-to-trails system.

Trails and greenways provide an essential link between community and the adjoining environment (ICMA 2002, 47). Community connection to the surrounding countryside, as exemplified by the adoption of rails-to-trails in many design communities, illustrates the importance of relating community and economic development to the smart growth principle of preserving open spaces and natural assets. This has been important in all of CDT cases, especially in those that serve as gateways to public lands in West Virginia, such as national forests and state parks. Because of the intergovernmental dynamic that exists in connecting community to adjacent public lands, considerable attention has been given to opening lines of communication and fostering cooperation between federal, state, and local governments—a critical practice in smart growth planning (ICMA 2002, 45). The CDT strongly encourages federal and state officials with jurisdiction over public lands and parks to participate in community-led presentations, interactions with the team, and follow-up efforts. Communities have been very responsive in this regard.

Conclusion

Smart growth planning strategies recognize that development success and sustainability depend on community-centered and community-led efforts. Outside expertise and assistance can assist and facilitate smart growth, but should not be relied on to provide leadership and direction. Higher education is particularly well positioned to facilitate smart growth and planning. The West Virginia Community Design Team has made important contributions to residents of small rural communities who are searching for ideas, resources, and plans to positively control the path and destiny of development. This experience, the focus of this chapter, can be summarized with a few observations.

First, a Community Design Team visit is more than a forty-eight-hour collaboration between university and community. As a result of a CDT effort, a relationship is forged between the community and team members. There can be a considerable lead-up time, starting with the application process and continuing through the screening process. Developing a planning relationship requires candidness and open communication. Some communities will require more team interaction than others, due to the complexity of issues involved (Loveridge and Plein 2000, 16–17). The final reports prepared after each visit have become important planning and discussion documents for each community. The follow-up visits allow communities to recognize accomplishments and renew contacts with university personnel and others.

Second, it is important to align expectations between communities and the CDT. Stakeholders should not expect to be led to success by the design team, nor should they expect the team to be responsible for follow-through. This should be established early in the process so that disappointment does not result. In addition, the community and the team must reach an understanding regarding the geographic scope and focus of the visit. The team is assembled ideally to reflect the composition of the issues identified by the community in the planning process. Geographic scope takes into account the area that will be the primary focus of the visit. In the CDT experience, this has ranged from a downtown business district to a twenty-five-mile corridor linking a series of coal camp towns. It is also important to align the expectations of team members with the task at hand. There are few off-the-shelf solutions to community problems or needs. Team members are reminded to keep a sense of perspective toward what is feasible and appropriate for the community.

Third, it is key to acknowledge and address community conflict in the smart growth activities associated with planning and development. From difficult experiences, the CDT has learned the importance of identifying and airing differences of opinion—healthy debate and discourse are key. A willingness to help should not lead to a failure to assess and perceive community conflict, which may not necessarily veto a visit or void its contributions. All too often, opposing sides agree to the ends but not necessarily to the means of achieving objectives. Part of the work of a community design team is to encourage various stakeholders to understand the positions of others and to recognize common ground and complementary viewpoints and desires.

Fourth, since the beginning of the CDT there has been an effort to learn from experience, both positive and negative, to improve the process. Self-assessment is key to improving community design programming and can be carried out through a variety of means (Mehrhoff 1999, 117–19). Evaluation is built in to the follow-up visits that are conducted in each of the CDT communities months after the team visit. In addition, research and analysis have reviewed dimensions of the approach (Stead 1998; Shannon 2003; Loveridge and Plein 2000; Loveridge 2002; and Plein 2003). An active steering committee allows for continued review and assessment. A statewide conference held in June 2003 brought together representatives from CDT communities to assess program effectiveness and to offer recommendations for improvement. The West Virginia CDT plans to hold similar meetings in the future.

Fifth, the West Virginia CDT has become a platform and inspiration to build other university outreach efforts. It helped in efforts to envision and secure foundation funding to pursue a university-wide service learning initiative (Loveridge 2002, 338). Starting in late 1999 the CDT partnered with the WVU School of Medicine's Recruitable Communities project to assist rural communities in attracting health care professionals to medically underserved areas of the state (Shannon 2003, 348). In 2001 the university launched an effort aimed at promoting a forest heritage area by linking small communities with ties to timbering and proximity to forested lands. The CDT program has figured prominently in this effort, allowing communities to explore how they fit into a shared region. The CDT has also helped in disaster response: after floods ravaged the southern part of the state in 2001 and 2002, a special initiative was launched utilizing design teams in assisting communities in two watersheds to develop plans and priorities for postflood recovery.

Circumstances related to the pressures of growth and sprawl helped give rise to smart growth approaches to community and economic development. Because of this, we can understand how urban and suburban areas have moved first toward these approaches. They have the need and the institutional capacity to engage in such activity (ICMA 2002, 73–76). We also understand how rural areas subjected to rapid change brought about through suburban encroachment or second home development have looked toward smart growth to help guide the future (Wells 2002, 9–12). The West Virginia CDT experience reveals how smart growth approaches, predicated as they are on proactive and community-based efforts in development, have a place in rural communities where the need for, rather than the pressures of, growth is prevalent. The experience shows how universities can play a vital role in providing the institutional capacity needed to help orient citizens toward smart growth strategies for community and economic development.

Note

1. Comments made by a round-table participant on the West Virginia Community Design Team Program at the 9th Annual Fall Continuing Education Conference, West Virginia University Division of Social Work, Flatwoods, WV, October 5, 2002. Examples of CDT community reports can be found online at www.wvu.edu/~exten/; click on "Communities," then "Community Design Team."

References

Arendt, Randall, with Elizabeth Brabec, Harry Dodson, Christine Reid, and Robert Yaro. 1994. *Rural by design.* Chicago: American Planning Association Planners Press.

Bacow, Adele. 1995. *Designing the city: A guide for advocates and public officials.* Washington, DC: Island Press.

Hoiberg, Otto. 1955. *Exploring the small community.* Lincoln: University of Nebraska Press.

International City/County Management Association (ICMA). 2002. *Getting to smart growth: 100 policies for implementation.* Washington DC: ICMA.

Lancaster, Lane W. 1952. *Government in rural America.* New York: D. Van Nostrand Co.

Lewis, Ronald L. 1998. *Transforming the Appalachian countryside.* Chapel Hill: University of North Carolina Press.

Loveridge, Scott. 2002. Keys to engaging faculty in service: Lessons from West Virginia's community design team. *Journal of Planning Education and Research* 21:332–40.

Loveridge, Scott, and L. Christopher Plein. 2000. Catalyzing local leadership and infrastructure development. In *Small town and rural economic development: A case studies approach*, P. Schaeffer and S. Loveridge, eds., 11–20. Westport, CT: Praeger.

Mehrhoff, Arthur. 1999. *Community design: A team approach to dynamic community systems.* Thousand Oaks, CA: Sage.

Plein, L. Christopher. 2003. The West Virginia community design team. *West Virginia Public Affairs Reporter* 20(3):2–7.

Plein, L. Christopher, David G. Williams, and Kenneth Green. 1998. Organic planning: A new approach to public participation in local governance. *Social Science Journal* 35(4):509–24.

Radin, Beryl, Robert Agranoff, Ann Bowman, C. Gregory Buntz, J. Steven Ott, Barbara Romzek, and Robert Wilson. 1996. *New governance for rural America.* Lawrence: University Press of Kansas.

Shannon, Ken. 2003. A community development approach to rural recruitment. *The Journal of Rural Health* 19(5):347–53.

Stead, Kevin. 1998. Community design team evaluation survey results. West Virginia University. Unpublished report.

Stewart, Kathleen. 1996. *A space on the side of the road.* Princeton: Princeton University Press.

Toner, William. 1979. Getting to know the people and the place. In *Rural and small town planning*, Judith Getzels and Charles Thurow, eds., 1–26. Chicago: American Planning Association Planners Press.

Wells, Barbara. 2002. *Smart growth at the frontier: Strategies and resources for rural communities.* Washington, DC: Northeast-Midwest Institute.

West Virginia Community Design Team. 1998. *Community design team manual.* Morgantown: West Virginia University Extension Service.

Williams, John A. 2002. *Appalachia: A history.* Chapel Hill: University of North Carolina Press.

Part 4

SMART GROWTH IN THE COMMUNITY

11

The University of North Carolina at Chapel Hill's Master Plan and Development Plan: Blueprints and Partners in Smart Growth

Richard Thorsten

Campus settings present challenges to integrating smart growth principles that are similar to those of the cities and towns in which they reside. Both places generally include a diverse mix of land uses, housing options, transportation and pedestrian networks, and built and less-built environments. University and municipal administrators are concerned both with fostering growth amid budget constraints, existing land uses and interest groups, and with the historic and natural character of the larger area. Frequently the demands of town-and-gown leaders overlap and sometimes conflict, requiring innovative techniques to harmonize smart growth designs between the academic and municipal environments.

In 2001 the University of North Carolina at Chapel Hill approved a new campus master plan, which culminated a four-year endeavor. The university also worked extensively that year with the town of Chapel Hill to pass a new development plan that allows capital projects contained in the master plan to move forward more quickly, in exchange for adhering to higher environmental and neighborhood standards. This chapter overviews the campus master and development plans, with a special focus on smart growth principles, processes, and outcomes. Sources of information include these two planning documents as well as interviews conducted by the author in May and June 2003.

The Carolina Community and the Challenges of Growth

The University of North Carolina was commissioned in 1789 as the first state university in the new United States of America. A board of trustees selected a rural village setting, Chapel Hill, for the school's location. The original map of the campus, from 1795, features three large buildings on top of a hill, which formed a three-sided space facing north to the town. This notion of a mall reflected the board's intention to build a "University of the People," a campus open to the outside world. In *Campus*, his history of campus planning, Paul Turner notes that the design may have resulted from the merger of a large village green (as Nassau Hall at Princeton showcased) with an axial design (found at the College of William and Mary) (Turner 1984). The selection of a rural location and the notion of the open mall later became popular at several other state institutions, including the University of Virginia.

The UNC campus grew from this spot (known today as McCorkle Place) westward along the north rim of the hill, although the first campus master plan (1920) envisioned a more orderly eastward and later southward expansion, sloping down the hill. The university and the town continued their parallel growth—the university served as the town's largest employer and owned its water, electric, and telephone systems. After World War II, European-influenced architects created new campus buildings that maintained a more separate relationship from their surroundings.

The university experienced high enrollment and funding increases as a result of postwar expansion. It developed specializations in public health and medicine, fueling campus growth farther south (Carolina Master Plan 2001). Cumulative floor area increased from 3.97 million square feet in 1962 to over 11.87 million square feet in 1997. Approximately 25,000 students now attend the university. The state has the eleventh largest population in the country; its growth ranked in the top ten between 1990 and 2000 (U.S. Census 2000). The university expects to enroll and accommodate an additional 8,400 new students and employees over the next ten years. According to planners at UNC, by the late 1980s the master plan no longer informed decisions on where to build, so in 1997 the university embarked on a master planning process. The original 1920 plan achieved build-out in 1962, and incremental updates to it could not keep pace with university growth. While momentum for expanding enrollment and research continued to escalate, Chapel Hill maintained a fixed cap on university build-out at 14 million square feet. The university needed to work with the town on adjusting that cap, while accounting for the town's genuine concerns about impacts.

The scholarly mission of the university also motivated the master planning process. Former chancellor Michael Hooker completed an Intellectual Climate Study in 1997, the same year that the administration set the master planning process in motion. The Chancellor's Task Force sought to identify ways in which UNC could become a leader among public universities by fostering the intellectual environment. In those meetings faculty members expressed their desire for building designs and locations that would encourage greater exchange between students and faculty. Moreover, the task force urged UNC to reconnect the north and south ends of the campus. It suggested that campus planners examine the Ram's Head and Bell Tower parking lots as future loci of student and staff activity.

Other issues required more immediate attention from the stakeholders. The university owns a 1,000–acre parcel of land northwest of campus known as the Horace Williams Tract, or Carolina North. In 1996 Chancellor Hooker visited the University of Michigan and North Carolina State University, two schools that leapfrogged to other tracts of land to grow, to decide whether UNC would pursue this growth strategy or infill and grow on the main campus (it ultimately chose the latter). Facing pressure from the town, Chancellor Hooker also pronounced that the university would provide a "bed for every new undergraduate head": every new student would have space to live on campus. This challenge required the university to construct new residence halls to accommodate projected enrollment increases. During the plan's adoption, UNC and the towns of Chapel Hill and adjacent Carrboro also engaged in discussions for a new regional transit system that included a fixed guideway from campus. The sloping topography of the university and its current built form makes planning for this guideway extremely challenging, particularly if some form of a rail system were introduced.

Development of the Carolina Master Plan

In 1997 university officials became interested in developing a new campus master plan, and Ayers Saint Gross (ASG) was hired to guide the planning process. The firm, which had worked previously on crafting plans for the University of Virginia and Emory University, among other institutions, was selected for its experience and its substantive, inclusionary approach to master planning. Toward the end of the spring semester 1998, the university convened its first formal meetings on the plan. A tiered system was developed, consisting of an administration team (that included deans and vice chancellors), a design and operations team (involving university members and the general public), and a steering committee that made final decisions. The architects and staff established four geographic groups to handle specific precinct needs. Group I studied potential locations of new science buildings, additions to medical and health facilities, and the Bell Tower parking lot in the central and western portions of the campus. Group II centered on the historic northern area of campus and focused on historic preservation and the creation of an Arts Commons. Group III examined additions to the Schools of Public Health and Dentistry, parking concerns, and open space and pedestrian connections in the southern and eastern sections of campus. Finally, Group IV considered undergraduate housing, athletics' needs, and parking and landscaping on the southern and eastern ends of campus. Ad hoc advisory committees also organized along specific issues, including transportation, bicycling, pedestrian mobility, and neighborhood impacts.

The committees collected information from a variety of sources. The university hired George Alexiou from the firm Martin, Alexiou and Bryson to serve as a special transportation consultant. He and his staff generated traffic projections based on enrollment growth and likely residential patterns. They also simulated parking assumptions and mapped areas where the university could establish park-and-ride lots. UNC's Facilities Department provided much of the information on utilities, building specifications, and needs. Later in the process, the environmental consultants Andropogon Associates and Cahill Associates provided environmental and storm-water management expertise. Both the university and the town faced more stringent regulations (Phase II) from the federal National Pollutant Discharge Elimination System (NPDES) program. The school had already dealt with serious flooding conditions on campus as a result of building over streambeds that trickled down the hill. Andropogon relied on and generated several data sources, such as campus walks, soil surveys, global information system (GIS) analysis of forested areas, mapping of original streambeds, and historic and aerial photographs.

The development of each component of the plan was highly iterative, and there was an even balance of university and community stakeholders on the committees. Later drafts of the plan reflected additional levels of detail and changes in design as a result of more than twenty public forums that gathered community input. David Godschalk, of the City and Regional Planning Department at UNC and chair of the building and grounds and the design and operations committees, notes, "Visual communication was imperative to these plans. People needed to see how the landscape would change." ASG conducted minicharettes, where participants in different committees would come up with ideas and the architects would sketch how these might appear in the landscape. The charettes gave the participants a chance to learn how various concerns related to one another, and helped committee members to better understand relationships between parking and traffic, housing and parking, and the environment and build-out.

After three years of meetings and revisions, the board of trustees approved the Campus Master Plan in March 2001; the final report was published in March 2002. The master plan incorporated several smart growth principles and objectives.

Figure 11.1 **University of North Carolina at Chapel Hill, existing campus**

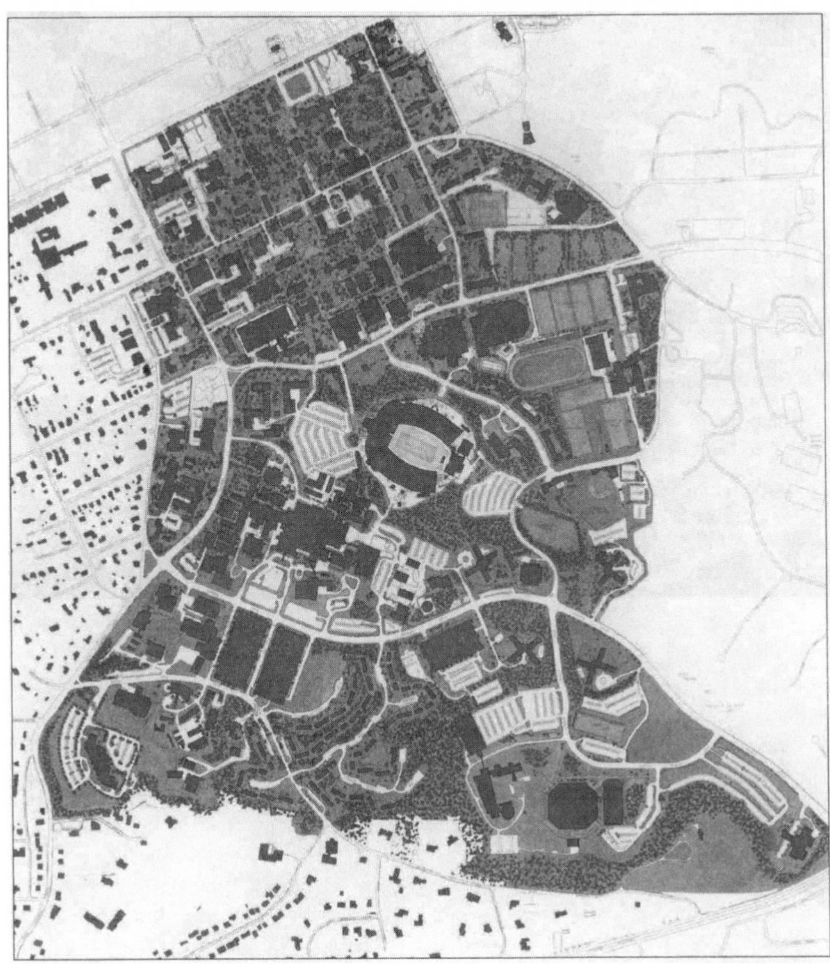

Promote Campus Infill

The committees and staff looked at several options for growth on the main campus and for the Carolina North property. The stakeholders decided to focus new building and growth on the existing campus, adding 5.9 million square feet over the subsequent ten-year period. Figure 11.1 represents the existing campus, while Figure 11.2 demonstrates the proposed campus layout under the master plan. The infill strategy carefully adds an Arts Com-

Figure 11.2 **University of North Carolina at Chapel Hill, proposed campus plan**

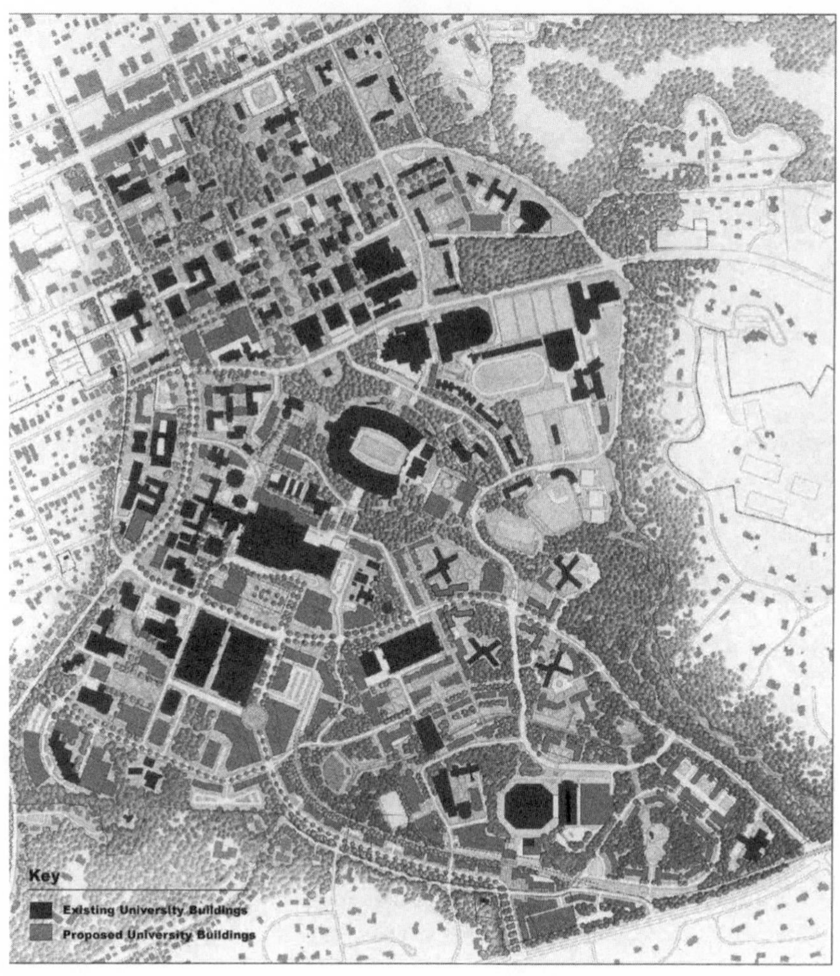

mons in the northwest corner of campus and a new Science Complex at the southwestern rim of the historic North Campus. The central and southern sections of campus undergo a greater transformation. The plan places new buildings on several existing parking lots and a few areas of unutilized paved open space. New parking decks will accommodate existing and planned vehicular traffic, while other areas will be reclaimed as open space.

The increases in campus density will help facilitate more interaction on campus, as called for in the Intellectual Climate study. The South Campus (where the majority of students live) will more closely resemble North Campus in its mixed-use character of buildings. The infill strategy also provides increased opportunities for multimodal forms of transportation.

Increase and Diversify On-Campus Housing

The master plan reflects the chancellor's policy that every undergraduate student will have a place to sleep on campus. The plan invigorates student life by locating new undergraduate and student family housing near existing residence halls, creating new quads and courtyards in the southeastern section of campus. Unlike the existing X-shaped, high-rise dormitories, the new undergraduate housing facilities will rise no more than four stories, which will complement the scale of the majority of buildings on campus. The buildings feature freshmen suites and upperclassmen apartments; a few will also site retail establishments on their ground floors. Student family housing will relocate into a one- and two-story courtyard area, separated from undergraduate housing and from their current location as a thoroughfare to hospital traffic. So far, the university has made good on these initial commitments. Four new dormitories opened in fall 2002 that include a mix of living options and high-speed Internet connections.

Provide a Range of Transportation Alternatives

Stakeholders quickly realized that enrollment and staff increases would overwhelm existing surface parking areas. At the same time, they had decided to remove approximately 5,500 surface spaces for new buildings and greenway restoration areas. Full build-out would require 11,500 new spaces, given commuting trends. In response, the master plan provides sites for approximately 8,500 new spaces, mostly within new parking decks. To accommodate future travel and parking needs, the stakeholders worked with consultants to limit single-occupancy vehicular travel to campus. Using GIS and travel demand models, they decided to place greater emphasis on public transit as a means of accounting for the net reduction in growth of surface parking. Committees identified four park-and-ride lots where employees and students could commute, as well as bike routes within the campus and improvements for potential cyclists, including showers, lockers, signage, and safety.

Consultants also sited a fixed guideway for a future regional transit system. The preferred alignment crosses the south edge of campus, taking advantage of a natural grade and paralleling a new road that entered into the master plan. It does not conflict with existing or planned campus development, although it does cross three properties not owned by the university. The plan incorporates several future high-capacity transit options, including a worst case scenario—heavy rail—which can only traverse certain slopes and requires wide sweeping turns. Shuttles would be available to take students to other parts of campus if the regional transit system becomes a reality.

Promote Walkability on Campus

While North Campus features a rich texture of pedestrian paths, the existing South Campus suffers from disjointed planning that confuses pedestrians hoping to reach North Campus or other South Campus buildings. The master plan reestablishes legible walking paths that reconnect the north and south ends of campus. It envisions a circulation system of paths that allows students who live in the medium-rise dormitories to have easy access to Kenan Stadium, the Schools of Medicine and Public Health, and the north end of campus. Features will include legible signage, lighted pathways, and new pedestrian bridges; their design will also enhance pedestrian activity. For example, the Ram's Head parking lot, near Kenan Stadium at the southern, lower end of campus, will be replaced by a small parking deck that will include a marked pedestrian bridge to campus on top of the structure. This provides commuters with easy access and reduces the grade uphill that pedestrians must travel to North Campus.

Mix Land Uses on Campus

Although campus settings offer students the chance to learn, live, consume, and play in a single environment, the northern and southern portions of campus differ in their diversity of uses. North Campus includes residential, academic, and public uses within the area, while South Campus spreads many of these functions across the landscape. The new plan calls for South Campus to integrate more of its roles. Two examples of this are (1) the Bell Tower surface parking lot, which will be converted to a major parking deck and a set of academic and support buildings that will serve UNC hospital employees and students alike; and (2) the Ram's Head area of South campus. In both areas, large parking decks will replace the surface lots. The top portion of the Ram's Head deck will feature a dining area, bookstore, recreational building, and a green roof to handle storm-water flow.

Foster Distinctive University Settings

While the plan harmonizes the traditional and newer areas of campus and creates new focal points for students, faculty, and staff, it also strengthens many of the unique attributes of the school. Representatives of older precincts sought to export many of the natural features and architectural scale of the old quadrangles to other areas. They also laid the groundwork for identifying new historical places on campus and listing the renovation needs of some of the older buildings. A set of design guidelines outlined preferred (and not preferred) building types that reflect Carolina's heritage and set more specific standards for new buildings on the priority list.

The plan essentially creates three academic villages: the historic North Campus area; the new Health Affairs Village to the southwest; and the new Housing and Student Life Village to the southeast. Most of the North Campus area remains intact. The Health Affairs Village centers new science and medicine buildings that surround the existing hospital and annex in the form of a quadrangle. A grid system unifies local roads, while open spaces are connected along its edges. The Housing and Student Life Village creates a more integrated community where most students live, and will feature diverse housing types, connected open spaces and plazas, and retail spaces (including a grocery store) that will allow students to interact more comfortably at this end of campus.

Preserve and Restore Natural Open Space

New buildings in the South Campus area will have distinct edges that will create open-space connectors between North and South Campuses. New roads will contain tree-lined sidewalks and landscaping. Along the southern and eastern edges of campus, the university will tear down older facilities and restore drainage channels, floodplains, and reforested areas. The university also intends to uncover and reclaim two buried streams on campus. These stream corridors will become part of the new pedestrian network on campus.

Protect Environmentally Sensitive Areas and Ecological Functions

The master plan includes an environmental component that evaluates the quantity and quality of land and water resources, protects and restores environmentally sensitive areas, and mitigates water-resource impacts of new construction. The plan focuses new construction away from the sloping, forested southeastern boundaries of campus. New construction also avoids disturbing the aesthetic and historic beauty of the North Campus.

One of the most dramatic pieces of the master plan aims to change how the university handles storm-water retention. Campus officials anticipate that their infill strategy will mitigate storm-water increases, and possibly even result in net losses. The plan calls for maximizing on-site infiltration to recharge groundwater and absorb floodwaters, capture and reuse rainwater, and ultimately result in no net gains in storm-water runoff. Techniques will include bioretention areas, "rain gardens," natural swales, and the reduction of lawn fertilizers.

Encourage Citizen and Stakeholder Participation

UNC conducted many public forums to present the new plan and gain input in its development. Students in particular adopted a unique and important role in shaping its characteristics. They initially formed their own committee and submitted their ideas to early stakeholder groups. Later, a few student leaders joined the committees, and a student task force also developed their own master plan. According to past student body vice president Emily Williamson, the final master plan addressed many student concerns, including more strategically placed parking, better transit and pedestrian connections, and a more mixed-use South Campus. In her opinion, students felt that the one weakness of the plan was its inattention to more recreational facilities.

The UNC Development Ordinance and Master Plan Implementation

The Development Ordinance

Before passage of the master plan, the town of Chapel Hill had developed standards that applied to the university. Floor-area requirements and storm-water guidelines and mitigation techniques were among those previously mentioned. The town periodically reviewed land use decisions on individual buildings, yet had not worked with the school to develop a land use plan that would guide future development. University officials wanted to implement their master plan, and this required a more integrated approach to working with town leaders.

UNC began to bump against the town's regulations for maximum floor area coverage just as it prepared to construct new facilities that would exceed that floor area. Raising the cap on the floor area would have solved the problem, yet it would have alarmed town residents concerned with the impacts of rapid growth. Moreover, the university wanted to avoid costly delays in new construction resulting from the prior permit process, where every permit received scrutiny and deliberation from planning staff, the town council, and the general public. University and town officials finally reached an agreement on town review of projects in the master plan. The UNC development plan requires the university to analyze and mitigate traffic, lighting, noise, and storm-water impacts for all new projects identified in the campus master plan before it applies for building permits. After examining this unified impact report and suggesting modifications, eventually the town council approved the development plan.

The town has created a special zoning district (Office/Industrial #4 or OI-4) for the university that outlines an alternative permitting process for individual university building permits. Projects that are included in the development plan receive expedited review and approval of the town manager, who certifies that each building permit meets the plan's objectives. The town council is not involved in the permit process, which is now restricted to fifteen working days. The town manager has approved all six applications within this time frame since passage of the development ordinance in October 2001.

Public consideration of the development plan was very robust. The university held several open presentations on their plan, and officials met with UNC staff to suggest revisions to it, such as a transition perimeter that protected adjacent neighborhoods from lighting and noise impacts. Council members held several meetings and requested information that the university furnished. Town councilors shared major concerns about the transportation plans (specifically cost commitments from the university for improved transit) and storm-water guidelines (e.g., the explicit technical verification of managing storm-water flows). Negotiations with the town proved beneficial on both counts. The university agreed to pay 40 percent of the cost of operating an expanded and fare-free transit service in conjunction with the towns of Chapel Hill and Carrboro. The university increased its contribution, and students voted to increase student fees toward this fund as well. Both university and town officials also hired professional consultants and designed new groundbreaking standards for performance and monitoring of storm water, according to several interviewees.

Town officials and nearby residents are concerned with UNC's plans for locating buildings and widening roads along the south edge of campus, known as Mason's Farm Road. Original plans called for neighborhood intrusions on both sides of the street, where several single-family homes are now located. Public hearings ultimately produced a decision to leave the south side of the street alone, while eventually intruding (either through purchase or eminent domain) on the properties of four houses on the north side. As of this writing, the university is constructing more than 300 units of student family housing along the road.

The UNC development plan and new zoning ordinance demonstrated several smart growth principles in action. These include:

- *Compact building design.* The new zoning district allows the university to increase its floor area ratio within the region. School officials can now construct infill development plans on the existing campus.
- *Housing on campus.* The zoning ordinance also allowed the university to construct four new dormitories, which opened in 2002. Others are planned for the future.
- *Transportation choices.* The fare-free, expanded bus system has increased ridership both from park-and-ride areas and along existing bus routes. Early results indicate 40 percent increases in the first year.
- *Strengthen existing communities.* The university must account and mitigate for environmental, noise, lighting, and other impacts on adjacent areas before introducing building applications. Neighborhood residents have a better idea of what conditions new projects must adhere to and may take those concerns to town planning officials.
- *Improve environmental protection.* Chapel Hill's storm-water management policy of no net increase is a rare and ambitious standard to achieve. However, the town and the university have established this as a major benchmark and have committed resources to make it happen.
- *Make development decisions predictable, fair, and cost-effective.* The development plan gives the university a predictable set of requirements that master plan projects must abide by to gain approval. Acceptance of the development plan occurred in a fair, open, and public process, while project approval requires timely town staff decisions. The compromise also ensures that, in most cases, the university and the town will not face costly legal battles and delays over project approval.

Despite these laudable goals, some challenges remain for town-gown relations. Chapel Hill contains a proactive neighborhood activist community that may well fight for tougher university dealings. For example, some residents of a neighborhood that borders the eastern edge of campus are currently attempting to block the construction of a utility chiller plant that was originally listed in the development plan. Some transportation issues also remain unsolved. Although both the master and development plans attempt to mitigate traffic, growth will continue to accelerate overall trips. UNC and Chapel Hill have yet to reach agreement on traffic flow along a few major intersections along the western edge of campus. The university will also encounter resistance if it attempts to move forward on constructing a six-lane road along Mason Farm Road or an additional heavy-rail transit guideway.

Neither university nor regional transit plans call for significant changes in the next few years, but the issue remains outstanding. The other major issue is the fate of Carolina North. The town council has seen three separate plans for that property in the last eight years. In 1995 the town worked with the university and an outside firm on guidelines for the property's development that called for a mixed-use village center, with housing and services for students and faculty, tied to the transit system. Yet deliberations continue on Carolina North's future.

The Campus Master Plan

Over the last two years the university has implemented elements of the master plan. UNC won passage in 2000 of a $3.1 billion state capital bond for higher education spending. Approximately $550 million of that bond is committed to the Chapel Hill campus to construct several new buildings and renovate many more. Planning and construction has also begun on School of Public Health additions, the student union, and a science complex. The Sonya Haynes Stone Black Cultural Center recently was completed. The university as well has invested its own resources toward plan implementation, and many new positions were created as a result of the planning process.

The university hired Cindy Shea in April 2001 as its first Sustainability Coordinator. Key responsibilities of the position include working with designers to make new buildings more energy and water efficient, promoting recycling and storm-water detention in existing facilities, and reviewing university curricula and purchasing policies to suggest more sustainable practices. In 2002 UNC hired Debby Freed, former manager of the Commuter Alternatives Program at Virginia Tech, to launch the Transportation Demand Management (TDM) program. The university had already taken some piecemeal TDM steps, such as offering emergency rides and carpooling and vanpooling permits. Freed's office now provides more comprehensive information on alternative forms of transportation to and from campus and on campus, coordinates park-and-ride permits, and just started a discount program, where local merchants agree to provide discounts for frequent nonauto commuters. She hopes to apply and continue some of the good work that Virginia Tech and other schools such as Stanford University and the University of California at Davis began. Historic preservation also received renewed attention after adoption of the master plan. The university maintains more than fifteen buildings and landmarks on the National Historic Register. Paul Kapp was hired by the UNC to serve as the Historic Preservation Manager. His office has begun to survey all the historic buildings on campus to identify specific needs. The university just completed a $6 million renovation of

Murphy Hall, and an additional $10 million has been committed for upcoming projects. The university also has hired a landscape architect and an engineer to focus on storm-water management.

Challenges remain on the horizon for the university as it implements the master plan. The UNC system, like many state institutions, faces budget cutbacks and the prospects of raising tuition. Fiscal cuts hit new offices especially hard. The Sustainability office lost 50 percent of its budget only two months after Shea arrived. And the TDM program operates on a limited budget, though Freed hopes that a state TDM grant will allow the program to expand.

Conclusion

The campus is an important laboratory for smart growth planning, particularly for larger and medium-sized institutions, where university decisions shape the towns and city neighborhoods in which they reside. Their campuses are microcosms of activities in the domain of planning—unique environments where employment, housing, design, transportation and mobility, and environmental protection needs and objectives intertwine and interact with the larger urban and social fabric.

Most of the UNC community and the consultants they worked with did not originally set out to create a smart growth master plan. They recognized that physical, academic, financial, and regional short-term needs and longer-term challenges had outstripped the ability of current plans to guide development and meet the university's mission. The 2002 master plan credibly responds to most of those issues, yet it also reflects smart growth principles and practices in action.

Infill strategies can represent responses to growth in the face of land use constraints. They may also reflect a strategy that stresses the redevelopment of existing areas. Both scenarios apply to the Carolina Master Plan, which, along with the UNC Development Plan allows the university to expand within the confines of its existing boundaries. The master plan also reshapes the university via an infill strategy that creates two new axes of campus life (academic villages) in addition to the traditional North Campus. This vision directs development toward existing areas and redesigns the southeast and southwest portions of campus as distinctive places where members of the university community will want to visit and interact. This strategy also promotes such interaction in distinct places by fostering another goal of smart growth: more walkable communities. Students and staff members who live and work in the southern ends of campus will be able to move across campus more easily using trails. The plan lowers the gradients that pedestrians must travel to reach the central and northern portions of campus and defines pathways to reach multiple destinations. These elements reduce the need for short automobile trips on campus and allow students living in South Campus housing units to feel more connected to the rest of the school.

Increases in on-campus housing contained in the plan also promote a more integrated campus and relieve pressure for off-campus housing (and the conflicts that erupt between students and neighborhood residents). Unlike more modernist planning efforts, though, the plan promotes a range of housing options to meet the needs of different student groups. The scale of new undergraduate dormitories has been reduced to harmonize with other areas of campus and create less daunting student settings. Apartments and suites have been added for upperclassmen and the population of foreign students on campus, and married student housing remains apart from both undergraduate clusters and the constant traffic of UNC Hospital.

The master plan represents a fundamental shift toward the integrated treatment of parking, transportation, and mobility. Although many walk, bike, or ride the bus to campus, incremental additions to surface parking have allowed others to drive and park during normal weekday hours. UNC recognized that this parking strategy has led to single-occupancy traffic gridlock during peak hours, while limiting facility expansion and detracting from campus beauty. The master plan does accommodate for some parking increases in structured, paid lots, yet also envisions less single-occupancy travel to campus. A multipronged strategy for travel demand has emerged—one that creates new park-and-ride lots off campus, offers expanded and fare-free bus service to and around campus, and actively promotes and incentivizes walking and cycling alternatives.

In the same manner, storm-water measures and open-space protection have received more systematic treatment. Storm-water management has moved from an incremental, building-based approach to one that sets high standards for university-wide compliance and offers new techniques for proposed buildings like bioswales and green roofs. Plans call for replacing lost open space due to expansion through reclaiming unused surface parking lots and providing greater buffers around the tree-lined streambeds at the eastern edge of campus. The storm-water management goals were reached in conjunction with the town of Chapel Hill as part of the UNC Development Plan.

The plan also reflects another equally valuable smart growth achievement—a cost-effective, predictable, and fair system of making town development decisions regarding master plan permits. UNC will not face costly, delayed consideration of master plan projects due to town indecision or political haggling. In return, town officials and community members have opportunities to review all project impacts and mitigation strategies even before UNC submits a permit application. While the school and town residents still have their problems, this compromise represents a new level of smart growth collaboration.

Can other universities and communities learn from and apply UNC's experience? Campus settings vary considerably, and the university's age and historical split of activities may be somewhat incomparable. Not all university communities harbor strong antigrowth sentiments, and, to be fair, some universities do not stress public service to the same degree as UNC. Nevertheless, some lessons are transferable to other institutions and localities. Passage of major proposals such as the master and development plans require early and frequent interaction of stakeholders. The university sought broad participation in crafting the master plan across the spectrum of UNC stakeholders. Both the master and development plans received considerable public scrutiny and revisions as a result of community input.

Although universities are large landowners, they frequently require a different regulatory environment than private developers. Expansion plans and local decisions take shape over a span of years; it is important to consider how best to meet those challenges before unproductive arguments surface that criticize the important societal roles that both neighborhoods and colleges play. Even in cases where universities are exempt from local zoning decisions, local governments and colleges frequently must reach agreement on planning decisions, such as transportation infrastructure and operations. Universities place high value on innovation. The development of smart growth plans and practices provide a competitive venue among schools for creative, constructive expression. This requires effective, visionary leadership from university administrators. Perhaps this challenge from former Mayor Rosemary Waldorf of Chapel Hill best sums up the importance of their role:

> Universities are revered institutions. They are lighthouses during dark and confusing times, dedicated to the improvement of civilization. We should expect that they should provide examples of good development, and deal with their towns with understanding and generosity. They must set higher standards as they attempt to grow and educate a growing populace.

References

Turner, Paul Venable. 1984. *Campus: An American planning tradition.* New York and Cambridge, MA: Architectural History Foundation and MIT Press.

University of North Carolina at Chapel Hill. 2001. Carolina master plan, available at www.fpc.unc.edu/CampusMasterPlan.

U.S. Bureau of the Census. 2000. *U.S. Census.* Washington, DC: Prepared by the Geography Division in cooperation with the Housing Division, Bureau of the Census.

12

A King's Ransom: Chattanooga's University Invests in Partnerships for Smart Growth in the Historic Martin Luther King District

Meredith Perry and John Schaerer

In 1886 the University of Chattanooga was founded by the city of Chattanooga and the Methodist Episcopal Church, through the kind of symbiotic partnership that has shaped the institution. In 1969 the University of Chattanooga merged with the University of Tennessee to form the University of Tennessee at Chattanooga (UTC). Built on a cornerstone of partnerships and assembled from the best aspects of higher education's public and private traditions, UTC emerged as a regional public institution. Even as UTC joined the statewide system, major social changes were under way that would influence the relationship between UTC and its central city neighbor, the Martin Luther King (MLK) District.

The MLK District has a rich cultural tradition dating back to the end of the Civil War, when the community served as the regional hub of African American commerce and the epicenter of fashionable African American society. Throughout the early twentieth century, southerners knew the district as The Big Nine (the main corridor, Ninth Street, was renamed Martin Luther King Boulevard). During this period the neighborhood's commercial district hosted a variety of establishments owned and operated by African American residents. However, the legacy of the MLK District goes beyond commercial prosperity. Once known as the Jewel of the South, the district was critical to the development of American blues music. World-renowned blues artist Bessie Smith grew up there and got her start in the speakeasies and after-hours establishments that catered to the glitterati of early twentieth-century African American society.

Ironically, desegregation hastened the end of the MLK District's prosperity, as more affluent African Americans migrated to the suburbs, eroding the

Figure 12.1 **Prior to redevelopment efforts, the block between the UTC campus (along the top of the photo) and the MLK community (along the bottom of the photo) served as a buffer separating the entities rather than as a gateway.**

tax base and clientele for businesses in the community. At this time, relations between the MLK District and UTC were strained. The tense relationship persisted throughout the 1970s and 1980s, when misguided land use policies and a variety of socioeconomic challenges continued to take their toll on the MLK District (see Figure 12.1).

During the late 1990s a new administration at UTC and a groundswell of support among local community organizations created the synergy to initiate major redevelopment activities within the MLK District. Among the challenges that UTC and the MLK District faced together were to design and implement campus expansion efforts, neighborhood revitalization, and commercial renewal that would be mutually beneficial.

This case study describes the successful initial phases of ongoing urban redevelopment within Chattanooga's MLK District. The first phase of the redevelopment included two initiatives designed to address district needs for residential and commercial growth and university needs for campus expansion. MLK residents, UTC representatives, and other public and private partners launched efforts with two interrelated goals: (1) increase population density in the MLK community, and (2) fund and construct a neighborhood-based school.

Background on the Problem

In the early 1990s the MLK community seemed caught in the grip of an irreversible decline. Two lanes each way of traffic sped through the community every day to get to the central business district and then back to suburban bedroom communities. The few manufacturing industries left in the area were in their death throes, and residents faced severe socioeconomic challenges. Meanwhile, the university's enrollment was increasing dramatically. While this was a proud accomplishment for the institution, it also presented a dilemma for a "landlocked" urban campus that desperately needed to expand. By the end of the 1990s there was simply not enough space to house and educate the student body. At the same time, leaders in the MLK District were seeking ways to increase business for merchants, to recruit new residents into the community, and to identify positive uses for vacant and abandoned properties. Residents and other stakeholders noted that a major obstacle in the community was the fact that neighborhood students were bussed to various low-performing schools. Bussing made it difficult for MLK parents to be involved with their children's educations and made the community unattractive to families with children.

Both of these problems appeared insurmountable because the UTC-MLK partnership lacked the funding and capital investments needed to support the new construction that the initiatives required. In addition, for the university to expand, it would have to acquire fifty-three properties in the MLK community and relocate ten households and the New Monumental Baptist Church. Given the historic tensions between residents and the university, the prospect of securing citizen support for the process seemed unlikely. Fortunately, the open channels of communication among UTC administrators, MLK leaders, and other stakeholders that had emerged during the 1990s helped all groups work together to develop interrelated plans that would meet each partner's needs.

Program Activity, Planning, and Collaboration

Literature, Research, and Data

Over a ten-year period approximately $5 million were spent on research, analyses, reports, and plans—with little or no positive benefits to the district itself. UTC administrators decided that, while they would take all existing research into account, the core of MLK-UTC partnership planning efforts would be face-to-face interactions with community residents.

The university sponsored more than one hundred planning engagements from 1997 to 2000, including charettes, community planning meetings, and visioning sessions to identify needs, brainstorm solutions, and reach consensus on strategies and action items. In addition, MLK residents, UTC, and community leaders visited the University of Pennsylvania's Center for Community Partnerships to gain insights into successful university-community partnerships.

Goals for the Parties Involved

In 1998 the UTC chancellor convened a forty-member Communications Task Force consisting of university faculty, staff, and students as well as community members, business owners, and other stakeholders. A subset of the Communications Task Force, the Client Committee was established to conceptualize and analyze community design options and oversee redevelopment efforts. The Client Committee's fifteen members included residents, UTC personnel, ministers, and elected officials. Both groups worked together to design plans for potential land use that would mutually benefit the MLK community and the UTC campus.

Even though much had been done to establish a strong partnership between the university and community stakeholders, a certain level of distrust lingered. Within this context, the initial goals of residents were to limit negative UTC exposure in the district and to block any development that they felt would hurt their community. As the relationship among the stakeholders grew, partners quickly came to see that they had little to fear from one another and much to gain from working together. The group adopted the following guiding principles: (1) the campus should be a microcosm of the city, with a wide variety of activities, uses, and people; and (2) the special identity of the city should be matched by the special identity of its university.

Program Activity Implementation

As in many smart growth initiatives, planning and implementation are difficult to approach as discrete activities. In the MLK redevelopment, identification and clarification of needs and planning were critical first steps, but the implementation process uncovered unidentified challenges as well as unnoticed opportunities that informed additional planning and implementation. In this case, strong planning and relationship building were critical, but constant monitor-

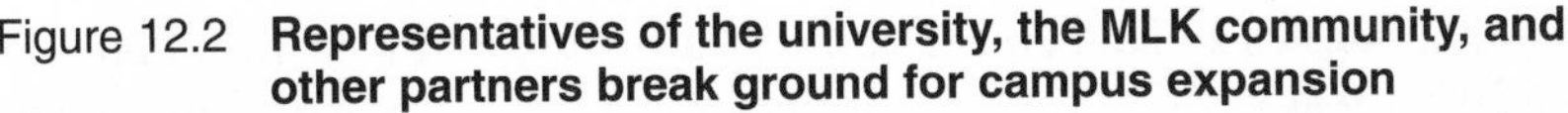

Figure 12.2 **Representatives of the university, the MLK community, and other partners break ground for campus expansion**

ing and adjustments of implementation were also necessary to achieve a flexible process. A brief overview of the implementation process reveals the ways in which planning and implementation spurred further development activities.

Overview of Implementation

In fall 2000 ground was broken for the first phase of UTC construction, which would eventually house one thousand students within the MLK community (see Figure 12.2). While dormers would significantly increase the neighborhood's population, students do not provide the same community benefits that come from stable homeowners. To support the goal of attracting homeowners, UTC partnered with the Lyndhurst Foundation (a local philanthropy) to offer home ownership incentives in the district. A package ($15,000 over five years) was developed to attract young families in particular, who would help increase the residential capacity of the community. Unfortunately, the community at that time offered few amenities (e.g., quality schools and child-care facilities) to draw homeowners. But fortunately, the precedent for UTC-MLK partnership activities had been set through successful consensus building on campus expansion and housing issues, and the partnership began work on a more ambitious agenda: securing community-based schools to serve district children and families.

Dr. Mary Tanner, dean of UTC's College of Education and Applied Professional Studies and a member of the local school district's Task Force for Buildings, learned that the school district had preliminary plans to construct one inner-city school but had not yet been able to identify a suitable site. The dean approached the chancellor with this information, and the university put forth a proposal: to build the proposed school on the UTC campus in a location adjoining the MLK community. The idea was taken to Client Committee members, some of whom were wary about the university's involvement in K-12 education (some voiced concerns that the students would be "experimented on"). Through consensus building and an open planning process, the initial misgivings and concerns were alleviated, and the decision was made to include a magnet elementary school in the proposed campus expansion plans.

Residential Infill

Smart growth researchers have long recognized the importance of residential infill to promote urban redevelopment and combat sprawl (Marquand 2001). Infill that fosters a mixed-income residential community is key to community health and has positive impacts on economic development, community advocacy, education, and crime and safety (U.S. HUD, Recent Research Results, 2000).

While the housing initiative was a great start, additional residential infill was necessary to promote the economic growth that was needed in the MLK community (see Figure 12.3). UTC also was desperate to deal with the rapidly growing residential student population. To address both partners' needs, the Task Force and Client Committee worked together to design UTC Place, a 1,500–unit student housing development located along the neighborhood's main thoroughfare. Throughout this process the Client Committee worked hard to ensure that residents had a strong voice in the design process and that new construction aligned with their needs and expectations.

The first phase of UTC student housing (undergraduate dormitories) has been completed, and nearly 1,000 students have moved into the community as a result. The second phase, which provides an additional 560 beds, was completed in the fall of 2004, and reached full occupancy by the end of October 2004. From both phases of housing, students will bring an estimated $6 million residual income annually into the MLK District. As a result of the incentives to promote home ownership, several new homeowners have already chosen to invest in the MLK community. It is estimated that an additional 100 homeowners will move into the district within the next two years.

Figure 12.3 **Before and after: dilapidated housing that contributed to blight (left) is replaced with student dormitories (right). Housing rehabilitation projects and new residential developments are under way to foster mixed-income residential infill.**

Elementary Schools

The UTC-MLK partnership engaged numerous participants to fund and construct two downtown magnet elementary schools. (One larger school was originally projected, but with UTC's involvement, two smaller schools were constructed.) H.H. Battle Academy of Teaching and Learning and Tommie F. Brown Academy of Classical Studies are fully equipped with early childhood learning centers so that they are able to serve students up to grade 5, creating a stable cohort of pupils and parents with an interest in community well-being (see Figure 12.4).

Establishing strong community schools within neighborhoods is a prime strategy for achieving community redevelopment (Passmore 2002, 2). All too often public schools act as a wick, drawing residents and other resources out of urban centers and creating sprawl (Steward 1999, 370). By locating new schools in the MLK District, the partners anticipate that the wicking effect will hold true—that the schools will draw residents and resources into the district. The schools have already been heralded by the Local Government Commission as models for smart growth partnerships (Local Government Commission 2002, 12–13).

Faculty, Staff, and Student Engagement

The UTC-MLK partnership has captured the imaginations and harnessed the intellectual and human resources of faculty, staff, and students who have made tremendous contributions to the success of partnership efforts. In 1999

Figure 12.4 **The Tommie F. Brown Academy is one of two new magnet schools that engage faculty and students to serve MLK families. Each school has the capacity to serve 450 students and attract residents from all over the city to visit the district daily.**

UTC secured federal funding from the Department of Housing and Urban Development to implement a Community Outreach Partnership Center (COPC) in the MLK District. The COPC has served as the hub for faculty engagement in MLK. Skeptical at first, faculty and staff have embraced Chancellor Bill Stacy's metropolitan focus and have been involved in numerous initiatives including the development of an MLK Commercial Land Use Plan, grassroots organizing and advocacy training for residents, a variety of youth empowerment programs, computer training classes, and health initiatives. Perhaps no campus unit has so completely internalized UTC's metropolitan mission as the College of Education and Applied Professional Studies, which staffs the new magnet elementary schools with its faculty and students. Faculty offer college courses and supervise practicum experiences on-site. This arrangement has created a remarkable learning exchange; school teachers are serving as adjunct faculty and lecturers and UTC faculty are offering unique learning experiences for elementary students. For example, the head of UTC's Teacher Preparation Academy is teaching an elementary-level class in Latin, making Brown Academy the only elementary school in the county to offer foreign language instruction.

Challenges That Arose During Implementation

The four main challenges that have been faced are issues associated with property acquisition, resident mistrust about UTC's motives and intentions, funding and revenue to support revitalization, and infrastructural issues within the community that had to be addressed.

Property Acquisition

The historic tensions between UTC and MLK made property acquisition, always a sensitive topic, a particularly delicate issue. To secure the land necessary to construct campus housing and other facilities without eminent domain action, UTC had to relocate approximately ten households and, more challenging, an entire church congregation. Initially, residents and churches were wary or even hostile about UTC's intentions; however, the households were relocated, and all of the residents involved were satisfied with the outcome. To ensure a positive experience, for the one homeowner to be relocated (the other households were renters), the university purchased a new house on an adjoining street within the neighborhood and swapped the new—and more valuable property—for the homeowner's previous residence.

Relocation on a larger scale involved moving the New Monumental Baptist Church. This was a major undertaking and entailed a substantial amount of trust building to be successful. At the initial meeting, the church felt that UTC had already determined to move them out of the neighborhood. During the course of the meeting, the chancellor reassured church leadership that the purpose of the meeting was for the group to develop a plan in collaboration. The two groups frankly laid out their needs, interests, and concerns: UTC desperately needed the New Monumental property for campus expansion; New Monumental needed to shore up its dwindling membership and better serve a congregation that had moved into the suburbs.

After several months of negotiations, Dr. Margaret Kelley, then vice chancellor for University Advancement, learned that a church in Brainerd (a suburban community where a large portion of New Monumental's congregation lived) was looking for a new facility. UTC's special assistant to the chancellor negotiated a $2.5 million deal where the University of Chattanooga (UC) Foundation bought the Brainerd Church and traded it to New Monumental in exchange for their MLK property. Property acquisition was difficult and time consuming—it took nine months to resolve the New Monumental move; however, by maintaining communication and demonstrating a good faith plan to help the community meet its needs, UTC eventually overcame the community's initial skepticism and gained the confidence of residents and other stakeholders.

Resident Mistrust/Suspicion of Motives

In addition to resident mistrust associated with property acquisition, there was at first a great deal of suspicion among residents and other MLK stakeholders about UTC's motives in the community. MLK business owners had fears that UTC would try to buy or force them out of the community. To alleviate this fear, UTC made a strong commitment to promote and support minority- and resident-owned businesses at planning sessions and community meetings.

The development of Brown Academy in the proposed expansion area also sparked signs of community mistrust among MLK residents. Because it was designed as a magnet school, residents feared that neighborhood children would be excluded and that the school would simply serve as a K-12 extension of the traditional "ivory tower." Inaccurate quotes published in local newspapers and rampant rumors exacerbated this perception. After deliberations, the schools established a system to guarantee that adequate space would be reserved for neighborhood children.

Funding

Without state or local government support, funding was a major challenge, but innovative partnerships and creative financing structures enabled the arrangements necessary to secure funding for partnership activities.

Campus Expansion

To finance the student housing and campus expansion efforts, the university embarked on a highly innovative public-private partnership. The only property suitable for campus expansion was owned by the UC Foundation, a nonprofit philanthropic institution that supports university efforts. Unfortunately, the state of Tennessee would not allocate funds to purchase this property. Chancellor Bill Stacy then suggested that the UC Foundation issue a request for proposals (RFP) to the private sector to build and finance housing for UTC expansion. The UC Foundation and UTC developed the RFP and selected a private-sector developer, Place Collegiate Properties, to manage the initial $18 million project.

To insulate the UC Foundation's endowment from liability and to facilitate the design, land lease, financing, and construction of UTC housing, a separate 501(c)(3) organization, Campus Development Foundation, Inc., was established by the UC Foundation under the leadership of past president Joe Decosimo and property committee chairman John Anderson. All property assembled for expansion was transferred to this new foundation, in exchange for two promissory notes totaling $3 million plus interest, a debt that will be paid from excess cash flow generated by the student housing.

Residential Infill and Home Ownership Incentives

To promote a stable homeowner base in the community, several community organizations have formed a partnership, MLK Tomorrow, to develop housing stock and to promote residential infill through a variety of incentive packages and confidence-building activities. New construction and renovations to the housing stock have been financed through traditional means; however, these housing investments are bringing tremendous resources into the community. Equally heartening are the many packages that partners have developed to encourage residential infill. The Lyndhurst Foundation and UTC partnered to form one of the earliest home ownership incentives: Lyndhurst contributed $100,000, which UTC matched with institutional funds to provide approximately twelve $15,000 homeownership packages for UTC faculty or staff.

Downtown Magnet Schools and Children's Center

Funding to construct the campus elementary school was a challenge for the partners. Initially projected to cost $8 million, the school actually cost just under $10.5 million—the difference was covered using the first phase of housing as collateral. An anonymous donor pledged $5 million, and the UC Foundation contributed the remaining $3 million through innovative financing strategies that capitalized in part on profits from the first phase of development. Battle Academy, the second downtown elementary school (located on the boundary of the MLK District) was financed through traditional bonds issued by the county to be retired via tax revenue.

Once the debt service has been met, the UC Foundation plans to utilize the $5 million pledged by the anonymous donor to endow a fund to support the UTC College of Education and Applied Professional Studies' efforts to enhance urban education. Although only one of the schools is located on the UTC campus, UTC and the Hamilton County Department of Education have developed a binding memorandum of understanding stating that the university will be involved in both schools' curriculum development, enrollment, and other aspects of school governance.

In addition, the university also secured funding to expand the services offered through UTC's Children's Center to include infant care and enlarged the Children's Center facilities to two sites housed within the two new elementary schools. UTC and the Community Foundation of Greater Chattanooga provided funds for this expansion.

Lack of Infrastructure

Typical of many older, urban communities, deficiencies within the MLK District's infrastructure consistently came to the fore as serious obstacles. The majority of structures and utilities in the MLK community were put in place in the early twentieth century; therefore, they needed major improvements to handle increased residential and business capacity and to meet the high expectations of current and potential residents and business owners. Major infrastructural issues included terrible problems with the district's sewer/storm-water run-off system, neighborhood traffic patterns, and street layout.

Sewer/Storm-water Run-Off

The existing sewage system combined storm-water run-off and sewage removal. It had deteriorated over the years, causing problems for neighborhood businesses, which had to contend with sewage backup and associated foul odors. University personnel approached the mayor about the problem; he employed a neutral third party to evaluate and assess the condition. The assessment confirmed the problem, and a $1.3 million sewage/storm-water system reconstruction was completed in September 2003.

Traffic Patterns

UTC has also been involved in efforts to revert to two-way the one-way streets that hinder pedestrian traffic and easy access to neighborhood businesses, residential areas, and churches. The university joined with the MLK Neighborhood Association and the MLK Task Force and requested that the mayor and the city council commission a study of converting the two one-way thoroughfares through the community (McCallie Avenue and Martin Luther King Boulevard) to two-way streets with on-street parking in order to promote commercial redevelopment and increase walkability for residents and visitors alike (Figure 12.5).

After much debate and particularly vocal criticism from suburbanites who had grown accustomed to driving to work at high speeds through the district, the city began converting the streets to two-way thoroughfares; this process was completed in late 2003, and residents and business owners anecdotally describe improved traffic and commerce patterns. The city has invested $1.2 million in the two-way conversion, which is estimated to bring tremendous economic development opportunities within the MLK District.

Streetscaping

In addition to the two-way conversion, UTC has also worked diligently with residents and other partners to enhance the streetscape of the MLK community. Only a short time ago the district, though centrally located within the city, was virtually isolated from the larger community, circumscribed by busy one-way streets and unsafe secondary streets lined by abandoned buildings and overgrown vacant lots, streets with few sidewalks and poor lighting.

Figure 12.5 **UTC and the MLK community worked to convert to two-way the one-way streets that hindered pedestrian traffic and easy access to neighborhood businesses, residential areas, and churches**

All campus construction has been accompanied by streetscape enhancements including sidewalks on both sides of the roads, which are lined with landscaping buffers. Intersections have been renovated with cobbled bricks to emphasize pedestrian thoroughfares, and streetlights line the sidewalks. These changes are already beginning to have an impact on the community, and the benefits of the pedestrian-friendly changes will increase as construction and conversion projects are completed. Walkability is a key tenet of the smart growth movement, and the partners view these pedestrian-friendly changes as a cornerstone of revitalization efforts, because they will increase accessibility, foster a stronger sense of community, boost commercial viability, and enhance the health of residents (Figure 12.6).

Nature of the Collaboration

What Was Learned

The partnership efforts between UTC and the MLK community have revealed a number of important lessons for university-community partnerships. The

Figure 12.6 **Before (left) and after (right) images of East 8th Street document the streetscape enhancements that have characterized revitalization efforts**

wealth of experience and knowledge that all of the stakeholders have gained is far too vast to enumerate here, but there are two key lessons that this process revealed.

Planning Must Be a Joint Enterprise

Many of the institution's initial concepts for campus expansion were not in line with the expectations of community residents and business owners. For example, original plans called for "fraternity row" to be moved into the MLK community, a step that was opposed by some community churches and residents. Because of their concerns, the campus decided to leave the fraternities in their current locations. In addition, the university had originally hoped to develop a community-wide sports and recreation facility that would include an Olympic-size track and soccer field. However, residents opposed this plan because of concerns about parking, traffic congestion, noise and light pollution, and community access. Working through the partnership structure, UTC and the MLK District collaborated to achieve individual and mutual goals while ensuring that no partner was exploited.

Efforts Must Be Cohesive, Comprehensive, and Sustained

No single redevelopment activity can be addressed in isolation from other issues. While it is critical to prioritize redevelopment activities and follow a shared set of milestones, the process also has to take into account the fact that the proper metaphor for a community is not a set of building blocks, but an organism where all of the elements (housing, education, business, crime, public space, health, etc.) are inextricably intertwined.

The Importance of Partnership

When Chancellor Stacy first approached the MLK community about redevelopment, he promised that the university would not come into the community unless it was invited. That statement set the tone for the UTC-MLK partnership efforts that followed. Whereas many partnerships are founded not on a carrot-and-stick model, where the organization with the most power utilizes rewards and penalties to achieve its goals, but on mutual trust. Dr. Stacy set out from the beginning to decentralize the power dynamic in the joint venture so that the community became the center of gravity within the collaborative framework.

The success of the partnership process itself has paved the way for collaborative opportunities and redevelopment activities that were beyond the best expectations of campus and community leaders. A quote from Arthur Moran, community member and MLK District advocate, best describes the overwhelming success of the UTC-MLK partnership efforts: "It used to feel like there were two or three people fighting a whole army; now it's like an army fighting two or three" (COPC Community Forum, June 5, 2003).

Conclusion

During the past five years the way that the MLK District is perceived by the larger Chattanooga community has changed dramatically. To borrow a metaphor from Wilson and Kelling's article "Broken Windows" (1982), the MLK District has changed from a community characterized by broken windows, indicating disarray, lack of normalcy, and criminal behavior, to a neighborhood that exemplifies the concept of mended windows, where residents are engaged in civic action and make investments in their community. This perception shifted due to changes in the physical environment championed by UTC and implemented by UTC-MLK partnership efforts, changes that created a tipping point within the MLK community.

Perspectives within the partnership have changed as well. When planning efforts first began in 1998, both partners had many of the assumptions and biases that so often stymie university-community joint venture. An anecdote from the early days of UTC-MLK planning efforts provides a potent metaphor for the shift in perspectives that has occurred. Driven by fears of crime and safety for UTC students and of community concerns about students' behavior, there were several suggestions early on that the university construct a wall to demarcate the campus from the community. Robert Frost, in his wonderful poem "Mending Wall," wrote, "Before I built a wall I'd ask to know what I was walling in or walling out" (Frost 1987, 33). The wall, in this case, never materialized, but the fact that it was suggested shows how drastically the perspectives on the campus-community relationship have changed.

Ongoing initiatives will further expand notions of community to include both the campus and the MLK neighborhood. Through the downtown schools that engage university faculty and students in community education, the federally funded Weed and Seed program, which promotes community policing and promotes joint efforts by Chattanooga and UTC police officers, the Community Outreach Partnership Center, which lends the weight of UTC's intellectual resources to community development efforts, and countless ongoing interactions between community residents and UTC faculty, staff, and students, the traditional boundaries that separated the UTC campus from the MLK community have been erased.

Possible Program Replication and New Opportunities

UTC and the Martin Luther King District have addressed the same kinds of challenges that institutions and communities face throughout the country. Nearly all mid- to large-size cities face issues associated with housing and quality urban education, issues that are widely recognized as key components of smart growth. By addressing these community needs, the UTC-MLK partnership has made significant progress toward smart redevelopment.

Perhaps the most important component to the success of program activities is the philosophy at the core of UTC-MLK efforts: people and partnerships are more important than projects and funding. UTC's concept of metropolitan engagement is not simply a potpourri of projects, but an ongoing relationship with the community and its residents. It is a critical point that the partnership predated any project or fund-raising activities, empowering all partners to meet on common ground as equals.

There were tremendous challenges associated with these initiatives that caused UTC and its partners to develop innovative solutions and to expand and strengthen partnerships to ensure success. Facing and overcoming these challenges has emboldened the partnership to pursue solutions to other difficult problems facing the community: traffic flow and neighborhood walkability, business development and support, streetscaping, green space and park development, and major construction and infrastructural initiatives are currently under way.

References

Frost, Robert. 1987. *The poetry of Robert Frost: The collected poems*. New York: Henry Holt & Company.

Local Government Commission. 2002. Case Study 4: The H.H. Battle and Academy of Teaching and Learning and the Tommie F. Brown Academy of Classical Studies. *New schools for older neighborhoods*, 12–13. Washington, DC: National Association of Realtors (January).

Marquand, Barbara. 2001. Infill development eases pressures of expansion. *Sacramento Business Journal* 18 (September 28): available at http://sacramento.bizjournals.com/sacramento/stories/2001/10/01/focus2.html.

Passmore, Sam. 2002. Translation paper number eight. *A symposium on smart growth and schools*. Charles Stewart Mott Foundation/Funders' Network for Smart Growth and Livable Communities (March).

Steward, Cecil. 1999. Case 13: Lincoln, Nebraska, public school systems: The advance scouts for urban sprawl. In *Under the blade: The conversion of agricultural landscapes*, Richard K. Olson and Thomas A. Lyson, eds., 370. Boulder: Westview Press.

U.S. Department of Housing and Urban Development (HUD). 2000. Inner-city neighborhood design report released. Washington, DC: Recent Research Results (June).

Wilson, James Q., and George L. Kelling. 1982. Broken windows. *The Atlantic Monthly* 249(3):29–38.

13

Universities as Participants in Planning Enabling Statute Reform

Brian W. Ohm

This chapter examines the role of the university in helping to reform state policy to support smart growth. Specifically, it is a case study about the collaborative process that led to the passage of Wisconsin's comprehensive planning and smart growth law in October 1999. It did not begin as a "smart growth project." Indeed, the term *smart growth* was relatively unheard of at the time. Rather, the project began as an effort to promote good local planning by updating the state's planning enabling laws. It is the result of a convergence of the University of Wisconsin's strong outreach tradition known as the Wisconsin Idea and the increasing visibility of land use as a public policy issue in the state. Because of the overlap between promoting good planning and the then emerging principles of smart growth, the project evolved into smart growth.

Smart growth is a reaction to the spatial pattern of development in the United States since World War II. While some attention is paid to federal and state governmental policies and private development practices that encouraged this form of development, smart growth places an increased emphasis on the role of local plans and regulations in shaping urban form. Since updating plans and regulations is not always a high priority for local governments, many existing local plans and regulations reflect the model of urbanization used in the 1950s and 1960s—the very model smart growth attempts to change. In addition, public acceptance of integrating new concepts such as smart growth into plans and regulations is frequently a slow process. As a result, local plans and regulations often present barriers to the implementation of smart growth principles.

States have an important role in smart growth as an enabler of land use planning and regulation by local governments. Enabling statutes influence the type and quality of local plans and regulations. Wisconsin's comprehensive planning and smart growth law begins to create an enabling law framework that can support smart growth and encourages local governments to update their plans and regulations. With the increased public awareness of smart growth principles in general, communities have an unprecedented opportunity to incorporate them into their plans and regulations.

The Wisconsin Idea Context

Most colleges and universities have a variety of outreach programs and activities extending their resources beyond campus grounds. At the University of Wisconsin–Madison, however, outreach is strongly influenced by the legends and aspirations of the century-old Wisconsin Idea, the guiding principle that, as a state-supported institution, university resources should benefit the people of Wisconsin and beyond (Elliott 2003). The University of Wisconsin is a pioneer in the field of outreach and has served as a model for other programs across the nation.

The university's outreach efforts originated in the 1880s when the school began to offer short courses in agriculture for Wisconsin's farmers. The university offered these classes as a political move in response to the legislature's threat of separating the College of Agriculture from the university. During the nineteenth century state-supported universities were often denounced as aristocratic. The University of Wisconsin struggled to meet the expectation that state universities should disseminate knowledge to the community at large. A legislative committee critical of the early university declared, "The farmers, mechanics, miners, merchants, and teachers of Wisconsin . . . have a right to ask that the bequest of government shall aid them in securing to themselves and their prosperity, such educational advantages as shall fit them for their pursuits of life" (Carstensen 1981, 9).

The Wisconsin Idea was named from a book published in 1912 documenting the contributions of faculty who assisted the state legislature with the formulation of state policies during the Progressive Era in Wisconsin government (McCarthy 1912). A hallmark of the Progressive Party, under the leadership of the governor and later the U.S. senator Robert M. LaFollette, was the theory that it is the state's duty to promote the common interest of all rather than the special interest of particular groups. The Progressives were influenced by the Jeffersonian ideals that humans ought to improve themselves and their society and that representative government could be maintained only if the whole population became literate and willing to be guided by knowledge (Carstensen 1981, 8). These ideals are also a theme of the current interest in smart growth (Scully 1999).

LaFollette embarked on a series of significant reforms, working with the support of the university's president Charles R. Van Hise, a friend and former classmate at the university. Van Hise promoted the use of faculty as technical experts for the state to help solve social and political problems. The reforms became models for other states, and included creation of the direct primary, workers compensation, regulation and taxation of railroads, the legislative reference library, and the University of Wisconsin Extension (UWE).

Events during this era helped establish the proud tradition of the Wisconsin Idea. Over the years the program has continued to influence the work of the university. During the 1930s national innovations such as unemployment compensation and Social Security were credited to the Wisconsin Idea. More recently the Wisconsin Idea has supported a wide range of activities involving faculty and students, including partnerships with the biotechnology industry and K-12 education. (University of Wisconsin–Madison 2002). Students are involved through a variety of means, including service learning courses and undergraduate fellowships that link students to community organizations and real-world issues. Many of these opportunities for civic engagement by students are coordinated by the Morgridge Center for Public Service.[1] State and local government leaders, businesses, and citizens are accustomed to turning to the university for assistance.

The budget for the University of Wisconsin System supports the Wisconsin Idea, primarily through its funding for the UWE. The University of Wisconsin System oversees the state's public higher education network, comprised of thirteen four-year campuses (including the University of Wisconsin–Madison), thirteen two-year colleges, and the UWE. Student enrollment in the university system exceeds 160,000; current state support is a little more than $1 billion, or about 27 percent of the university system's biennial budget. At several of the University of Wisconsin campuses individuals hold joint appointments as faculty of a campus department and as a specialist in certain academic areas with the UWE. The joint appointments allow faculty the time to lend their expertise to address issues specific to the needs of Wisconsin, ranging from working with at-risk youth, agricultural production, economic development, and natural resource preservation to leadership development. The Wisconsin Idea, therefore, provides a strong rationale for these and other faculty to get involved in real-world issues facing the state, such as land use.

The Land Use Issue

As in many states, land use emerged as a significant public policy issue in Wisconsin during the 1990s. The amorphous nature of the forces shaping land use was apparent in the various organizations that began to explore the topic. Several state agencies issued reports on land use (Wisconsin Department of Transportation 1993; Wisconsin Department of Natural Resources 1995), as did local governments (Preserve Dane Task Force 1994). Environmental groups produced reports on land use in Wisconsin (Hulsey 1996), and agricultural interest groups reported on the loss of farmland in the state (American Farmland Trust 1994). The mayor of Milwaukee, John Norquist, became an advocate of new urbanism, promoting the strong sense of place embodied in the urban fabric of the city while criticizing the placelessness of many of Milwaukee's suburbs. Such other issues as affordable housing and historic preservation also became more prominent.

In fall 1994 Republican governor Tommy Thompson issued an executive order creating a land use council comprised of state agency officials and a task force of various interest groups and local government officials to assist the council (State of Wisconsin, Office of the Governor 1994). The executive order charged the council with recommending consistent land use policy objectives for state agencies and ways to coordinate state agency efforts to achieve those objectives. The executive order would later serve as a model for the American Planning Association's Growing Smart research project (Meck 2002, I-22–I-25).

In 1996 the council issued its report *Planning Wisconsin* (State of Wisconsin, State Interagency Land Use Council 1996), which, rather than focusing on state agencies, included many recommendations related to local government such as making substantial changes to local planning authorities. The report's recommendations are consistent with the observation that states are more willing to direct local government to undertake growth management than to advocate and support such planning by their own agencies (Porter 1992, 176). Following the council's report, the Wisconsin legislature initiated a study of it. Local government interests expressed concern about the report's recommended changes to local land use authority. After wading into the issue, the legislative study concluded that there was "virtually no consensus" on land use in Wisconsin (State of Wisconsin, Joint Legislative Council 1998, 5).

Wisconsin's local government structure is often at the heart of the lack of consensus over the land use issue. Wisconsin has more than 1,900 local units of government—395 villages, 1,265 towns, 190 cities, and 72 counties. Every square inch of the state falls within the jurisdiction of a county. Within counties, all land also falls within the jurisdiction of a city, village, or town. Cities and villages are "incorporated" areas that cover approximately 5 percent of the land area of the state and house approximately 70 percent of the state's population. Towns (often called townships in other states) encompass the "unincorporated" areas—the remaining parts of the county outside the borders of cities and villages. The other 95 percent of the state's land area and 30 percent of the state's population fall within a town. Cities and villages have broader authority than towns. They generally have independent authority for land use planning and the power to annex land from towns and use tools such as tax increment financing. Towns do not have these authorities. Towns and counties generally have overlapping land use regulatory authorities dating from the days when towns were unpopulated and had limited financial resources. Today, while towns are still mostly rural, there are some very urban towns. The largest town has a population of 23,614 people; the smallest city has a population of 611. The tension created by differing visions for the urban/rural nature of towns, the broader authority of cities and villages, and the overlapping regulatory authorities of towns and counties creates a complex challenge for land use planning.

Like similar reports before it on land use, *Planning Wisconsin* did not result in any substantial change to the local planning framework in the state. However, the legislature did act on one recommendation from the report, by creating the Wisconsin Land Council, with a small staff, within the state's Department of Administration, though it placed a sunset date on the council of 2003, now extended to 2005. The council is meant to be an advisory body to the governor on computerized land information and other land use issues. It consists of state agency officials, local government officials, and private-sector interests.

In addition to the various studies on land use conducted in the 1990s, an increasing number of land use disputes were making their way through the Wisconsin courts. One, *Lake City Corp v. City of Mequon,* decided by the Wisconsin Supreme Court in early 1997 (207 Wis.2d 156, 58 N.W.2d 100 [1997]), involved a challenge to the denial of a proposed subdivision by the city plan commission based on an inconsistency with the city's master plan. The subdivision, however, was consistent with the city's zoning ordinance. The Wisconsin high court upheld the plan commission's denial of the proposed subdivision. The ruling affirmed the authority of an appointed plan commission to deny a proposed subdivision based on a master plan adopted by the plan commission, as provided under Wisconsin's land use enabling statutes, without (1) a public hearing on the plan, and (2) approval of the master plan by the governing body. The decision also elevated the commission's master plan over the conflicting zoning ordinances adopted by the elected local governing body.

The Lake City case is a classic example of the courts deciding land use cases on a narrow reading of the statutory requirements, thereby avoiding any appraisal of the value judgments expressed in the local action (Mandelker 1971, 58). The proposed subdivision called for a mixture of uses and a higher density that could have provided a range of housing types and more affordable housing. In a regional context, the case raises issues related to the difficulty of building affordable housing in suburban communities and the growing socioeconomic disparities between central cities and their surrounding suburbs. Milwaukee is one of the most economically and socially segregated metropolitan areas in the United States (Jargowsky 1997, 50–51). Mequon is one of Milwaukee's wealthiest suburbs.

The outcome of the Lake City case led the Wisconsin Builders Association and Wisconsin Realtors Association (WRA) to initially push for legislation to eliminate the statutory authority to reject a subdivision based on a master plan. The proposed legislation met with strong resistance from local government organizations and environmental groups. The Builders and Realtors then focused on the planning process and proposed an amendment to the bill clarifying that it would only apply to master plans not adopted by the governing body. Nonetheless, local government and environmental interests prevented the bill from advancing. Frustrated by the land use issue, the Realtors turned to the university.

Program Activity Planning and Collaboration

Given the persistence of the land use issue but the lack of consensus on what to do about it, the WRA approached the author during the summer of 1998 because of his research on the need to update Wisconsin's antiquated planning and zoning enabling statutes for local governments (Ohm and Schmidke 1998; Ohm 1995, 1996, 1997). The research was undertaken while serving as a state specialist in land use law for the UWE and was meant to help inform the discussions of the various organizations examining the land use issue at the time. Members of WRA had read some of the research and found that updating the state's planning and zoning enabling laws made sense for problems their members were experiencing in the state.

The need to update Wisconsin's planning laws was first raised almost forty years ago in a study that found local planning enabling laws antiquated and lagging behind other states' (Beuscher and Delogu 1966). Like many states, Wisconsin's local planning and zoning enabling laws still closely follow the 1920s-era model promulgated by the U.S. Department of Commerce: Standard State Zoning Enabling Act and Standard City Planning Enabling Act. Early observers of local zoning and planning practices under state laws based on these model acts began to identify problems with the model acts and local practices shortly after World War II. For example, the acts added to the confusion over the relationship between planning's general policy-making framework and the detailed legal instrument of zoning (Haar 1955; Kent 1964; Scott 1969, 350). Additional problems with the model acts included their failure to define the elements of a comprehensive plan; the allowance of the plan to be adopted in parts, separate from the complete plan; and the plan's adoption by the independent plan commission, not the elected governing body (Black 1968, 353–54). Other problems were related to the effects of local zoning practices, primarily socioeconomic exclusionary zoning practices that adversely impacted the affordability of housing (Williams 1955; Sager 1969). Wisconsin law was not immune from these criticisms. They were some of the same complaints the WRA had with Wisconsin law in the 1990s.

More recent criticisms of the model acts and local zoning practices focus on their impact on the physical form of suburban areas (Epstein 1997; Duany and Talen 2002). Indeed, the original purposes of these acts are contrary to smart growth principles. The Standard State Zoning Enabling Act, for example, was meant to promote local zoning that would stop the mixture of land uses such as the "[i]nvasion of apartment houses by stores on their ground floors" (Bassett 1936, 25). Following similar state enabling laws, local governments adopted zoning ordinances that divided cities into districts, separating different uses of land. Today these zoning ordinances often inhibit smart growth principles such as promoting mixed-use development (Talen and Knaap 2003). These problems were a concern for 1000 Friends of Wisconsin (1000 Friends). Established in 1996 as a land use advocacy organization modeled after 1000 Friends of Oregon, 1000 Friends of Wisconsin was a critical organization to the program, along with the Realtors.

The WRA suggested meeting with 1000 Friends to see if they would be willing to cooperate on a land use program. 1000 Friends previously had gone head-to-head with the Realtors on different pieces of legislation. The WRA had been successful in defeating legislative proposals of 1000 Friends, and 1000 Friends had been successful in defeating the land use legislative initiatives of the Realtors. The Realtors had important political influence on the Republican administration and the Republican-controlled assembly; 1000 Friends was influential with the Democratic-controlled senate. The land use issue was important to both organizations, and both wanted to make some progress on the issue.

A meeting between the WRA and 1000 Friends was facilitated, and all parties agreed to try a consensus-building process involving key land use stakeholders. Stakeholder participation is a principle of smart growth and is also an important part of planning practice (Susskind and Cruikshank 1987). The author served as a neutral facilitator for the program, and the WRA and 1000 Friends agreed to be the main supporters. In contrast to the unsuccessful formal state processes that had studied the land use issue, it was agreed that this would be a very informal grassroots process. The following organizations were identified to be involved: the Wisconsin League of Municipalities, the Wisconsin Towns Association, the Wisconsin Counties Association, the Wisconsin Alliance of Cities, the Wisconsin Builders Association, the Wisconsin Chapter of the American Planning Association, the Wisconsin Council of Regional Planning Organizations, and the State Department of Administration. The consensus process operated with the ground rule that any agreement would not modify the governance structure for land use decision making. All of the identified stakeholders agreed to participate.

The WRA was also successful in getting a commitment by the secretary of the state's Department of Administration, Mark Bugher, that if the group could agree on a planning proposal, it would be placed in the state budget bill, the main legislative initiative of the governor. Secretary Bugher, who served on the plan commission for a suburban Madison community, had a strong interest in land use issues. The initial goal for the program was to try to collectively update and simplify Wisconsin's local land use planning enabling laws. An appropriate place to begin was with the definition of a comprehensive plan.

Program Activity Implementation

Beginning at the end of summer 1998, the consensus group met for three hours every other week for almost six months to develop a comprehensive plan definition and discuss related land use planning issues. While the initial meeting was held on the university campus, subsequent meetings were conducted in Madison at the offices of the Wisconsin Builders Association. Each stakeholder sent one or two representatives. The participants' time was the major resource commitment made by the organizations. Other than incidental expenses, no financial contribution was needed from any of the participants or the university. The facilitator's time was paid as part of his responsibilities with the UWE.

During this period the American Planning Association (APA) began to publish draft chapters of its research project *Growing Smart*. The realtors and builders found the chapter related to local planning to be credible because it included recommendations for approaches that addressed their concerns, such as the adoption of comprehensive plans by the governing body, a process accepted as good planning theory (Meck 1998). The background research summarized in the APA materials proved invaluable to the process and the participants. It provided a short course in the history of planning enabling legislation, academic literature on such legislation, and a selection of alternative approaches, recognizing that legislation will need to vary from state to state. On several occasions the model legislation offered a starting point for discussion. In the end, however, the comprehensive plan definition was crafted word by word by the participants based on their experiences unique to Wisconsin.

The participants ultimately agreed on a definition that would apply uniformly to villages, towns, cities, counties, and the regional planning commissions. It included nine elements: issues and opportunities; housing; transportation; utilities and community facilities; agricultural, natural, and cultural resources; economic development; intergovernmental cooperation; land use; and implementation. The elements incorporated such smart growth principles as creating housing opportunities and choices for a range of household types, family sizes, and incomes; preserving open space, farmland, and critical environmental areas; and providing a variety of transportation choices. The elements also reflected fundamental views on comprehensive planning such as those articulated by T.J. Kent in his 1964 book *The Urban General Plan.* Kent wrote that the comprehensive plan must address the essential physical elements of the community and their "relationships with all significant factors, physical and nonphysical, local and regional, that affect the physical growth and development of the community" (1964, 98–99).

Since Wisconsin's planning enabling laws never defined a comprehensive plan, agreement to the comprehensive plan definition addressed that problem with Wisconsin law. After developing the definition, the group then set about addressing other problems with Wisconsin's planning laws. To correct the piecemeal nature of the plan's adoption, the group agreed that the comprehensive plan should be implemented in its entirety, and that the governing body, not just the plan commission, should adopt the plan. Finally, the group agreed that zoning and other plan implementation tools should be consistent with the plan, and that state funding for local planning should be made available. Because of the timing of the state budget bill, the group did not have sufficient time to work out the specific language. As a result, only the comprehensive plan definition and $2 million for local comprehensive planning grants were included by Governor Thompson in the state budget bill (1999 Wis. Senate Bill 45, 1999 Wis. Assembly Bill 133).

Senator Brian Burke, a Democratic legislator representing part of the city of Milwaukee, who supported the comprehensive planning language, wanted to build upon this language in the budget bill to create a smart growth proposal. 1000 Friends took the lead in working with the members of the consensus group to expand the planning package. Senator Burke then successfully offered an amendment to the bill that added many of the process requirements the group had discussed: adoption of the comprehensive plan in its entirety and by the governing body; and making a comprehensive plan a prerequisite to implementing actions by requiring consistency between implementing actions and the plan. In addition the amendment included the following provisions: $3.5 million for local planning grants; local comprehensive planning goals (see Table 13.1) to prioritize funding for the state planning grants; encouraging

Table 13.1

Wisconsin's fourteen local comprehensive planning goals

a. Promoting the redevelopment of lands with existing infrastructure and public services and the maintenance and rehabilitation of existing residential, commercial, and industrial structures.
b. Encouraging neighborhood designs that support a range of transportation choices.
c. Protecting natural areas, including wetlands, wildlife habitats, lakes, woodlands, open spaces, and groundwater resources.
d. Protecting economically productive areas, including farmland and forests.
e. Encouraging land uses, densities, and regulations that promote efficient development patterns and relatively low municipal, state governmental, and utility costs.
f. Preserving cultural, historic, and archaeological sites.
g. Encouraging coordination and cooperation among nearby units of government.
h. Building of community identity by revitalizing main streets and enforcing design standards.
i. Providing an adequate supply of affordable housing for individuals of all income levels throughout each community.
j. Providing adequate infrastructure and public services and an adequate supply of developable land to meet existing and future market demand for residential, commercial, and industrial uses.
k. Promoting the expansion or stabilization of the current economic base and the creation of a range of employment opportunities at the state, regional, and local levels.
l. Balancing individual property rights with community interests and goals.
m. Planning and development of land uses that create or preserve varied and unique urban and rural communities.
n. Providing an integrated, efficient, and economical transportation system that affords mobility, convenience, and safety and that meets the needs of all citizens, including transit-dependent and disabled citizens.

Source: Adapted from Wisconsin Statutes Section 16.965(4)(b).

state agencies to use the local comprehensive planning goals to take a more balanced approach in some of their programs and to integrate other state planning requirements into local comprehensive planning requirements; citizen participation requirements; new plan adoption procedures; a smart growth dividend aid program as an incentive for local governments to adopt comprehensive plans that provide for more dense development and affordable housing; and, finally, a provision requiring cities and villages with populations of at least 12,500 to adopt a traditional neighborhood development ordinance.

The WRA and 1000 Friends took the lead in lobbying for the comprehensive planning and smart growth provisions in the budget bill. Other members of the consensus process played a lesser role in lobbying for the planning provisions. Not all the stakeholders agreed to the provisions added by Senator Burke, but they held the position that they would not oppose the legislation. The comprehensive planning and smart growth provisions in the state budget bill passed the legislature, and the bill was signed into law by the governor in October 1999 (1999 Wis. Act 9).

The Nature of Collaboration

Without the collaborative efforts of everyone involved in the consensus process, it is doubtful the planning legislation would have passed. Presenting the legislature with the proposed language produced and supported by such a diverse set of stakeholders was critical. The stakeholders involved in the project have a long history of disagreement over land use issues. With this proposal they were in agreement for perhaps the first time. The goodwill among the participants established during the consensus process also led some of the participants to accept Senator Burke's amendments. Opposition by even one of the organizations might have been enough to defeat the proposal. University involvement helped facilitate the group, provide credible research, and explore various alternatives. The stakeholders supported the law because it was tailored to their interests. For example, through the housing element, the Realtors and builders would get local governments to address housing issues, something that many communities had not planned for in the past. Local government interests supported planning at the local level as an alternative to their fear of losing local control and having the state somehow dictate a plan for them.

Since the passage of the law, the continued support of all the organizations has been critical to educating their membership and citizens around the state about the legislation and in assisting in local planning efforts. Because of the collaborative process by which the legislation was put together, many stakeholders have a greater ownership of the legislation, which strengthens their support. The continued involvement by the stakeholders has also been important to attend to proposals to weaken the planning legislation. The WRA in particular has had to work hard to convince certain Republican legislators not to repeal the law. The work of the Realtors in Wisconsin resulted in their pushing the National Association of Realtors to establish a smart growth task force to provide research and positions on smart growth activities nationally and in the states.

Outcomes

Comprehensive Planning

Wisconsin now has an updated planning enabling law that reflects a collaborative, integrated, and continuing planning process (Wis. Stat. § 66.1001). The law attempts to balance competing interests on a complex set of issues that encourages comprehensive planning that follows a consensus-building model with meaningful involvement by citizens and interest groups (Innes 1996). The law also provides an unprecedented opportunity for local governments to update their plans and ordinances, adopt smart growth innovations, and remove barriers to smart growth. The new law attempts to move beyond many of the older growth management programs that were "unbalanced and incomplete" because of their limited focus on the environment (Bollens 1993, 215). These programs often ignored other important issues, such as affordable housing (Mandelker 1989, 204; Kushner 1994, 74–75).

The law requires that local land use actions be consistent with the local comprehensive plan beginning on January 1, 2010. As a result, hundreds of local governments across the state are in the process of preparing comprehensive plans. This raises several significant challenges for the state. One is the number of plans that need to be prepared, given the many local governments in Wisconsin. Not all local governments will need to have a comprehensive plan, because there are parts of the state where local governments do not take any action affecting land use and, hence, do not need a comprehensive plan upon which to base those actions. General zoning, for example, is not mandatory in the state, and parts of the state remain unzoned. Nonetheless, with more than 1,900 local governments, Wisconsin could end up with more local comprehensive plans than any other state. Prior to the passage of the law, only 29 percent of Wisconsin local governments had a land use plan and many were outdated (Ohm and Schmidke 1998). And, of those, few had a plan approaching the multidimensional comprehensive plan contemplated by the new law. For most local governments, however, the comprehensive planning process is their first attempt at planning.

A related challenge is the need to build a planning culture among many local governments that have never planned; for them, zoning is planning. This has created tremendous educational demands and challenges in helping citizens and local officials understand comprehensive planning and smart growth. The law has heightened the need for local assistance. Several state agencies, the UWE, and some of the stakeholders' groups have cooperatively published educational guides, fact sheets, and other materials to assist local governments in their planning efforts.[2] The University of Wisconsin–Madison's Land Information and Computer Graphics Facility developed a Web site, Community Planning Resource, to assist local planning efforts.[3] The Web site includes online educational modules; Web-based geographic information system (GIS) tools; models for assessing land use impacts, including scenario building; population allocation and growth projection tools; and examples of the relevant digital data needed to prepare the comprehensive plan elements and links to online data repositories and procedures for customized local area data development.

Another challenge is that in some parts of the state, the concept of comprehensive planning has brought out the antigovernment fringe faction. Citing smart growth rhetoric collected from around the country, that faction mistakenly applies the smart growth label as a one-size-fits-all conspiracy aimed at taking away private property rights. These individuals blame the comprehensive planning and smart growth law for a range of unrelated state activities that affect the use of land. The ungrounded fears that they raise in citizens in the more rural parts of the state have helped undermine some local planning efforts there.

Challenges arise even within the planning community. The Southeastern Wisconsin Regional Planning Commission was the only organization that asked the governor to veto the law because it did not fit with its model of planning. Some of the stakeholders promoting the law had difficulty understanding why planners would oppose a law supportive of their practice. Nevertheless, the response from some reflects the diversity in the field of planning and the lack of consensus over some fundamental issues, many of which are not new. For example, there is no consensus that states should mandate planning (Mandelker 1978; Susskind 1978), nor is there agreement about what constitutes a "good" plan (Baer 1997). Planners also do not have a uniform understanding of what it means for zoning to be consistent with a comprehensive plan (DiMento 1980). Finally, there is no consensus among planners whether sprawl itself is a problem (Miller 1999). With planners unable to agree on these issues, it is impossible to expect local officials and citizens to agree.

Despite these challenges, as of May 2004, 645 local governments had received $11.5 million in comprehensive planning grant funds; many are still in the planning process. Other local governments are preparing comprehensive plans using alternative sources of funding from state and local entities. Ninety-five local governments funded through the grant program have adopted their comprehensive plans, and an additional 44 local governments have completed their comprehensive plans using other funds (local and state). Because of the preference for intergovernmental cooperation in the law, a majority of the plans funded through the comprehensive planning grant program are multijurisdictional planning efforts. This level of intergovernmental cooperation is unprecedented in the state. It allows for a bottom-up approach to addressing some regional issues. As communities update their plans and ordinances, many are incorporating smart growth principles into their plans (City of Green Bay 2003; Village of Maple Bluff 2003; Town of Freedom 2003; City and Town of Brillion 2003).

Traditional Neighborhood Development Ordinances

In addition to the comprehensive planning activities, the law requires that cities and villages with populations of at least 12,500 adopt traditional neighborhood development ordinances (Wis. Stat. § 66.1027). This requirement furthered the university's involvement in the project. To provide guidance to cities and villages in meeting this mandate, the legislation requires that local ordinances be "similar" to a model traditional neighborhood development ordinance that the University of Wisconsin Extension prepared. The university's involvement was now in direct response to a legislative mandate; Wisconsin does not have a state planning office, which would ordinarily be responsible for preparing the model ordinance.

Traditional neighborhood developments have the potential to embody many of the principles of smart growth: (1) mix land uses; (2) take advantage of compact building design; (3) create housing opportunities and choices; (4) create walkable communities; (5) foster distinctive, attractive communities with a strong sense of place; (6) preserve open space, farmland, natural beauty, and critical environmental areas; (7) strengthen and direct development toward existing communities; (8) provide a variety of transportation choices; (9) make development decisions predictable, fair, and cost-effective; and (10) encourage community and stakeholder collaboration in development decisions. They are an integral part of the new urbanism movement (Congress for the New Urbanism n.d.).

The traditional neighborhood development ordinance mandate affects approximately sixty cities and villages in the state. The mandate is the outcome of efforts to "legalize" traditional neighborhood developments. The idea to mandate these development ordinances originated from 1000 Friends. As justification for the mandate, 1000 Friends cited the difficulties related to the approval process for a traditional neighborhood development called Middleton Hills designed by Duany Plater-Zyberk & Company, located in Middleton, Wisconsin, a suburb of Madison. Middleton Hills was proposed in 1993 as a planned development district, as provided in the city's ordinances. The city, however, wanted to apply many of its conventional standards, such as street widths and minimum lot sizes, to the project. After considerable delay and heated debates in the local papers, the project was approved. However, the project made people aware of the challenges presented by local ordinances to "new" models of development. These are the same challenges that innovative developments face elsewhere in the country (Talen and Knaap 2003). The Wisconsin law is intended to remove the disincentive to traditional neighborhood development existing in many local ordinances. The traditional development ordinance is meant to provide an option for developers seeking an alternative approach to conventional development.

The legislature provided the UWE with $20,000 to finance the preparation of two ordinances—the model traditional neighborhood development ordinance and an ordinance for a conservation subdivision. Unlike with the traditional ordinance, the legislature did not mandate that local governments adopt the conservation subdivision ordinance. It was meant purely as a local assistance tool. The UWE administration asked the author to prepare the two ordinances, along with Professor James LaGro, a landscape architect with the department, and two student research assistants. Because of the mandate, this discussion focuses primarily on the traditional neighborhood development ordinance.

Drafts of the ordinance were based on Wisconsin development practices and emerging national approaches to traditional neighborhood development ordinances (see Table 13.2). The drafts were reviewed by all the stakeholders involved in the original legislative work group and by other interested parties, including staff from several state agencies. Changes were made to the ordinance to reflect the comments received. As required by the law, the model ordinance was presented to the legislature at the end of 2000 for referral to the appropriate standing committee of each house. If the ordinance was approved, the committee would not schedule a meeting on the model ordinance. The senate did not schedule any meetings, thereby giving approval to the ordinance. However, the Assembly Committee on Natural Resources scheduled a hearing for late February 2001, at which both the sample conservation subdivision ordinance and the model traditional neighborhood development ordinance were the subject. No one testified in opposition to the model traditional ordinance and the associated mandate. However, the conservation subdivision ordinance, with no associated mandate, became a concern for several metropolitan Milwaukee area builders. The assembly committee withheld approval of the traditional ordinance until after some of the builders' concerns were considered. A few minor modifications were also made to the traditional neighborhood development ordinance.

The assembly committee finally approved the traditional ordinance on July 25, 2001 (Ohm, LaGro, and Strawser 2001). With the approval, the mandate for cities and villages to adopt the ordinances became effective. The delay in approval by the assembly made it very difficult for most cities and villages to meet the January 1, 2002, statutory deadline for adopting the ordinance; there is no penalty, however, for failing to meet the deadline.

Most cities and villages that fall under the mandate have now adopted traditional neighborhood development ordinances. The legislation provides express enabling authority for such developments, thereby removing questions about permitting mixed-use developments, given the requirement for

Table 13.2

Elements of a traditional neighborhood development ordinance

a. *Mixed use.* Traditional neighborhood developments must be comprised of different areas, such as a residential area, neighborhood or employment center area, and open space areas. Mixture of housing types (such as single-family and multifamily) and sizes to accommodate households of all ages, sizes, and incomes. Consistent with the variety of uses, lots sizes and densities within the residential and commercial areas of the traditional neighborhood development may also vary.
b. *Compact development.* Some of the fundamental building blocks of the neighborhood—street widths, block lengths, and lot sizes—are smaller than allowed under conventional zoning.
c. *Pedestrian orientation.* Walking distances are a fundamental design component for the neighborhood. Focal points, such as the neighborhood center, are within a five-minute walking distance (or one-quarter mile) of the majority of residents. Narrow streets and other "traffic calming" techniques help slow traffic down to promote pedestrian safety. Required amenities, such as street trees, are also meant to encourage walking.
d. *Street and parking standards.* Standards for narrower streets and different parking requirements than found in conventional ordinances. Need for an interconnected network of street system within the neighborhood and with streets in areas adjacent to the neighborhood. Shorter blocks arranged in a traditional grid or modified grid pattern that creates multiple routes and more direct ones for motorists. Required independent network of sidewalks and bikeways to complement the street network.
e. *Emphasis on design.* Building height limitations and requirements for front porches on residences.

Source: Ohm, Brian W., James A. LaGro Jr., and Chuck Strawser. 2001. *A model ordinance for a traditional neighborhood development.* Madison: University of Wisconsin Extension.

uniformity within zoning districts in Wisconsin's zoning enabling laws. The requirement has helped to educate local officials, planners, and citizens about traditional neighborhood developments and caused them to reexamine local standards for development. At least one city went beyond the requirements of the law and mandates traditional neighborhood developments for certain parts of the city (City of River Falls 2002). Nevertheless, many people remain skeptical of the traditional neighborhood development concept.

Smart Growth Dividend Aid Program

The smart growth dividend aid program outlined in the law remains unfunded, and the specific components of how it would function have not been developed. Given the structural budget deficit facing the state, it is unlikely Wisconsin will be able to develop funding to support the program in the near future. It is an unfulfilled promise of the legislation.

The budget problems affecting the state have also distracted participants from focusing on the seemingly more mundane issues of land use enabling law reform. The comprehensive planning and smart growth law only updated the state's planning enabling legislation. Some of the state's other land use enabling laws are also in need of updating. The various zoning laws, for example, have been pieced together over the decades and are in need of an overhaul. In addition to having to deal with other such issues as the budget, the enormous amount of energy spent by some of the stakeholders on working with legislators and constituent groups educating about the comprehensive planning and smart growth law has limited their ability to concentrate on further reform efforts.

Conclusion

It is still too early to fully evaluate the effectiveness of Wisconsin's comprehensive planning and smart growth law. Nevertheless, the law has created important opportunities for research on a range of issues, from the role of citizen participation to the state's role in promoting smart growth, from comprehensive planning's part in promoting smart growth to traditional neighborhood developments. There are no perfect models for promoting smart growth. Some communities will do better than others. But it is important to learn from these efforts and appreciate the progress that has been made, given the challenges in the state.

In retrospect, it is difficult to identify what could have been done differently. Maybe additional organizations should have been part of the consensus-building process, but if the group were too large it would be unmanageable. Also, it is not clear how the addition of others would have affected the dynamics of the group. The wording of the legislation is awkward in places, but particular phrases were important for certain stakeholders. There are many unresolved issues, and there is no consensus on how to deal with them. They will need to wait for another opportunity. Finally, the university and the extension could have provided greater financial and administrative support, but that did not necessarily detract from the process.

This case study highlights the importance of building a strong coalition of diverse stakeholders to support reform. Despite differing personalities and opinions of the stakeholders, they were able to work with one another and avoid personality clashes. The participants respected the views of others. The project also benefited from timing. It started when interest in land use was high. Stakeholder groups such as the WRA and 1000 Friends were ready to do something about land use. There was interest in the issue from at least one official in the executive branch, Secretary Bugher, and a strong advocate in the legislature, Senator Burke. The state budget was healthy, so the state was willing to help fund comprehensive planning. Much has changed today. The state is in a fiscal crisis and many of the original advocates are gone. It is not clear that the exact program could be replicated in Wisconsin. Nonetheless, at a general level Wisconsin's experience is transferable. Universities can play a central role in working with stakeholders at the state level to address the complex series of fiscal, social, and environmental issues attributed to the spatial patterns of development commonly called *sprawl*. However, to assume that role, universities must have the capacity to assess the unique issues and opportunities that exist in their state. There is no one way to promote smart growth. Universities must have the credibility as a neutral party and be aware of the mechanics of everyday land use issues and problems to help frame the issue in a coherent manner. The key to success is determining the mixture of variables that will make the project work, given its dynamic context.

Notes

1. Additional information about the Morgridge Center is available at http://www.morgridge.wisc.edu/servicelearning.html.

2. Example resources include: *Housing Wisconsin: A guide to preparing the housing element of a local comprehensive plan* (2000), http://www.wisc.edu/urpl/people/ohm/projects/housingf/index.html; *Transportation planning resource guide: A guide to preparing the transportation element of a local comprehensive plan* (2001), http://www.dot.wisconsin.gov/localgov/docs/planningguide.pdf; *Planning for natural resources: A guide to including natural resources in local comprehensive planning* (2002), http://www.dnr.state.wi.us/org/es/science/landuse/smart_growth/urbplan_bk.pdf; *Planning for agriculture in Wisconsin: A guide for communities* (2002), http://www.doa.state.wi.us/dir/documents/ag_guide.pdf; *A guide to smart growth and cultural resources planning* (2003), http://www.doa.state.wi.us/dir/documents/cultural_guide.pdf; and *Intergovernmental cooperation: A guide to preparing the intergovernmental cooperation element of a local comprehensive plan* (2002), http://www.doa.state.wi.us/dir/documents/wi_intergovernmental_guide.pdf.

3. University of Wisconsin–Madison, Land Information and Computer Graphics Facility, *Community planning resource*, available at http://www.lic.wisc.edu.

References

American Farmland Trust. 1994. *Farming on the edge: A new look at the importance and vulnerability of agriculture near American cities*. Washington, DC: American Farmland Trust.

Baer, William C. 1997. General plan evaluation criteria: An approach to making better plans. *Journal of the American Planning Association* 63:329–44.

Bassett, Edward M. 1936. *Zoning: The laws, administration, and court decisions during the first twenty years*. New York: Russell Sage Foundation.

Beuscher, Jacob H., and Orlando Delogu. 1966. *Land use controls*. Madison: State of Wisconsin, Department of Resource Development.

Black, Alan. 1968. The comprehensive plan. In *Principles and practice of urban planning*, William I. Goodman and Eric C. Freund, eds., chapter 13. Washington, DC: International City Managers Association.

Bollens, Scott A. 1993. Restructuring land use governance. *Journal of Planning Literature* 7:211–26.

Carstensen, Vernon. 1981. The emergence of the Wisconsin Idea. *The Wisconsin Idea: A tribute to Carlisle P. Runge (colloquium proceedings)*. Madison: University of Wisconsin Extension.

City and Town of Brillion, Wisconsin. 2003. *City and town of Brillion coordinated comprehensive plan.* http://www.omnni.com/ArchivedProjects.htm.

City of Green Bay, Wisconsin. 2003. *Smart growth 2022.* http://www.ci.green-bay.wi.us/geninfo/plan/smartgrowth.html.

City of River Falls, Wisconsin. 2002. *Traditional neighborhood development ordinance.* http://municipalcodes.lexisnexis.com/codes/riverfalls/_DATA/TITLE17/Chapter_17_112__TRADITIONAL_NEIGHB/index.html.

Congress for the New Urbanism. n.d. *Smart solutions to sprawl.* San Francisco: The Congress for the New Urbanism.

DiMento, Joseph F. 1980. *The consistency doctrine and the limits of planning.* Cambridge, MA: Oelgeschlager, Gunn and Hain, Publishers.

Duany, Andres, and Emily Talen. 2002. Transect planning. *Journal of the American Planning Association* 68(3):245–66.

Elliott, Erin. 2003. A century-old legacy: Influence of Van Hise lives on through Wisconsin idea. *Wisconsin Week* 17(15):1 ff.

Epstein, Lee R. 1997. Where the yards are wide: Have land use planning and law gone astray? *William and Mary Environmental Law and Policy Review* 21:345–79.

Haar, Charles M. 1955. In accordance with a comprehensive plan. *Harvard Law Review* 68:1154–75 .

Hulsey, Brett. 1996. *Sprawl costs us all.* Madison, WI: Sierra Club Midwest Office.

Innes, Judith E. 1996. Planning through consensus building: A new view of the comprehensive planning ideal. *Journal of the American Planning Association* 62:460–72.

Jargowsky, Paul A. 1997. Metropolitan restructuring and urban policy. *Stanford Law and Policy Review* 8:47–53.

Kent, T.J., Jr. 1964. *The urban general plan.* San Francisco: Chandler Publishing Co.

Kushner, James A. 1994. Growth management and the city. *Yale Law and Policy Review* 12:68–92.

McCarthy, Charles. 1912. *The Wisconsin Idea.* New York: Macmillan. http://www.library.wisc.edu/etext/WIReader/Contents/Idea.html.

Mandelker, Daniel R. 1971. *The zoning dilemma: A legal strategy for urban change.* Indianapolis: Bobbs-Merrill.

———. 1978. Should state government mandate local planning? . . . Yes. *Planning* 44(6):14–16.

———. 1989. The quiet revolution—Success and failure. *Journal of the American Planning Association* 55(2):204–205.

Meck, Stuart, ed. 1998. *Growing smart legislative guidebook: Model statutes for planning and the management of change (Phases I and II interim edition).* Chicago: American Planning Association.

———. 2002. *Growing smart legislative guidebook: Model statutes for planning and the management of change*. Chicago: American Planning Association.

Miller, D.W. 1999. Searching for common ground in the debate over urban sprawl: As policy makers charge ahead, research findings offer no road map. *Chronicle of Higher Education* (May 21):A15.

Ohm, Brian W. 1995. A context for reforming Wisconsin land use law. *Perspectives on planning* 1(3):1–2.

———. 1996. A critical review of Wisconsin's current planning and zoning enabling law. In *The inaugural Wisconsin land use law conference* (published proceedings). Madison: University of Wisconsin Law School, Continuing Legal Education for Wisconsin.

———. 1997. *The need to update Wisconsin's planning enabling legislation* (Extension Report Series, 97–4). Madison: Department of Urban and Regional Planning, University of Wisconsin–Madison/Extension.

Ohm, Brian W., James A. LaGro Jr., and Chuck Strawser. 2001. *A model ordinance for a traditional neighborhood development*. Madison: University of Wisconsin Extension. http://www.wisc.edu/urpl/people/ohm/projects/tndord.pdf.

Ohm, Brian W., and Erich Schmidke. 1998. *An inventory of land use plans in Wisconsin* (Extension Report Series 98–3). Madison: Department of Urban and Regional Planning, University of Wisconsin–Madison/Extension.

Porter, Douglas R. 1992. Issues in state and regional growth management. In *State and regional initiatives for managing development: Policy issues and practical concerns*, Douglas Porter, ed., chapter 7. Washington, DC: Urban Land Institute.

Preserve Dane Task Force. 1994. *Final report*. Madison: Office of the Dane County Executive.

Sager, Lawrence. 1969. Tight little islands: Exclusionary zoning, equal protection, and the indigent. *Stanford Law Review* 21:767–800.

Scott, Mel. 1969. *American city planning since 1890*. Berkeley: University of California Press.

Scully, Patrick. 1999. Democracy in action: Engaging the whole community in smart growth. *Getting Smart* 2:1ff.

State of Wisconsin, Office of the Governor. 1994. *Executive order no. 236, relating to the creation of the State Interagency Land Use Council and the Wisconsin Strategic Growth Task Force*. Madison, WI.

State of Wisconsin, State Interagency Land Use Council. 1996. *Planning Wisconsin: Report of the State Interagency Land Use Council to Governor Tommy G. Thompson*. Madison, WI.

State of Wisconsin, Joint Legislative Council. 1998. *Report of the Joint Legislative Council's Special Committee on land use policies*. Madison, WI.

Susskind, Lawrence. 1978. Should state government mandate local planning? . . . No. *Planning* 44(6):17–20.

Susskind, Lawrence E., and Jeffrey Cruikshank. 1987. *Breaking the impasse: Consensual approaches to resolving public disputes*. New York: Basic Books.

Talen, Emily, and Gerrit Knaap. 2003. Legalizing smart growth: An empirical study of land use regulation in Illinois. *Journal of Planning Education and Research* 22:345–59.

Town of Freedom, Wisconsin. 2003. *Town of Freedom comprehensive plan*. http://www.omnni.com/ArchivedProjects.htm.

University of Wisconsin–Madison. 2002. *The Wisconsin Idea in action: The University of Wisconsin–Madison and its partners.* Madison: University of Wisconsin–Madison.

Village of Maple Bluff, Wisconsin. 2003. *Comprehensive plan.* http://www.villageofmaplebluff.com/landuse.html.

Williams, Norman, Jr. 1955. Planning law and democratic living. *Law and Contemporary Problems* 20(2):317–50.

Wisconsin Department of Natural Resources. 1995. *Common ground: Report of the DNR Land Use Task Force.* Madison, WI.

Wisconsin Department of Transportation. 1993. *Statewide Land Use Task Force final report.* Madison, WI.

About the Editors and Contributors

Editors

Wim Wiewel is the Provost and Senior Vice President for Academic Affairs at the University of Baltimore. Previously he served as Dean of the College of Business Administration and the College of Urban Planning and Public Affairs at the University of Illinois at Chicago. He is a past president of the Association of Collegiate Schools of Planning. His publications include *Suburban Sprawl: Private Decisions and Public Policy, When Corporations Leave Town: The Costs and Benefits of Metropolitan Job Sprawl,* and *Urban-Suburban Interdependencies.*

Gerrit-Jan Knaap is Professor of Urban Studies and Planning and Director of the National Center for Smart Growth Research and Education at the University of Maryland, College Park. He earned his BS from Willamette University, his MS and PhD from the University of Oregon, and received postdoctoral training at the University of Wisconsin–Madison, all in economics. Knaap is the coauthor or coeditor of four books: *Land Market Monitoring for Smart Urban Growth, The Regulated Landscape: Lessons on State Land Use Planning from Oregon, Spatial Development in Indonesia: Review and Prospects,* and *Environmental Program Evaluation: A Primer.*

Contributors

Thomas T. Ankersen is a Legal Skills Professor and Director at the University of Florida Conservation Clinic and Codirector of the Summer Environmental Law Program at the University of Florida/University of Costa Rica Joint Program in Environmental Law, Gainesville.

James R. Cohen is Lecturer and Director of Graduate Studies in the Urban Studies and Planning Program at the University of Maryland, College Park.

Christine Danis, AICP, is Project Manager of the National Center for Neighborhood and Brownfields Redevelopment, at the Edward J. Bloustein School of Planning and Public Policy, Rutgers, the State University of New Jersey, New Brunswick.

Nancy Frank is Associate Professor of Urban Planning at the University of Wisconsin–Milwaukee.

Priscilla Geigis is Director of Massachusetts State Parks and formerly the Director of Community Preservation for the Executive Office of Environmental Affairs, Massachusetts.

Michael J. Greenberg, PhD, is Professor and Associate Dean for Faculty at the Edward J. Bloustein School of Planning and Public Policy, and Director of the National Center for Neighborhood and Brownfields Redevelopment, both at Rutgers, the State University of New Jersey, New Brunswick.

Michael Greenwald is Assistant Professor of Urban Planning at the University of Wisconsin–Milwaukee.

David W. Gross, PhD, is a conservation program development consultant in Ithaca, New York, and was formerly a member of the Department of Natural Resources, Cornell University.

Elisabeth Hamin is Assistant Professor in the Department of Landscape Architecture and Regional Planning, University of Massachusetts–Amherst.

Richard W. Jelier, PhD, is Associate Professor at the School of Public and Nonprofit Administration at Grand Valley State University in Grand Rapids, Michigan.

Nicole C. Kibert is an attorney at Carlton Fields in Tampa, Florida.

Edward W. LeClear is Special Projects Coordinator for the Pennsylvania Downtown Center in Harrisburg, Pennsylvania.

Greg Lindsey is Director of the Center for Urban Policy and the Environment and is the Duey-Murphy Professor of Rural Land Policy, School of Public and Environmental Affairs, Indiana University–Purdue University Indianapolis (IUPUI).

Henry Mayer, PhD, is Executive Director of the National Center for Neighborhood and Brownfields Redevelopment, Edward J. Bloustein School of Planning and Public Policy at Rutgers, the State University of New Jersey, New Brunswick.

Jeremy Morris is at West Virginia University, Morgantown.

Brian W. Ohm, JD, is Associate Professor in the Department of Urban and Regional Planning, University of Wisconsin–Madison.

John Ottensmann is Associate Director of the Center for Urban Policy and the Environment and Professor of Public and Environmental Affairs at the School of Public and Environmental Affairs, Indiana University–Purdue University Indianapolis (IUPUI).

Jamie Palmer is Planner/Policy Analyst at the Center for Urban Policy and the Environment, School of Public and Environmental Affairs, Indiana University–Purdue University Indianapolis (IUPUI); President of the Indiana Planning Association; and Chair of the Indiana Land Use Consortium.

Robert Parker, AICP, is Director of the Community Planning Workshop, Department of Planning, Public Policy and Management, University of Oregon, Eugene.

Meredith Perry is Community Outreach Specialist in the Office of Grants and Program Review, University of Tennessee at Chattanooga.

L. Christopher Plein, PhD, is Associate Professor of Public Administration at West Virginia University, Morgantown.

John Schaerer is Special Assistant for External Affairs at the University of Tennessee at Chattanooga.

Linda Silka is Director of the Center for Family, Work, and Community; Professor in the Department of Regional Economic and Social Development; and Special Assistant to the Provost for Community–University Partnerships at the University of Massachusetts–Lowell.

Laura Solitare, PhD, is Research Associate at the National Center for Neighborhood and Brownfields Redevelopment, Edward J. Bloustein School of Planning and Public Policy, Rutgers, the State University of New Jersey, New Brunswick, and is also Assistant Professor of Urban Planning and Environmental Policy at the Barbara Jordan/Mickey Leland School of Public Affairs, Texas Southern University, Houston.

Richard Thorsten is a PhD candidate at the University of North Carolina, Chapel Hill.

Carol L. Townsend is Community and Economic Development Agent at the Michigan State University Extension and Urban Component Coordinator, United Growth for Kent County, Kent/Michigan State University Extension, Grand Rapids, Michigan.

Joseph Tutterrow is Director of the Indiana Land Resources Council and was formerly an Assistant State Forester at the Indiana Department of Natural Resources.

Kendra C. Wills is Land Use Extension Agent at the Michigan State University Extension and is Project and Rural Coordinator, United Growth for Kent County, Kent/Michigan State University Extension, Grand Rapids, Michigan.

Jeffrey Wilson is a scholar at the Center for Urban Policy and the Environment, School of Public and Environmental Affairs, and Assistant Professor in the Department of Geography, Indiana University–Purdue University Indianapolis (IUPUI).

About the Lincoln Institute of Land Policy

The Lincoln Institute of Land Policy is a nonprofit and tax-exempt educational institution established in 1974 to study and teach land policy, including land economics and land taxation. The Institute is supported primarily by the Lincoln Foundation, which was established in 1947 by Cleveland industrialist John C. Lincoln. He drew inspiration from the ideas of Henry George, the nineteenth-century American political economist, social philosopher and author of the book, *Progress and Poverty.*

The Institute's goals are to integrate theory and practice to better shape land policy decisions and to share understanding about the multidisciplinary forces that influence public policy in the United States and internationally. The Institute organizes its work in three departments: valuation and taxation, planning and development, and international studies, with special programs in Latin America and China.

The Lincoln Institute seeks to improve the quality of debate and disseminate knowledge of critical issues in land policy by bringing together scholars, policy makers, practitioners and citizens with diverse backgrounds and experience. We study, exchange insights and work toward a broader understanding of complex land and tax policies. The Institute does not take a particular point of view, but rather serves as a catalyst to facilitate analysis and discussion of these issues—to make a difference today and to help policy makers plan for tomorrow.

L LINCOLN INSTITUTE
OF LAND POLICY
113 Brattle Street
Cambridge, MA 02138–3400 USA

Phone: 617–661–3016 x127 or 800–LAND-USE (800–526–3873)
Fax: 617–661–7235 or 800–LAND-944 (800–526–3944)
E-mail: help@lincolninst.edu
Web: www.lincolninst.edu

Index